Machine Learning Interviews
Kickstart Your Machine Learning
and Data Career

Susan Shu Chang

Beijing · Boston · Farnham · Sebastopol · Tokyo

Machine Learning Interviews

by Susan Shu Chang

Published by O'Reilly Media, Inc., 1005 Gravenstein Highway North, Sebastopol, CA 95472.

O'Reilly books may be purchased for educational, business, or sales promotional use. Online editions are also available for most titles (*http://oreilly.com*). For more information, contact our corporate/institutional sales department: 800-998-9938 or *corporate@oreilly.com*.

Acquisitions Editor: Nicole Butterfield	**Indexer:** Sue Klefstad
Development Editor: Sara Hunter	**Interior Designer:** David Futato
Production Editor: Beth Kelly	**Cover Designer:** Karen Montgomery
Copyeditor: Shannon Turlington	**Illustrator:** Kate Dullea
Proofreader: Piper Editorial Consulting, LLC	

December 2023:   First Edition

Revision History for the First Edition

2023-11-29:   First Release

See *http://oreilly.com/catalog/errata.csp?isbn=9781098146542* for release details.

978-1-098-14654-2

[LSI]

Table of Contents

Preface

Machine learning (ML) is an integral part of our day to day, whether we're aware of it or not. Each time you go on sites like YouTube and Amazon.com, you're interacting with ML, which powers personalized recommendations. This means that the way the products are displayed on the sites is based on what ML algorithms think suit your taste and interests. And not just that—there's ML-based comment moderation to flag spam or toxic comments, review moderation, and more. On sites like YouTube, there are ML-generated captions and translations.

ML is also present in aspects of our lives beyond shopping and entertainment. For example, when you send a money transfer online, ML algorithms are checking to see whether it's fraudulent. We live in an age of software that is built on a foundation of data and ML algorithms.

All of this software requires specialized talent to design and build, which has created a demand for software skills and has elevated ML careers in recent years. The pay for technology roles has also risen as a result. These are just some of the many factors that make an ML career enticing: building the products and product features that are so integral to our lives. Since ML techniques power AI advancements, this discussion similarly applies to "AI careers."

Entering the ML field is challenging, however. ML jobs have a reputation for requiring higher academic credentials, with most of the jobs in the 2010s requiring a PhD. Even if the credential requirements on job postings have decreased since the late 2010s, the advice I still commonly see online is to have at least a master's degree. Even those with ample credentials can struggle to find a role in the data and ML fields. Is the advice given online wrong, or is it too generalized and vague?

I've interviewed for numerous ML jobs, and I've been successful at entry level, senior level, and the staff+[1] and principal[2] levels. Throughout the process, I've experienced firsthand the same difficulties and frustrations that aspiring candidates encounter during ML interviews. I've sent out endless resumes only to get no replies. I've failed phone screens, suffered the anxiety of waiting for responses, and even failed an on-site after they'd flown me to San Francisco from Toronto. I've applied for data scientist and machine learning engineer (MLE) jobs only to be confused when the interviewers seemed to be looking more for a data engineer or data analyst.

Apart from my experience as an interviewee, I've built years of experience as an interviewer. As part of my jobs in the ML field, I've reviewed and filtered hundreds of resumes, conducted numerous interviews, and served on many decision-making committees. As part of technical leadership (principal level at two companies), I've reviewed job descriptions and interviewed co-ops, interns, and entry-level candidates as well as senior and staff+ hires. I've included tips in this book based on mistakes made by job candidates that resulted in my fellow interviewers and me deciding not to pass them on to the next round. "If only the candidate had done this other thing," we said. "They were quite promising otherwise." This book will help you avoid some of these obvious mistakes.

The truth is that there are a lot of unspoken criteria for job seekers. For example, having good communication and teamwork skills may not be included in some job descriptions. Expectations such as these aren't omitted from job descriptions because of malice but because those in the industry see them as minimum requirements. I have more recently seen ML job postings from major companies clearly list "communication skills" at the very top of their lists of requirements in an attempt to improve the clarity of job descriptions.

In addition to these hidden expectations for new and experienced job seekers alike, the interview process can be confusing because it differs so much from role to role and from company to company. Even Randy Au, a writer who's worked in data at Google for years, said that "things are … different"[3] when, out of curiosity, he looked at current data scientist and ML job postings.

Many people wish for a roadmap, a full step-by-step for how to enter the ML field, guaranteed. For example, what are the best university majors and internships? What are the best side projects, and what Python libraries should you learn? I can relate to

---

1 *Staff+* refers to roles that are above the senior level.

2 The job levels in tech often progress from entry/intermediate level → senior level → staff level → principal level, although there are minor differences depending on the company. For example, some companies combine the staff and principal levels.

3 Randy Au, "Old Dog Revisits the DS Job Market out of Curiosity," *Counting Stuff* (blog), December 1, 2022, *https://oreil.ly/yzIsx*.

this—I've asked many friends for as much information as possible along each step of my job interview journey. I worried about whether I should send a follow-up email after an interview and looked in multiple online forums to see if I should. Would I annoy the interviewers, or would they be expecting it? Such a small thing caused me a lot of anxiety, and I wished there were just a clear answer instead of "it depends" or "it probably won't hurt." This is the book I wish I'd had back then to refer to for all those questions!

Now that I've been on the other side as an interviewer, I've learned what the hiring side prefers in job candidates in various scenarios. I now have firsthand answers to many questions I had in the past, and more of a roadmap to entering the ML field. Although even if there were such a guaranteed roadmap, it won't be the one you are imagining. By the time I learned about the ML and data science fields, I had long ago chosen my university major, graduated, and was partway through a master's degree in economics. I didn't have any internships during university; instead, I made and played video games and socialized in my spare time. If anything, the roadmap to an ML job is quite flexible, and even if you start a bit later, *there is no such thing as being too late.*

When I was searching for my first ML job, I didn't do all the most straightforward things, but I was somehow able to make my way through job interviews as a student who had never done an internship. I probably knew less about the interview process than many people did, but that's why I've been able to write from a perspective of someone who didn't do all the *right* things and was still able to thrive in the ML field. Indeed, there are no *right* things, only the things that are right for your situation.

I won't tell you things like, "Just major in [SUBJECT] at your university and then get an internship at [COMPANY], and you'll be set." I'd need to write a separate book for each different type of person. A one-size-fits-all, prescriptive roadmap will fail when you encounter a point not already on the map. If you learn how to navigate without being glued to a map, you can create your own maps, regardless of the situation.

In this book, I'll show you how to be a navigator and create your own roadmap, whether you are a non-STEM[4] major, a STEM major without internship experience, have no relevant work experience, have ML work experience or non-ML work experience, and so on. As long as you stick with it, it'll be fine if you majored in something that's not often recommended. It's OK if you have previous job experience that you don't think is directly relevant to ML. I'll walk you through how to enhance and make use of your past experiences as well as how to gain additional relevant experience.

---

4 Science, technology, engineering, and mathematics.

I advocate for flexible and tailored career roadmaps based on your own scenario because in my own career I've encountered many scenarios in which there wasn't one single roadmap:

- Landing an entry-level data scientist (ML) job as an economics master's degree student at a large, public company[5]
- Landing a job with a more senior role at a startup with about 200 employees when I joined, and about 400 employees at peak
- Landing a job at a new, mid-large public company as a principal data scientist

Depending on the industry, the company size, the ML team size, and the company's lifecycle stage (e.g., startup), employers had different expectations that I needed to learn about. If I had only followed online advice or advice from people who interviewed at companies that used a different job-interview process, I might have failed (no, I would have failed). Each time, I've had to change up the way I prepare and the way I interview in order to succeed. Through all my personal experiences and (literally) hundreds of ML interviews, I've found patterns for how to ace ML and data science job interviews and be a successful candidate. With my experiences and the lessons I've learned, it's now possible to write this book to help aspiring job candidates.

Successful job candidates know what each step in the interview process is trying to assess in their scenario. Unfortunately, simply showing up and having the technical skills isn't always enough. It's like exams at school—people who look at the syllabus carefully and understand the scope of each exam are more likely to succeed. In this case, you try to reverse engineer a syllabus for each of the jobs you are applying for.

As I gained more and more experience in ML, I also got more and more questions from aspiring job seekers. I've taken on many coffee chats (100+ at this point) and to help even more people, I've written career guides for my blog *susanshu.com* for years. When the opportunity to help even more people with this book came up, the decision for me was clear.

Why Machine Learning Jobs?

I've spoken about how ML is prevalent in our day-to-day lives, whether we know it or not, and whether we like it or not. You may have had some experiences in your own life that caused you to become curious and pick up this book! I'll also outline my experiences, which may reinforce your motivations or bring even more attractive aspects of the ML field to your attention.

---

5 A *public company* means it has publicly traded stocks.

As someone working in tech, I think ML is a great area to develop high-value products that can affect millions of users. I had the chance to work on such a project in my very first job out of school, and I think that I might not have had that responsibility and opportunity so early in my career if I hadn't been skilled in machine learning.

In my opinion, ML is a fun and fulfilling area. I enjoy learning about new technologies and research, and if you relate to that, you'll enjoy that facet of working in ML too. There is a flip side to the fast-paced innovations in our field. For example, it can be exhausting to continuously learn about new advancements when trying to focus on family or other important aspects of our lives. Nowadays, even if I'm very focused on other activities such as socializing or writing this book on the weekends, I still take the opportunity to learn without spending too much time. I also take some time during work hours to listen to talks online or read books. This isn't exclusive to ML, but I've heard from many people that the pace of continuous learning for ML is a bit faster than for other tech-related jobs that require learning new frameworks.

Of course, there is also the aspect of pay. On average, ML jobs are well compensated. I've been able to provide for myself and even accomplish many financial goals that enhance my life and the lives of my loved ones. This is something I'm very grateful to my ML career for enabling. On another note, I've been able to achieve so much because of the ML field and community: I've been flown around the world to speak at conferences (so many of them that I've had to rain check for future years). Meeting cool people working at cool places in ML and seeing advancements in the ML and AI space firsthand are all perks of working in this industry.

No matter what your motivation for picking up this book is, I hope that I can successfully share with you the skills and tools for you to succeed at ML job interviews and to overcome roadblocks along the way.

In this book I'll help you understand the following:

- The various types of ML roles and which ones you'd be most likely to succeed at
- The building blocks of ML interviews
- How to identify your skill gaps and target your interview preparation efficiently
- How to succeed at both technical and behavioral interviews

I'll be adding commonly asked questions from the online live training I've taught at O'Reilly as well. Consider it a coffee chat with me and the various sources I've gained supporting insights from:

- How to succeed as a candidate with a less "typical" educational or career background
- How to greatly increase the chances that your resume will clear the initial screening

- What ML interviews for senior and higher roles look like

And more.

Who This Book Is For

Before I dive into the chapters, I want to outline the following scenarios that you might find relatable; this is the audience I've written this book for:

- You are a recent graduate who is eager to become an ML/AI practitioner in industry.
- You are a software engineer, data analyst, or other tech/data professional who is transitioning into a role that focuses on ML day to day.
- You are a professional with experience in another field who is interested in transitioning into the ML field.
- You are an experienced data scientist or ML practitioner who is returning to the interviewing fray and aiming for a different role or an increased title and responsibility, and you would like a comprehensive refresher of ML material.

You could also benefit from this book if the following scenarios describe you:

- Managers who want to get inspiration for how to conduct their ML interviews or nontechnical people who want to get an overview of the process without wasting too much time on scattered online resources
- Readers who have a basic knowledge of Python programming and ML theory and are curious to explore if entering the ML field could be a future career choice

What This Book Is Not

- This book is not a statistics or ML textbook.
- This book is not a coding textbook or tutorial book.
- While there are sample interview questions, *this book is not a question bank.* Code snippets will be brief and concise since they become outdated quickly.

Since I can't cover every concept from scratch, I assume that readers have a rudimentary familiarity with ML (a high-level understanding is enough). But don't worry, as I will cover the basic definitions as a quick reminder. I also assume the audience has some familiarity with the Python programming language, such as running scripts on Jupyter Notebooks, since Python is popular in ML interviews and on the job. However, I do include a brief section on learning Python from scratch if you happen to not be familiar with it.

In addition, this book provides a substantial library of links to external practice resources to help you with preparing for ML interviews; but first, I'll help you identify what is most helpful for you to practice and learn beyond your current knowledge and skill level.

Thus, instead of listing a bunch of questions and answers to memorize, with this book I'm aiming to teach you how to fish. As an interviewer, many candidates I've seen who didn't pass the interview *wouldn't* have been saved if they had just practiced some more questions. Rather, they didn't even know what their gaps were. I'll teach you how to identify your strengths and gaps and how exactly you can use the resources in this book to close those gaps.

Conventions Used in This Book

The following typographical conventions are used in this book:

Italic
> Indicates new terms, URLs, email addresses, filenames, and file extensions.

`Constant width`
> Used for program listings, as well as within paragraphs to refer to program elements such as variable or function names, databases, data types, environment variables, statements, and keywords.

`Constant width bold`
> Shows commands or other text that should be typed literally by the user.

`Constant width italic`
> Shows text that should be replaced with user-supplied values or by values determined by context.

> This element signifies a tip or suggestion.

> This element signifies a general note.

This element indicates a warning or caution.

O'Reilly Online Learning

O'REILLY® For more than 40 years, *O'Reilly Media* has provided technology and business training, knowledge, and insight to help companies succeed.

Our unique network of experts and innovators share their knowledge and expertise through books, articles, and our online learning platform. O'Reilly's online learning platform gives you on-demand access to live training courses, in-depth learning paths, interactive coding environments, and a vast collection of text and video from O'Reilly and 200+ other publishers. For more information, visit *https://oreilly.com*.

How to Contact Us

Please address comments and questions concerning this book to the publisher:

O'Reilly Media, Inc.
1005 Gravenstein Highway North
Sebastopol, CA 95472
800-889-8969 (in the United States or Canada)
707-829-7019 (international or local)
707-829-0104 (fax)
support@oreilly.com
https://www.oreilly.com/about/contact.html

We have a web page for this book, where we list errata, examples, and any additional information. You can access this page at *https://oreil.ly/ML-interviews*.

There is a supplemental website that includes bonus content not found in the book: *https://susanshu.substack.com*.

For news and information about our books and courses, visit *https://oreilly.com*.

Find us on LinkedIn: *https://linkedin.com/company/oreilly-media*

Follow us on Twitter: *https://twitter.com/oreillymedia*

Watch us on YouTube: *https://youtube.com/oreillymedia*

Acknowledgments

Many people's wisdom and encouragement helped make this book become a reality!

A big thanks to the reviewers who read and reviewed this book as a work in progress: Margaret Maynard-Reid, Serena McDonnell, Dominic Monn, and Suhas Pai. All your early feedback and comments have helped make this book so much better. I'd also like to thank folks who reviewed select chapters: Eugene Yan, Prithvishankar Srinivasan, Ammar Asmro, Luis Duque, Igor Ilic, Jeremy C., and Masoud H. I'm super grateful and humbled by how you all graciously took the time to look over the book at varying stages of completion and answer my questions!

Everything I have written in this book has been accumulated throughout my career, so I'd be remiss if I didn't mention the friends, mentors, and organizations that have greatly affected my career who haven't already been named: Nick Miles, Denis Osipov, Amir Feizpour, Shannon Elliott, the Python Software Foundation, PyCons around the world, and many more amazing colleagues in the teams I've worked with. You rock!

Of course, big thanks to the O'Reilly team: the awesome development editor Sara Hunter, who's been encouraging me and helping me stay focused through this intense year of writing; production editor Elizabeth Kelly; copy editor Shannon Turlington; and acquisitions editor Nicole Butterfield, who gave me a lot of encouragement and originally reached out about teaching the O'Reilly "Machine Learning Interviews" online training—which eventually kicked off this book!

Thank you to my loved ones who have supported me through thick and thin, no matter what random adventure I'm on. My family, who has always been there for me, and even more so during the writing of this book, is a source of motivation and inspiration. Thank you to mom, dad, my brother, and my grandparents. Thank you, Susan, for being my sun. Thank you to my friends who have been my support system and warmth since university days.

Lastly, I'd like to thank my instructors, peers and lifelong friends at the University of Waterloo and the University of Toronto for fostering an inspiring, rigorous, yet flexible environment for me to explore my curiosity and interests. This freedom led me to my career in machine learning, and I wouldn't be here without that environment in which to chase my dreams.

## CHAPTER 1

Machine Learning Roles and the Interview Process

In the first part of this chapter, I'll walk through the structure of this book. Then, I'll discuss the various job titles and roles that use ML skills in industry.[1] I'll also clarify the responsibilities of various job titles, such as data scientist, machine learning engineer, and so on, as this is a common point of confusion for job seekers. These will be illustrated with an ML skills matrix and ML lifecycle that will be referenced throughout the book.

The second part of this chapter walks through the interview process, from beginning to end. I've mentored candidates who appreciated this overview since online resources often focus on specific pieces of the interview but not how they all connect together and result in an offer. Especially for new graduates[2] and readers coming from different industries, this chapter helps get everyone on the same page as well as clarifies the process.

The interconnecting pieces of interviews are complex, with many types of combinations depending on the ML role you're aiming for. This overview will help set the stage, so you'll know what to focus your time on. For example, some online resources focus on knowledge specific to "product data scientists," but will title the course or article "data scientist interview tips" without differentiating. For a newcomer, it's hard to tell if that is relevant to your own career interests. After this chapter, you'll be able to tell what skills are required for each job title, and in Chapter 2, you'll be able

---

1 This book focuses on industry applications of ML as opposed to jobs with a primary focus on researching the ML algorithms themselves, publishing in conferences, and so on, which mostly require a PhD.

2 Also referred to as "freshers" in some regions. In this book, I will use the term "new graduates" or "new grads."

to parse out that information yourself from job postings and make your resume as relevant to the job title and job posting as possible.

Overview of This Book

This chapter focuses on helping you differentiate among various ML roles, and walks through the entire interview process, as illustrated in Figure 1-1:

- Job applications and resume (Chapter 2)
- Technical interviews
  - Machine learning (Chapters 3, 4, and 6)
  - Coding/programming (Chapter 5)
- Behavioral interviews (Chapter 7)
- Your interview roadmap (Chapter 8)
- Post-interview and follow-up (Chapter 9)

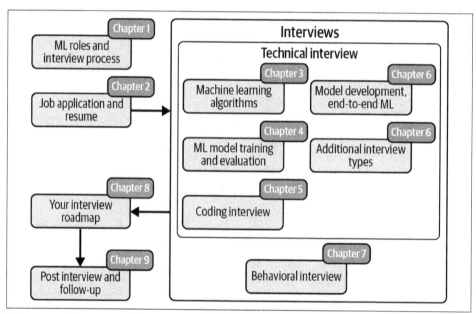

Figure 1-1. Overview of the chapters and how they tie into the ML interview process.

Depending on where you are in your ML interview journey, I encourage you to focus on the chapters and sections that seem relevant to you. I've also planned the book to be referenced as you go along; for example, you might iterate on your resume multiple times and then flip back to Chapter 2 when needed. The same applies to the other chapters. With that overview, let's continue.

The companion site to this book, *https://susanshu.substack.com*, features bonus content, helper resources, and more.

A Brief History of Machine Learning and Data Science Job Titles

First, let's walk through a brief history of job titles. I decided to start with this section to dispel some myths about the "data scientist" job title and shed some light on why there are so many ML-related job titles. After understanding this history, you should be more aware of what job titles to aim for yourself. If you've ever been confused about the litany of titles such as machine learning engineer (MLE), product data scientist, MLOps engineer, and more, this section is for you.

ML techniques aren't a new thing; in 1985, David Ackley, Geoffrey E. Hinton, and Terrence J. Sejnowski popularized the Boltzmann Machine algorithm.[3] Even before that, regression techniques[4] had early developments in the 1800s. There have long been jobs and roles that use modeling techniques to forecast and predict. Econometricians, statisticians, financial modelers, physics modelers, and biochemical modelers have existed as professions for decades. The main difference is that there were much smaller datasets compared to the modern day (barring simulations).

It was only in recent years, just before the 21st century, when compute power started to increase exponentially. In addition, advances in distributed and parallel computing created a cycle in which "big data" became more readily available. This allowed practitioners to apply that advanced compute power to millions or billions of data points.

Larger datasets started being accumulated and distributed for ML research, such as WordNet,[5] and, subsequently, ImageNet,[6] a project led by Fei-Fei Li. These collective

---

[3] David H. Ackley, Geoffrey E. Hinton, and Terrence J. Sejnowski, "A Learning Algorithm for Boltzmann Machines," *Cognitive Science* 9 (1985): 147–169, *https://oreil.ly/5bY2p*.

[4] Jeffrey M. Stanton, "Galton, Pearson, and the Peas: A Brief History of Linear Regression for Statistics Instructors," *Journal of Statistics Education* 9, no. 3 (2001), doi:10.1080/10691898.2001.11910537.

[5] The official WordNet website (*https://oreil.ly/91k2g*) provides more information.

[6] Jia Deng, Wei Dong, Richard Socher, Li-Jia Li, Kai Li, and Li Fei-Fei, "ImageNet: A Large-Scale Hierarchical Image Database," *2009 IEEE Conference on Computer Vision and Pattern Recognition*, Miami, FL, USA (2009): 248–255, doi:10.1109/cvpr.2009.5206848.

efforts laid the foundation for even more ML breakthroughs. AlexNet[7] was released in 2012, achieving high accuracy in the ImageNet challenge,[8] which demonstrated that deep learning can be adept at humanlike tasks at a scale that had not been seen before.

Many ML practitioners see this as a time when machine learning, deep learning, and related topics increased by leaps and bounds in terms of recognition from the broader population, not just the AI community. The recent popularity of generative AI (such as ChatGPT) in 2022 and 2023 didn't come out of nowhere, nor did the deepfakes, self-driving cars, chess bots, and more that came before it; these applications were the results of many advances over recent years.

"Data scientist" as a job title began as an umbrella term, when the ML and data fields were less mature. The term "data scientist" on Google Trends (*https://oreil.ly/0emY4*), which measures the popularity of search terms, surged in 2012. That was the year when *that* article was published by *Harvard Business Review*: "Data Scientist: The Sexiest Job of the 21st Century."[9] By April 2013, the search popularity of "data scientist" was already tied with "statistician" and subsequently surpassed it by magnitudes, as shown in Figure 1-2. Back in those days, there wasn't a narrow divide between infrastructure jobs and model training, though. For example, Kubernetes was first released in 2014, but companies have taken some time to adopt it for orchestrating ML jobs. So now there are more specific job titles for ML infrastructure that didn't exist before.

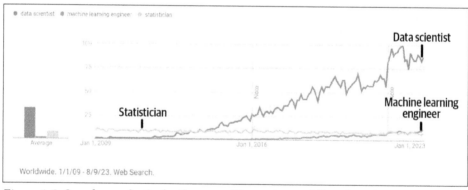

Figure 1-2. Search popularity for the terms "data scientist," "machine learning engineer," and "statistician" on Google Trends (retrieved August 9, 2023).

7 Alex Krizhevsky, Ilya Sutskever, and Geoffrey E. Hinton, "ImageNet Classification with Deep Convolutional Neural Networks," *Advances in Neural Information Processing Systems 25* (NIPS 2012), *https://oreil.ly/iFMkq*.

8 Krizhevsky, Alex, Ilya Sutskever, and Geoffrey E. Hinton, "ImageNet Classification with Deep Convolutional Neural Networks," *Communications of the ACM* 60, no. 6 (2017): 84–90, doi:10.1145/3065386.

9 Thomas H. Davenport and DJ Patil, "Data Scientist: The Sexiest Job of the 21st Century," *Harvard Business Review*, October 19, 2022, *https://oreil.ly/fvroA*.

As social media, web recommender systems, and other modern use cases increased, companies started gathering much more granular data, such as *clickstream data*, which is data collected as a user browses a website or app. Another recent advancement is an average corporation being able to store the sheer amount of telemetry from machines and Internet of Things (IoT) devices. Previously, data scientists may have worked with data that was updated weekly or daily. Now, as many applications update more frequently or in real time, more infrastructure is needed to serve ML functionality in web products and apps, so more jobs have been created around those functions as well.

In short: as the *machine learning lifecycle* grew more complex, more job titles were created to describe the new skills that a full ML team now requires. I'll elaborate more on the job titles and ML lifecycle later in this chapter.

All of this happened within the last decade, and companies don't always change their job titles to reflect how the roles have become more specialized. Regardless, as a candidate, knowing this history can help reduce confusion and frustration from applying for a job and finding the role is different from another company's job with the exact same title. See Table 1-1 for previous trends in ML-related job titles and Table 1-2 for current trends in ML job titles.

Table 1-1. Previous trends of ML and data job titles

ML and data job title	Previous trend for the job title
Data scientist	Do everything
Data analyst	Specifically responsible for data analysis related to business decisions

Table 1-2. Current trends of ML and data job titles

ML and data job titles	Current trends for the job titles
Data scientist Machine learning engineer Applied scientist …and so on	Train ML models
Machine learning engineer MLOps engineer, AI engineer Infrastructure software engineer ML software engineer, machine learning …and so on	MLOps and infrastructure work
Data analyst (Product) data scientist …and so on	Data analysis, A/B testing
Data engineer Data scientist in a startup Analytics engineer …and so on	Data engineering

With that history to explain why you will encounter different job titles, I'll elaborate on each of these job titles and their responsibilities.

Job Titles Requiring ML Experience

Here is a nonexhaustive list of job titles for ML (or closely related) roles:

- Data scientist
- Machine learning engineer
- Applied scientist
- Software engineer, machine learning
- MLOps engineer
- Product data scientist
- Data analyst
- Decision scientist
- Data engineer[10]
- Research scientist
- Research engineer[11]

As I discussed "A Brief History of Machine Learning and Data Science Job Titles" on page 3, each role is responsible for a different part of the ML lifecycle. A job title alone does not convey what the job entails. As a job seeker, be warned: in different companies, completely different titles might end up doing similar jobs! As illustrated in Figure 1-3, your ML job title will depend on the company, the team, and which part(s) of the ML lifecycle your role is responsible for.

To give specific examples of how job titles can depend on the company or organization that is hiring for the job—based on real people I've spoken to, job descriptions, and job interviews—the person responsible for *training* ML models but not for building the underlying platform might be called the following:

- Software engineer (ML) or data scientist (Google)
- Applied scientist (Amazon)
- Machine learning engineer (Meta, Pinterest)

---

10 ML and data science use data; data engineers are unlikely to use ML techniques themselves, but their work and collaboration are integral to ML workflows.

11 Serena McDonnell (lead data scientist and ex-Shopify) pointed out that in the field of hedge funds, "research scientist" and "research engineer" are used to refer to ML roles.

- Data scientist (Elastic, the team where I work)
- Data scientist (Unity)

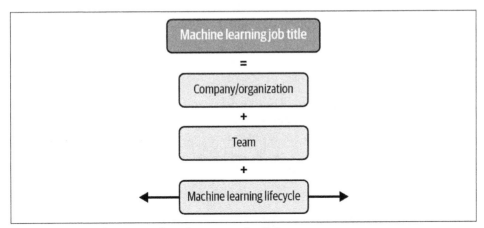

Figure 1-3. What's in a machine learning job title?

By the time this book is published, any of the job titles within these companies and teams may have changed. Regardless, it demonstrates the point that ML titles may vary between companies and even between different teams in the same company.

The job title also depends on the organization, the department, and so on. Some departments in Google have the data scientist[12] job title, and some don't. At the companies where I've worked, my teams had data scientists train ML models while MLEs built the infrastructure (working all day in tools such as Kubernetes, Terraform, Jenkins, and so on). In some other companies, MLEs are the ones who train ML models.

As a personal example, my work experience has heavily involved ML model training, so I apply for jobs that have the title "machine learning engineer" or "data scientist." I'll provide more examples of skills and roles that could be a good fit for your interests and skills in the following sections.

---

12 I've also seen research scientist job postings at Google, but these roles are specifically for researching ML, are responsible for publishing at large conferences, and require a PhD degree.

Machine Learning Lifecycle

In industry, it is an expectation for applied ML projects to eventually improve the customer experience—for example, a better recommender system that shows the user more relevant videos, news, and social media posts. In industry, "customer" can also mean internal customers: people within the same company or organization. For example, your team builds ML models that predict demand, which helps your company's logistics department better plan its shipment schedules. Regardless of whether the user is external or internal, many components are involved in building a full-fledged, end-to-end ML product. I'll walk through a simplified example.

First, there needs to be data, as most ML is trained and tested with large amounts of data. Someone needs to make sure the raw data is brought in (ingested) so that it's easily accessible later on for data analysis, ML, reporting and monitoring, and so on. This is illustrated by step A (data) in Figure 1-4.

Next, with the data in place, someone with knowledge of ML algorithms and tools will use the data to start ML development. This is illustrated by step B (machine learning development) in Figure 1-4. This involves feature engineering, model training, and evaluation. If the results aren't great, there is a lot of iteration in step B, and this person might enhance their feature engineering or model training, or even go back to step A and request that more data be ingested.

Once there are somewhat satisfactory results, they'll move on to step C (machine learning deployment), which connects the ML models to customers. Depending on the type of ML project, it could be deployed to a website, app, internal dashboard, and so on. Of course, they'd like to make sure the ML is working properly, so any good team will have a way to monitor the results. In ML there are two main types of potential issues. The first is that something in the software layer doesn't work, such as bugs in the code. The second is a data or ML model issue—for example, in the model-development phase, the model outputs normal results, but after deployment/release, there is data imbalance, so then the model results become undesirable. From step C onward, there can be more iteration back to step B to improve the models and run more experiments in step C again.

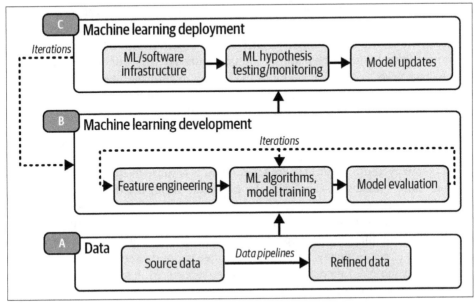

Figure 1-4. Machine learning lifecycle (the graph is simplified for understanding).

In the machine learning lifecycle I just walked through, a lot of skills are required. Data pipelines, model training, maintaining continuous integration and continuous deployment (CI/CD): as a job candidate, what should you be learning to prepare for the interview? Thankfully, as I mentioned in "A Brief History of Machine Learning and Data Science Job Titles" on page 3 companies nowadays *might* hire people who have a subset of these skills. For example, they need some people specialized in step A (data engineering), some specialized in step B (ML development), some in step C (ML deployment), and so forth. I emphasize the *might* since it still differs depending on the company or team; I will walk through some scenarios.

Startups

Startup roles will usually wear more hats, meaning they will need to do the jobs in multiple steps in the machine learning lifecycle as illustrated in Figure 1-4. Here's an example:

We were a team of 5–25 ML engineers and regularly had to participate in setting up data labeling jobs, QA testing, and performance improvements (on mobile devices), plus setting up demos.

—Dominic Monn, CEO of MentorCruise (previous six years in ML startups)

Usually, startup companies have the goal of shipping[13] an end-to-end product, but because they have fewer customers they might care less about the scale and stability (at an early stage). Hence, it's more likely that the person developing and training ML models is the same person doing data analysis and presenting to stakeholders, or even the same person building the platform infrastructure. An ML team in a startup might simply have fewer people. For example, the startup might have 30 software engineers and data people in total, whereas larger corporations could have a team of data analysts alone numbering 30 people to disperse the workload.

Larger ML Teams

If the company and/or team has grown enough, it is more likely the ML roles have become more specialized. Generally, the larger the team, the more specialized the role. If the "machine learning engineer" at a larger company trains models, then it's likely they don't wear two or three hats at once, as they might at a startup. Instead, the big company hires more people to fill those roles. That isn't to say the work is simpler at a larger company. In fact, there's often more data, more scale, and more downsides if the ML functionality goes down, so each MLE's time could be completely tied up wearing only one hat.

 Larger company size often corresponds to larger ML teams, but it depends. For example, a large company in a traditionally nontech industry, might have its first ML team hires operate in more of a startup-like environment while they figure out how ML best works for the company.

Let's go one level deeper and add more details of ML or data responsibilities. Figure 1-5 expands on the machine learning lifecycle from Figure 1-4 to reflect teams or companies with more fine-grained roles. (It's worth repeating that even if this list is a useful and common enough heuristic, it's still a bit simplified for illustration purposes since there will always be exceptions and outliers.)

---

13 *Ship* is a common term in software and, by extension, ML, that refers to releasing something, such as a software product or code update.

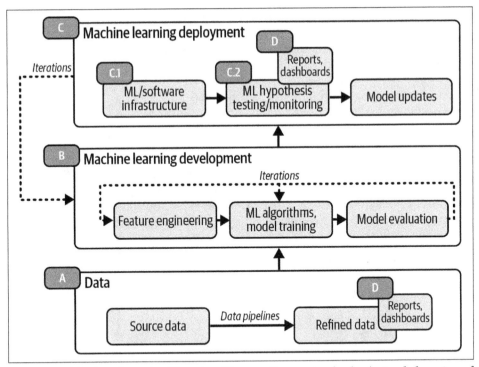

Figure 1-5. Machine learning lifecycle with more fine-grained roles (extended version of Figure 1-4).

Here's an example of what your role might be responsible for within these more fine-grained roles, as illustrated in Figure 1-5:

- You build the data pipelines for analytics and ML (step A).
- You train ML models (step B).
- You build the infrastructure for ML models to be deployed (step C.1).
- You design and conduct hypothesis testing, often A/B tests, for new ML product features (step C.2).
- You do data analysis, build reports and dashboards, and present to stakeholders (step D).

Figure 1-5 is often referred to in later chapters, so save or bookmark it!

The Three Pillars of Machine Learning Roles

To set the stage for the rest of the book, I'll go over what I call the three pillars of ML and data science roles:

- Machine learning algorithms and data intuition
- Programming and software engineering skills
- Execution and communication skills

These are the broad categories of skills that you will be evaluated on during ML job interviews. This book focuses a lot on helping you understand these skills and bridge any gaps between your current experiences and skills and those under these three pillars (see Figure 1-6). All these skills will be expanded on in the following chapters.

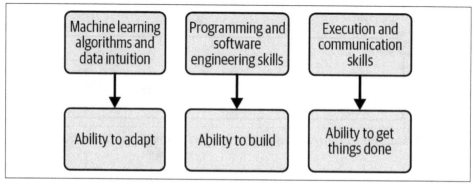

Figure 1-6. Three pillars of machine learning jobs.

Machine Learning Algorithms and Data Intuition: Ability to Adapt

You're able to understand the underlying workings of ML algorithms and statistics theory and their respective trade-offs—which is essential when you're faced with an open-ended question in a real-world ML project at work. You're not just following steps as you would for a school assignment.

Having data intuition means that when you're faced with a new problem, you know how to use data to solve it; and when you encounter new data or data sources, you know how to dive in to evaluate them. You ask yourself, is this data suitable for ML? What types of ML models might it be suitable for? Are there any issues with the data before you can use it for ML? You know what to ask and how to find the answers.

In the ML job-interview process, various types of interviews and interview questions are aimed at assessing a candidate's knowledge and readiness in this pillar, which I'll cover in Chapters 3 and 4.

Programming and Software Engineering: Ability to Build

While working on a project, you have the programming skills required to deliver, such as manipulating data with Python or using an internal deploy process so that another team can use the results from the ML model.

Even if you know the theory well, without the programming or software engineering[14] sense, you can't make ML materialize out of thin air. You need to use code to connect the data with ML algorithms, which are also implemented with code—that is, you must convert theory to practice.

Other programming skills in high demand for ML roles are the (software) engineer's ability to transition from prototype to production—that is, the ML is integrated and released. Some roles are responsible for end-to-end ML: from researching and training models to deployment and production. Some ML roles, such as MLOps engineers, are responsible for building software infrastructure that can handle the demands of processing large amounts of data to send ML responses to users in seconds or even milliseconds.

In the ML job-interview process, various types of interviews and interview questions assess a candidate's skills in this pillar, which I'll walk through in Chapters 5 and 6.

Execution and Communication: Ability to Get Things Done in a Team

You're able to work with people who aren't in the same role as you. In ML, we work with software engineers, data engineers, product managers, and many other colleagues. The ability to get things done in a team encompasses a few soft skills such as communication and some project management skills.

For example, being unable to communicate with team members is a real blocker[15] for projects and could cause your ML projects to languish or even be deprioritized. Even in cases where you work with only one person (say, your boss), you still need to be able to report on your projects, which requires communication skills. Consequently, in the ML field a highly in-demand skill is being able to communicate technical concepts with nontechnical stakeholders.

You'll also need some project management skills to keep your tasks on track. We all learn to how manage our to-do lists and calendars during the process of education or self-learning, but it's more chaotic since now your project calendar depends on others' calendars and priorities. Even if you have a project and/or product manager to keep the team on track, you still need to manage yourself to some extent.

---

14 In the more specialized roles where you deal with on-device or edge ML, some basic knowledge of hardware can also make a difference.

15 Business speak for something that blocks another thing from happening, usually a project or timeline.

Without soft skills, things don't get done, full stop. Don't be that candidate who focuses only on technical skills but neglects building and demonstrating their soft skills in interviews. I'll delve into the details of how ML interviews evaluate candidates on this pillar in Chapter 7.

Clearing Minimum Requirements in the Three ML Pillars

Growing your skills in all three ML pillars is a tall order, and for entry-level roles you're usually only expected to have a minimum (such as a 3/10) for each pillar, as illustrated in Figure 1-7. For example, a job candidate who has some exposure to programming, even if they aren't skilled or experienced, can be taught to improve. Ideally, you'd be stronger on at least one pillar (such as 5/10 for programming) that is most related to the particular ML role in order to stand out from other job candidates.

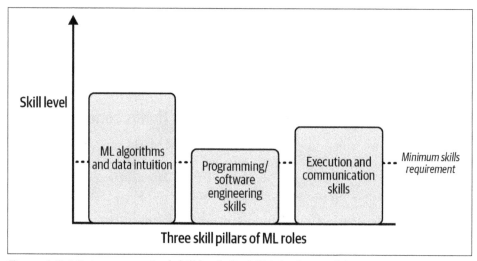

Figure 1-7. Minimum required skill levels for ML jobs (example).

For senior roles, the bare minimum requirements are higher, but a similar rule of thumb applies: clear the minimum skill requirements. From then on, you'll be compared with other candidates on the skills that you are great in, depending on the role. Data scientists who only train ML models but don't deploy them might not need to develop their programming skills as much as their ML theory and communication skills.

For entry level roles, I'd argue that the communication pillar has a lower requirement (but not 0/10, please!) because it takes the hard-earned experience of working with a larger group of people, including nontechnical teammates, to raise it higher. This also gives some candidates an edge in this pillar: for those with a nontraditional background, such as candidates who are self-taught or switching from software engineer roles or another field, the ability to adeptly tell a story and showcase a portfolio can set them apart from other candidates.

Now that you've had an overview of the three pillars, you can use this mental model to stand out.

Machine Learning Skills Matrix

Congratulations! You've made it to the end of a pretty dense section! Now that you've gone through the overview of the machine learning lifecycle and three pillars of ML skills, it's time for you to map your interests and skills to job titles.

Table 1-3 will give you a rough idea of what skills you will need to learn in order to succeed in specific roles. On a scale from one to three stars, one star represents a skill of lower importance, and three stars represents a highly important skill.

Table 1-3. Machine learning and data skills matrix

Skills	Job titles				
	Data scientist (DS)	ML engineer (MLE)	MLOps engineer	Data engineer	Data analyst
Data visualization, communication	★★★	★★	★	★	★★★
Data exploration, cleaning, intuition	★★★	★★★	★	★★★	★★★
ML theory, statistics	★★★	★★★	★★	★	★
Programming tools (Python, SQL)	★★★	★★★	★★★	★★★	★
Software infrastructure (Docker, Kubernetes, CI/CD)	★	★ to ★★★	★★★	★	★

> Table 1-3 is often referred to in later chapters, so save or bookmark it!

Taking a look at these skills, you can roughly map them to the three pillars of ML skills in the previous section, as shown in Table 1-4.

Table 1-4. Machine learning and data skills mapped to the three pillars of ML jobs

Pillar	ML and data skills
Pillar 1 Machine learning algorithms and data intuition: ability to adapt	Data exploration, cleaning, intuition Machine learning theory, statistics Data visualization
Pillar 2 Programming and software engineering skills: ability to build	Programming tools (Python, SQL) Software infrastructure
Pillar 3 Execution and communication skills: ability to get things done in a team	Communication and so on

It's OK if you aren't completely sure what each type of skill might entail just yet. In Chapter 2, we will revisit this matrix, and there will be details and a checklist for self assessment.

Tip for New Graduates

You don't need to worry about every single skill; companies are aware that they are responsible for training up new grads. But you can stand out from other job candidates by showing that you are more easily trainable and can learn fast. An easy way to demonstrate this earlier in your ML career is to gain high-level (not necessarily deep) exposure to topics that you don't have experience with yet. For example, even if you haven't worked much with version control, it's a bonus to be familiar with. You can achieve this by watching some videos (30 minutes) and installing/testing it out on a project (one hour).

Now, let's tie all this together. We've looked at the machine learning lifecycle (Figure 1-5) and machine learning skills matrix (Table 1-3). What's left is to see what jobs are best for *you* to apply to now or to gain the skills for! To do so, let's connect everything to the current trend of ML and data job titles (Table 1-2). This is illustrated in Figure 1-8.

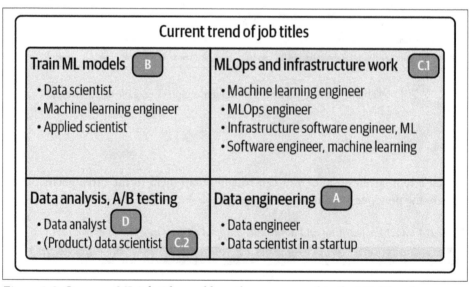

Figure 1-8. Common ML job titles and how they correspond to the ML lifecycle.

The alphabetical annotations in Figure 1-8 can be mapped to those in Figure 1-5, listed here for convenience:

- (A) Data
- (B) Machine learning development
- (C.1) ML/software infrastructure
- (C.2) ML hypothesis testing/monitoring
- (D) Reports and dashboards

 Figure 1-8 is often referred to in later chapters, so save or bookmark it!

When you see a job title and check the details of the job posting, you can map it to what that job is likely responsible for in the day to day. In addition, based on what part of the ML lifecycle you're interested in, you can better prepare and target your job applications, so you don't accidentally bark up the wrong tree.

Exercise 1-1

Go to a job board of your choice, such as LinkedIn, Indeed, or others listed in Chapter 2. Search "machine learning," "data scientist," "data," "AI," "generative AI," and so on. What are you seeing? Do you see different types of jobs being advertised that all use ML?

Introduction to ML Job Interviews

Now that I've introduced many job titles that might be of interest to you, it's time to go through all the steps and types of interviews you will encounter during the process! This book is called *Machine Learning Interviews*, but interviews are so much more than just interview questions. There are job applications and your resume, which are how you get interviews in the first place. If you don't increase your chances of getting more interviews, then you won't even get the chance to answer any interview questions! I'll be covering the process from beginning to end, including how to follow up after the interview (Chapter 9).

Machine Learning Job-Interview Process

Now let's get into the entire job-interview process. You'll start by applying to jobs, then interviewing, and then, after some rounds of interviewing, finally receiving offers. This process is detailed in Figure 1-9.

Figure 1-9 is often referred to in later chapters, so save or bookmark it!

---

16 Wayne Duggan, "What Happened to FAANG Stocks? They Became MAMAA Stocks," *Forbes*, September 29, 2023, *https://oreil.ly/JzMys*.

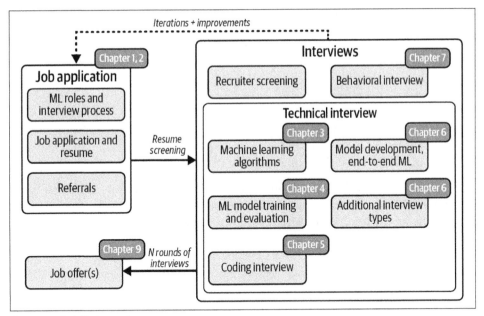

Figure 1-9. ML interview process.

Applying for Jobs Through Websites or Job Boards

Let's imagine that you're just starting out and applying for an ML role at a company with an established HR[17] and hiring process. You can begin your application in a few ways: by cold applying through the company website or job board (discussed in Chapter 2) or through a referral from someone within the team or company. You can also get interviews through cold messaging on LinkedIn or by emailing recruiters. Usually, at companies that have an HR-tracking software system, even if someone refers you, you'll still need to upload a standard application into the online portal, which means you'll need to prepare an updated resume and fill in your information.

You may also choose to supplement your job-search efforts by working with a third-party recruiter, which is *different* from an in-house recruiter who works or contracts specifically for the hiring company. Third-party recruiters often work with multiple companies at once. Professional peers I know recommend working only with specific trusted third-party recruiters but warned me to beware those who make too many unrealistic promises or aren't reputable. You can read more about third-party recruiters in this *Forbes* article (*https://oreil.ly/Z2LuQ*).

---

17 Human resources or equivalent department in the company.

Resume Screening of Website or Job-Board Applications

Using the first method—cold applying through company websites or third-party job boards—you've been browsing job boards like Indeed[18] as well as going directly to the career pages of companies you're interested in working for. In this scenario, you don't have someone referring you to the team or company (I'll cover that in "Applying via a Referral" on page 22). You've seen some ML-related jobs that seem relevant to you, and you clicked the links to apply. After you submit your application and the company has your information and resume, an HR member, recruiter, or whoever is in charge of resume screening, will proceed with the next step.

The reality is that jobs have many applicants, and you should assume the first batch of applicants will be filtered before the hiring manager sees them. The *hiring manager* is the manager you'll work with and report to if you join the team. So you can usually assume that a generalized HR partner or internal or external recruiters will be reading your resume first. These recruiters may be somewhat familiar with the roles they are screening resumes for, but they are still predominantly generalists, not as specialized as the engineers and ML professionals you'll actually be working with. This part of the screening process leads to several hidden criteria for your resume, which is why it might be baffling when your resume doesn't clear this step even if you have a relevant background.

It's important to remember that these generalists will likely pass along your resume to the hiring manager if they:

- See key technologies or experiences on your resume based on the job posting
- See years of experience in key technologies or experiences or, in the case of entry-level or new-grad jobs, sufficient evidence that you can be easily trained
- Understand that your skills and accomplishments are relevant, in plain language

To determine whether your resume meets the criteria, the recruiter will likely be searching for keywords and comparing your resume to the job posting. They will not automatically "translate" skills on your resume for you. For example, if the job description says "Python" and your resume says "C++," at this step they will likely not consider that, since both programming languages are object oriented, you could probably learn Python quickly if you put in the effort.

---

18 I provide a much longer list and overview in Chapter 2.

Do Applicant Tracking Systems Automatically Reject Your Resume, Even If You Are Qualified?

There has been some debate at this stage on *ATS*, which is an acronym for *applicant tracking system*. While companies do use systems such as Workday to manage applications, there hasn't been concrete proof (*https://oreil.ly/603SA*) that companies are using them to programmatically filter *out* resumes at this step for each job posting (Figure 1-10).

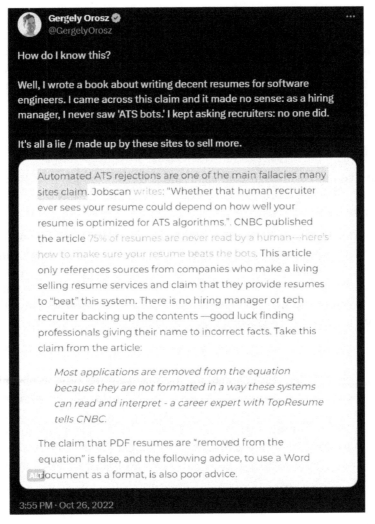

Figure 1-10. Gergely Orosz (founder of The Pragmatic Engineer publication and former manager at Uber) on ATS (screenshot via Twitter).

In practice, recruiters use them at most to filter resumes *into* a selection to fulfill existing criteria on the job posting, such as those mentioned on the previous page. I also haven't seen ATS automatically filter out *qualified* candidates during full-time work experience, and once I was responsible for manually reading a PDF containing more than 50 resumes. However, I don't want to claim that automated ATS rejections are fully untrue. To be safe, in this book I assume both standpoints have some truth to it. So even if ATS is an issue, the steps in this book will help you, since I'll teach you the principles for how resume selection is conducted. (You can read more on ATS on *thetechresume.com* (*https://oreil.ly/PRx9H*).)

If you're able to describe your experiences at a level that HR recruiters can understand is relevant to the job posting, you will increase your chances at the resume-screening step. HR and recruiters, by nature of the role, are aware of higher-level technologies and what's popular with the roles they're hiring for but not the details, so it's important for your resume to be optimized well. (Read more on how to optimize your resume in Chapter 2.)

Applying via a Referral

Now that I've walked through cold applications directly via job boards or websites without any referral, I'll provide some examples of how referrals can help you fast-track the process.

Let's say you're interested in an ML job at ARI Corporation.[19] You know an alum of your university who works on the ML team. You catch up with them and express your interest in the job. During the chat, you show the alum some of your personal ML projects, which are relevant to the ML job you're interested in. The school alum agrees to refer you and gives you instructions for how to be referred, something that depends on the way the HR system of the company is set up.

Since this alum knows you and is willing to vouch for your skills after seeing your personal projects, you get your resume to the "top of the pile." Depending on the strength of the referral/recommendation, you may skip the resume screening altogether and get a highly guaranteed callback from a recruiter or even bypass the recruiter directly and get to the rest of the interview rounds. This is illustrated in Figure 1-11. Note that I say "highly" guaranteed here since it still depends on various factors such as timing. As an example: maybe you got referred, but the job posting has coincidentally just been filled. Thus, you didn't get to the rest of the interview.

I will cover more on referrals and how to get them via professional networking in Chapter 2.

---

19 Fictional name, but I wanted to try using something other than ABC Corp. or Acme Corp.

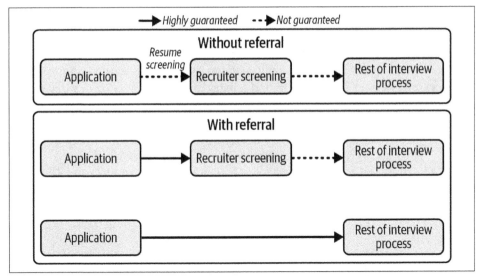

Figure 1-11. The interview process can be shortcut with a strong referral.

Preinterview Checklist

You've been invited to an interview! How do you perform your best? Maybe time is limited; what do you do to ensure that you can maximize your outcome?

Review your notes and questions that you fumbled

My personal tactic is to first narrow down the types of questions that might be asked. For example, in the first round of an Amazon interview, the recruiter has outlined the format and it will focus on statistical theory questions. I will read online resources, skim over my notes, and see what topics I'm the weakest on. I will focus less on the questions that I know I can answer confidently and more on those that seem more likely to be asked but that I don't know well. As to how I "guess" what will likely be asked, that is based mostly on conversations with the recruiter and my follow-up questions to the recruiter or hiring manager. I'm not super accurate at guessing, and this is similar to trying to guess what will come up in a university exam—it could work well, or it could backfire!

Either way, there's the trade-off between knowing a subset of questions well or knowing all questions roughly but not as well (depth vs. breadth). When reviewing my preparation notes, I personally go for breadth, but your results may vary depending on how well you know the material already.

Scheduling the interview

Depending on your location and your interviewers' location, there may be time zone differences. I try to find the time when I have the most energy possible. Sometimes the available interview time slots aren't ideal, so I choose the lesser of the evils (for example, interviewing from GMT+8 and talking to someone in GMT-4 while traveling abroad).

 To make it easy to figure out time zones for candidates invited to an interview, it's common for HR-scheduling software to have a calendar feature where you can input your preferred times and it will account for your local time zones. However, sometimes the time will be set via back-and-forth emails, and tools such as Calendly or Cal.com can help.

As both an interviewer and interviewee, I am wary of scheduling right at the beginning of a workday. This is so that I have more time to prepare after I wake up. But of course, if no other time slots are available, then I will select the early time.

Preinterview tech prep

As an interviewer, I've seen countless candidates' interviews start late because of connection issues or using a new web-conferencing software—for example, not being able to set up Zoom on time because they hadn't used it before. As a candidate, I've been tripped up and wasted time when needing to use Microsoft Teams because on my personal computers I only had Zoom and Google Meet. In the end, I used the browser version, but there was an issue with my login since my Microsoft student account had expired. We finally got it sorted out, a few minutes later. This could have been avoided if I had tried to sign in a bit earlier or on the day before the interview.

Here are some tips to help your interview go more smoothly:

Try your best to be in a quiet environment.
Some software, such as Zoom, has pretty good built-in noise canceling, as do some wireless headphones.

Check your audio and video beforehand.
Video-wise, make sure the lighting is good and your camera lens is clean. Sound-wise, make sure your mic sounds clear. On Windows and Mac, there are built-in camera and voice recording apps that I use. You could also start a new Zoom, Google Meet, or Teams session and run a test.

Keep a mental list of backup options.
Did the internet at your home suddenly go down before the interview? Is there a nearby cafe with (preferably secure) internet that you could go to? Can you use your phone data? Are there dial-in options via phone on the calendar invite?

Knowing these things beforehand can help you a lot. I've had to dial in once to an interview, and thankfully, I knew that I had the option to.

Recruiter Screening

Congrats, your resume has made it past the resume screening! Now let's go through an example to illustrate what might happen next.

Let's imagine that there were 200 applicants for the role. The recruiter has gone through them and removed 170 that either lacked relevant experience or for some reason didn't seem to fit the role. Recall that this is based on the impression your resume gave the recruiter; it's possible that with the same job title and same recruiter team, an improved resume would have passed. If you had a good referral, your resume might have already moved forward. Now that there are 30 applicants, the recruiter will call each of them; this is usually a shorter interview, 15 to 30 minutes long. We refer to this as the "recruiter screening" or "recruiter call."

Generally, the recruiter wants to see what you're like as a person and if you're easy to work with. If someone blatantly claims to have experience that they don't, the call could reveal fabricated work or school experiences. There are other logistical issues to screen for, such as location, salary expectations, and legal status.

 The recruiter screening is more of a "smell test" instead of an in-depth test of your technical skills and experience.

My tip for success is to optimize for one thing: that the *recruiter* understands that you are a good candidate, that your experience is relevant (or you can learn fast), and that you can fit well into the team and role they are hiring for. This is *different* from convincing a hiring manager of the same things, or an interview panel of senior MLEs. Instead, you will succeed here if you make the additional effort to connect your resume to the job description on this call.

Here's an example of some bullet points in a job description:

- "The candidate has experience with recommender systems."
- "Experience with data processing such as Spark, Snowflake, or Hadoop."
- "The candidate has experience with Python."

A bad example of explaining your experience on the recruiter call for this job is: "For that past project, I used the ALS algorithm, which was implemented with PySpark."

A better example of explaining your experience on the recruiter call for this job is: "For that past project, I used the alternating least squares (ALS) algorithm, which is a *recommender systems* algorithm based off of matrix factorization, and I used PySpark, which is *Spark* that's wrapped with a *Python* API." Note that the italicized phrases also appear in the job description.

The better example allows a recruiter to match up more of your skills to the job description, whereas the bad example doesn't match up to the posted skills in an obvious manner. When you're writing your resume, you have limited space; the real-time conversation of an interview is a chance for you to fill in gaps that the recruiter may not have noticed.

It's also important to expand on acronyms. This is true for interviews conducted with technical people too. I'm relatively specialized in recommender systems and reinforcement learning, but I don't work with computer vision tasks in my day-to-day work. I appreciated it when a candidate I interviewed was talking about computer vision projects and generally explained the more niche techniques. You can (and should) do this in a way that's not condescending to your interviewer, whether they are a recruiter or part of your future team.

The recruiter call is a good time for you as the candidate to assess the job as well. You can ask questions that you care about, to see if you should continue to interview. For example, I might ask about the team size and if this job focuses more on ML or data analyst responsibilities. You can also prepare some questions about the company and their products. For example, is the team's current project focused on improving the click-through rate or long-term engagement? If you're a user of the product, you might have a lot of ideas and questions to discuss. This is also a chance to show your enthusiasm and knowledge of the company.

Overview of Main Interview Loop

On to the next step. Good news: the recruiter cleared you! You explained your previous experience well, and the recruiter was able to understand your past work and how it connects to the job description they have on hand.

But it's not over yet. You're among 15 other candidates who succeeded at the first recruiter screening. The recruiter informs you of upcoming technical interviews which include ML theory, programming, and a case study interview. There are also behavioral interviews sprinkled throughout. If you pass those, you'll make it to the on-site interview, which is often the final round. These days, there are also virtual on-sites/final rounds. If you pass the final round, you'll be extended an offer.

Technical interviews

Let's break down the various types of interviews that take place after the recruiter screening, the first being technical interviews. Technical interviews are typically conducted with technical individual contributors (ICs), such as an MLE or a data scientist.

There may be multiple rounds of technical interviews; there could be one that is a data-focused coding round or one in which the interviewer presents some fictitious example data and asks you to use SQL or Python pandas/NumPy (sometimes there are multiple questions, and you use various programming tools throughout the interview). I'll expand more on this type of interview structure and interview questions in Chapter 5.

Apart from ML and data-focused programming interviews, you might be asked brainteaser-type questions. For this type of interview, you might use an interview platform such as CoderPad or HackerRank, where the interviewer presents you with a question and you code in the online integrated development environment (IDE) that both you and your interviewer can see in real time. Sometimes you'll get other formats, such as technical deep dives, systems design, take-home exercises in a private repo or Google Colab, and so on. I'll elaborate on how to prepare for these types of interviews in Chapters 5 and 6.

These subsequent interview rounds could further reduce the number of candidates before the final round. In our example, fifteen candidates passed the recruiter screen, and eight passed the first round of technical interviews. After the second round of technical interviews, we're left with three candidates who will proceed to the on-site interview.

Behavioral interviews

Interspersed during the interview process are questions meant to assess how you react in certain situations. The intent often is to use past experience to predict future performance and understand how you react to high-stress or difficult situations. In addition, these questions assess your soft skills, such as communication and teamwork skills. You'll want to prepare a few past experiences and relay them in a storytelling fashion.

For example, during your first recruiter call, the recruiter might ask about a time when you dealt with a difficult timeline on a project. Once you've responded you won't be out of the woods yet. During the on-site, an hour is often dedicated to behavioral questions. And in some technical interviews, you might be asked a couple of questions that are a mix between a purely technical question and a behavioral question. I'll help you succeed with behavioral interviews in Chapter 7, which also has tips on company-specific preparation, such as Amazon's Leadership Principles (*https://oreil.ly/Q6GC-*).

The on-site final round

For many companies there is an "on-site" final round or the virtual equivalent. These are usually back-to-back interviews. For example, starting in the morning, you might meet with a technical director for a case study interview and then a senior data scientist for a programming interview. After a lunch break, you might meet with two data scientists who ask about ML theory, and then the hiring manager asks more behavioral questions and probes about your past experiences. In addition to technical interviewers, you may speak with a stakeholder (e.g., a product manager on an adjacent team that the team you're interviewing for works closely with). In several final-round interviews I've been through, there was a product manager interviewer or someone from another department that the ML team worked closely with, such as marketing or advertising.

Some companies will have an additional mini round after this, such as a quick chat with a skip level (your manager's manager).

Summary

In this chapter, you've learned about various ML roles, the ML lifecycle, and the different responsibilities that map onto the ML lifecycle. You've also seen how you make your way from the beginning of the process to the final round of interviews. There's a lot to prepare for and to learn about, but now you have an overview and hopefully some thoughts on how you can target your preparations.

Now that this chapter has set the foundation, I'll walk through a detailed job application guide, including a resume guide, to help you greatly increase your chances of getting interviews.

## CHAPTER 2

Machine Learning Job Application and Resume

To successfully land job offers in the field of machine learning, not only do you have to prepare for the interviews themselves, but you must first get interviews. During the application process, there are many opportunities to make your profile stand out from the crowd and increase the number of interviews you get. If you are currently struggling with getting callbacks from your applications, this chapter teaches you how to optimize your applications for much better and relevant results. If you're just starting out, this chapter provides an in-depth walkthrough of the process that will help you avoid mistakes going in.

Where Are the Jobs?

You want to find an ML job, but where? You may know of online job boards such as LinkedIn or Indeed, but there are other places where I and countless other ML professionals have found jobs, too. Table 2-1 provides a list of additional job sites and informal methods of learning about job listings.

Table 2-1. Methods for learning about job listings with examples

How to learn about job listings	Examples
Online job applications (all types)	LinkedIn (*https://www.linkedin.com*) (the "easy apply" option is convenient)
	Indeed (*https://www.indeed.com*)
	Dice (*https://www.dice.com*)
	Directly on company sites since they may not post to the major job sites
	Regional job sites, if international sites like LinkedIn aren't popular in your area
	Job listings shared during community events or on Slack or Discord channels

How to learn about job listings	Examples
Online job applications (startup focused)	Wellfound (*https://wellfound.com*) (previously known as AngelList Talent (*https://www.angellist.com/*)) Work at a Startup (*https://www.workatastartup.com*) Regional startup job sites Directly on the startup's career page
Networking	Word of mouth Informational interviews Coffee chats Cold messaging

ML Job Application Guide

This section will walk you through choosing a strategy for applying for jobs, and the following resume guide will help you create an optimized job application.

Your Effectiveness per Application

Some folks have had success getting jobs without any networking. In fact, my second job was a cold application; I didn't know anyone working at the company at the time. But from a probability standpoint, I would need to send out more applications and do more interviews if I applied only to companies where I didn't have any referrals. The following is a mental equation I use to assess this:

$$\text{Applications} \times \text{Effectiveness per application (EPA)} \rightarrow \text{Interview invites}$$

The more applications you send out, regardless of EPA, the more you increase your chances of getting an interview. Indiscriminately sending out a vast number of applications—a "spray and pray" approach—might be able to make up for a low EPA.

On the other hand, if you want to have the same number of interviews but submit fewer applications, you'll need to increase your EPA on average. Filtering through job postings for suitable ones or tailoring your resume can increase your EPA. You'll need fewer applications to get the same number of interviews (most of the time).

So which type of strategy should you choose? You *don't* have to get referrals or tailor your resume, but be prepared to send out more applications in this scenario. It's your choice! If you prefer the mass-application approach, feel free to skip the following sections, though I recommend reading them.

Here are some strategies to increase your EPA, which I'll elaborate on in the following section (see Figure 2-1):

Get job referrals.
> Get referred for ML jobs and use networking to increase your chances of being referred.

Vet jobs before applying.

   If you invest the time to find and apply for jobs that your skills are more suitable for, that can increase your EPA.

Tailor your resume.

   In conjunction with vetting jobs, you can rearrange your resume to highlight keywords and skills that are most relevant to your target jobs.

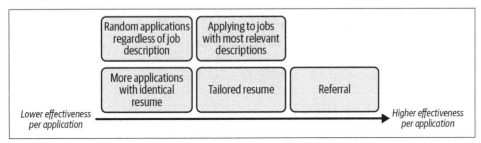

Figure 2-1. Job applications and their effectiveness per application.

Diversify Your Investments, I Mean, Job Applications

I have had good success applying to jobs that I've had referrals for, but does that mean I apply only for jobs when I have a referral? To be honest, no. I also send out resumes for jobs that may not be the best fit, and do not always tailor my resume. You don't have to *maximize* your EPA for every *single* application, but as long as you are getting some referrals, you are increasing your EPA on average. You can mix and match depending on your time commitments; sometimes I just don't have the time or energy to reach out to someone to ask for a referral, or don't feel that I know the connection at the company well enough to ask. So I just cold apply.

Job Referrals

In Chapter 1, I mentioned that job referrals can help you rise to the top of the "stack of resumes" or even guarantee that you get a recruiter call. In some cases, if you're a referred (i.e., recommended) candidate, you can even bypass the initial recruiter call and skip to a later stage of the interview process, as illustrated in Figure 1-11. In this chapter, I mention how referrals are one way to improve your EPA. I personally think it's great to make use of referrals when possible. This does require that the person referring you is willing to put their reputation on the line, because by referring you, they are suggesting that you will be successful once you are hired.

The following are three examples, with screenshots, of reaching out for referrals, coffee chats that led to a referral, and informational interviews.

A common misconception is that referrals are a silver bullet to getting hired. This is not true since a referral often only gets you through the first round of the process; the rest is up to you. The subsequent interview rounds will still put you through the wringer.

Job referral example 1: Successful intern networking and outreach

Here's an example of an intern candidate I once referred to my team. We had met when he attended an ML journal club meetup that I had coorganized called AISC (Figure 2-2). After another event I hosted, I reached out to him because he had presented a great five-minute "lightning" talk. We had a brief back and forth that concluded the conversation, after which we didn't speak for another two years!

Figure 2-2. Referral example 1: brief conversation after meeting at an ML journal club.

Later, in 2022, he reached out to me to chat about a role in the company where I was working. Since I recognized him from when he attended the ML journal club a few years ago and remembered our conversation, I gladly referred him (Figure 2-3).

Figure 2-3. Referral example 1: referring an intern job candidate.

This is a good example of reaching out when you've known each other and are professional acquaintances, which could result in a referral, interview, or job offer down the road.

Job referral example 2: Warm outreach to learn more about a job posting

Here's another example of a "warm"[1] outreach (Figure 2-4). This person messaged me, mentioning a conference we had both attended. We had spoken only briefly at the conference, but even that mention was enough to get my attention in a crowded inbox. I agreed to have a quick call and answer some questions about the job posting.

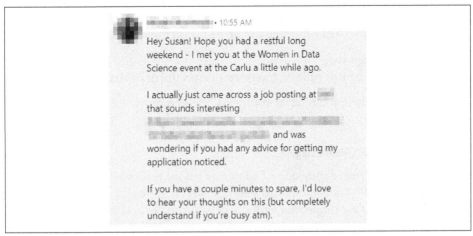

Figure 2-4. Referral example 2: warm reachout to ask about a job posting.

During the call, I asked the person about their past experiences. After hearing about their relevant data experience, I offered to refer them before they explicitly asked (Figure 2-5).

Figure 2-5. Referral example 2: A message where I referred a job seeker.[2]

---

1 As opposed to "cold," where both parties don't know each other at the time of reaching out.

2 At the company where I worked at the time, the way referrals worked was that the applicant could put in the employee ID themselves on the job portal. However, I've worked with other HR systems where the referrer (in that case, me) would have to put the person I'm referring into the system myself. Once again, it depends! Double-check with your referrer.

Here are some reasons I agreed to speak to the candidate and to refer them:

State a connection.
They stated where they had met me before. In some cases, job seekers mention reading my blog or seeing me speak. They may mention something as simple as seeing one of my LinkedIn posts (it's important to be specific about which one).

Be specific.
They linked the job posting or mentioned details about why they were reaching out. Sometimes I get very broad questions, such as "How do I enter data science?" In those situations, even if I have a coffee chat with them, I'll be duplicating and repeating information that they could get in one of my blog posts, or from this book! A call or meeting should be meant for a deeper conversation.

Politeness goes a long way.
They weren't pushy or rude and were very respectful of my time.

The intern candidate in job referral example 1 also demonstrated these traits in their reachout.

Job referral example 3: Cold message

Here's an example where someone I hadn't met before reached out for a coffee chat (Figure 2-6). Note that she mentioned seeing a specific LinkedIn post I wrote, which echoes the tip to *state a connection* with the person you're reaching out to. This message was for a general chat, not a specific job posting, but the fact she brought up both AI and game development, which are specific niches I'm interested in, was enough to prompt me to set up a meeting. This was relatively easy to do as we were both based in the downtown Toronto area at the time.

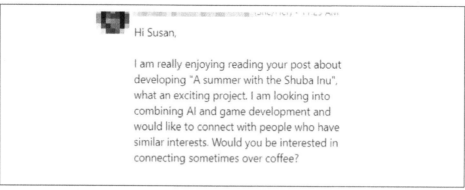

Figure 2-6. Referral example 3: coffee-chat request.

During the meeting, we chatted in depth about various ML and AI topics and game development, which gave me the confidence that this was someone I could keep in mind to refer. In fact, my team was hiring at the time, which I mentioned. Sadly, she had recently started a new job, so I wasn't able to refer her, but in an UNO Reverse[3] situation, she offered to refer *me* to her new employer (Figure 2-7)!

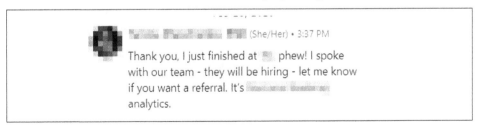

Thank you, I just finished at ▓ phew! I spoke with our team - they will be hiring - let me know if you want a referral. It's ▓▓▓ ▓▓▓▓ analytics.

(She/Her) • 3:37 PM

Figure 2-7. Referral example 3: UNO Reverse referral offer.

Networking

As you can see from these three examples, you can get referrals with a thoughtful message. Attending events and conferences can increase the number of warm connections you can reach out to when the time comes.

Many experienced leaders in the industry are proponents of referrals. Here are some examples:

> A significant amount of hiring occurs through channels such as cold-emailing managers, warm introductions via referrals, or networking events. In fact, I advise my mentees to never apply through the job board/company website unless it is absolutely necessary.
>
> —Suhas Pai, CTO of Bedrock AI

> In some roles, you can shortcut the resume screening and recruiter call if you're a trusted referral.
>
> —Eugene Yan, Senior Applied Scientist at Amazon

So, how do you "network"? When I was a student, this term *greatly* confused me. "Say I go to conferences and meetups, so what? People don't want to refer me to jobs just by meeting me once..." If you think that, then you're probably right—people usually won't refer you unless there's a reason for them to do so.

Luckily, many companies, especially big tech and larger companies, give referral bonuses. This means that if an employee refers someone who gets hired, they receive money or rewards. Usually, there is a requirement that the new hires have to stay for six months or so to prevent abuse of the reward system. Referral programs incentivize employees to find people in their networks to refer to job openings.

---

3 In the card game UNO, there is a card you can play that allows you to reverse the order in which people take turns. It can also refer to a situation where the intended action or consequence is turned back on the initiator!

In addition, ML is in high demand, so some companies even struggle to hire. Many companies and teams source qualified candidates through referrals from friends, former colleagues, university peers, and more. So even if you don't have a strong network (yet), people do have an incentive to keep an eye out for suitable job candidates.

These are the steps I use:

1. Look at meetups, conferences, and the like happening in person or online.
2. Go to events (usually free).
3. At each event, meet just one new person.

With this small goal, over time you will meet more people working at various companies. Even if you go to only one event per month, over the course of a year you will have met 12 people who may be willing to vouch for you when you apply to their employer in the future. Or you may even meet startup founders who can hire you more easily because they know you.

Networking is a long-term investment, and the rewards will appear over the long-term horizon. One misconception that people have is that networking only encompasses this scenario: you *first* find some jobs you're interested in and then reach out to people related to that company or job. If you're networking *only* when you're already applying, you will be stressed out and stretched thin on time—not to mention, it might be too late.

If you've been meeting people and know people from other companies, or even alumni from your university, bootcamp, and so forth, you can reach out when you see a job posting at their company. If you aren't sure how to start, refer to the successful examples in the previous section.

 Even if you don't think you're "good at" meeting new people, it's a skill that can be learned and practiced. Set the small goal of meeting just one new person when you go to any networking event, meetup, or conference. It really adds up.

Beyond getting referrals, there are strong benefits of networking. Here is an example from when I was a new graduate: I met two final-round interviewers (director level) at two different companies before I even applied to their job postings, merely by attending conferences and meetups.[4] I got both offers. Neither of them referred me, but I still got the benefit of networking since both had interacted with me at some

---

4 You can read the full details in my blog post: "Why Networking Is Like Investing in an Index Fund—How I Met Multiple Interviewers by Attending Events" (*https://oreil.ly/bKizY*).

point; they were warm connections, rather than interviewers I was meeting for the first time in the interview.

Machine Learning Resume Guide

I mentioned tailoring your resume as a way to increase your EPA, but whether you plan to tailor your resume or not, you'll still need at least one version of it. This section will guide you through creating your first resume. If you already have one, you can skim this section for tips and best practices, then head to the part where you tailor your resume or other sections you're interested in.

Take Inventory of Your Past Experience

Before you start writing your resume, you should jot down an inventory of what you've done in the past. This inventory includes past work experience, ML projects at school or at work—anything that could be relevant to ML and data science. If you don't have any personal or school projects or work experience outside of ML, you can still take an inventory; this will help you figure out what else you need to learn to close the gap between your current skills and your target ML role.

As an example, when I was a new grad (with less than one year of working experience), my inventory looked like this:

University
- Econometrics research paper about video game prices on Steam, with data I scraped myself
- Econometrics research paper about Reddit engagement, with data I scraped myself

First full-time job
- ML churn model I built

Exercise 2-1

Write down a list of jobs or major projects (school, personal, etc.) that you've done. Feel free to focus on ML-related ones, but at this stage, anything loosely related can count. (Did you do data cleaning? Use Python? Add it.) Include your education, certificates, anything relevant. These don't have to be in resume-bullet form; they can just be an unformatted text list or jotted on a notepad. Set a timer for 30 minutes, do it, and come back. This book will miss you but needs you to do this!

From the inventory that you listed in "Exercise 2-1" on page 37, pick three to five experiences you feel are most relevant to ML roles in general. Refer to Table 1-3, the ML and data skills matrix, again. For your targeted ML roles, are the experiences on your list relevant so far or not? If you feel that you don't have three relevant ML or data experiences, you can temporarily pad out three experiences with the work or school experiences that were the most substantial and "impressive." Don't worry about it being perfect at this stage; you can always go back to your longer inventory and pick another one later.

Next, list everything you did related to those top three experiences: this includes not only technical parts related to coding, ML, or data but also soft skills, such as presenting the results to your team or organizing a group chat to coordinate teammates.

To continue using the example from my own initial, unrefined inventory, here's what I would include:

University student experience example

> *Econometrics research paper about Reddit engagement, with data I scraped myself*
> - Scraped Reddit with Python
> - Cleaned data with Python
> - Performed statistical modeling with Python, Stata
> - Visualized results with Python
> - Created presentation of project with LaTeX
> - Presented project overview and results to seminar class of 10 people and professor

First job (less than one year experience) example

> *My first ML churn model*
> - Exploratory data analysis (EDA) with SQL, Python
> - Cleaned data with SQL
> - Trained logistic regression model with SAS on tabular data; created ensemble model in SAS
> - Ran model evaluation and analyzed results with SAS, SQL, Python
> - Created simplified and cleaner visualization to use in presentation with Excel, PowerPoint
> - Presented the results with PowerPoint
> - Collaborated with ML engineer to put the model in production

Overview of Resume Sections

Now that you have a starter list of your past experiences to refine, let's look at the sections of a resume. These are the core sections of your resume:

- Experience
- Education

These are optional sections:

- Skills summary
- Volunteering
- Interests
- Other sections (your name of choice)

Don't worry about filling in the optional sections yet; doing so will depend on what you have in your core sections and whether they are already lengthy.

Experience

Use the top three experiences you provided in your inventory for "Exercise 2-1" on page 37. You should also gather the following pieces of information:

- Job title
- Place where you worked
- Time frame you worked there (e.g., May 2018 to November 2021)
- Bullet points of your responsibilities from "Exercise 2-2"
- Any other information that might be expected in your region, industry, or work culture

An example of a section of your *initial* resume might look like this:

Data Scientist, ARI Corporation (May 2021 to Present)

- Design and develop collaborative filtering models for web page personalization

- Develop ETL[5] production code that aggregates predictive model scores according to user specification
- Develop predicting ensemble model to optimize marketing campaign planning and touchpoints

You don't need to format your resume in a template just yet; it's more efficient to pin down the contents first before you deal with formatting (sometimes adding just one word breaks your beautiful layout and you spend more time than it's worth to fix it...). Note that I'll link to some common templates at the end of this section.

Here are some more tips to improve your initial bullet points:

Use action verbs to start the sentences.
For example, instead of writing "Image recognition with TensorFlow," write "*Developed* image recognition model with TensorFlow." (The action verb is italicized for illustration; you don't need to italicize it on your resume.) This can help clarify what you *did* during your experience, not just the outcome (which was likely a team effort).

 You can find a larger list of action verbs from the University of Washington: Action Verbs for Resume Writing. (*https://oreil.ly/NsWMe*)

Specify your impact, ideally in a way that's quantified and easy to understand.
[*Original*] Design and develop collaborative filtering models for web page personalization

[*Modified*] Design and develop collaborative filtering models for web page personalization, resulting in 2x engagement rates compared to baseline

Add tools and programming languages you used.
[*Original*] Design and develop collaborative filtering models for web page personalization

[*Modified*] Design and develop collaborative filtering (ALS) models with PySpark and MLlib for web page personalization, resulting in 2x engagement rates compared to baseline

At some point, the word count might become too long, and you'll have to cut down on what you've written. Tinker around with the wording to see what the most essential information is to keep.

---

5 *ETL* refers to extract, transform, and load data.

Education

The points here are pretty similar to the Experience section; you should also include the following pieces of information:

- School/institution you attended
- Location, country (optional but recommended)
- Time frame when you studied there (e.g., May 2018 to November 2021)
- Bullet points of major projects and assignments related to ML or data
- Any other information that might be expected in your region, industry, or work culture

The following is a example of what this section might look like:

University of Waterloo

Waterloo, Canada, 2010–2015

- Scraped and cleaned sales data with Python, pandas
- Forecasted video game prices with ARIMA time-series model

Now that you have the core sections, take a look at the optional sections. Do you have a lot of projects and experience in your core section? If you do, then you may not have space to add volunteering. For example, when I was a new graduate, I added a skills summary and volunteering experience section to pad out the space since I barely had any experience.

 If you have other experience, I suggest that you focus first on refining your existing bullet points before you start padding your resume with irrelevant content. Too much additional content might only serve to distract recruiters and hiring managers from noticing the most crucial and important skills that you have.

Exercise 2-3

Take a look at your Experience and Education sections so far. Do they look robust and relevant enough for any of the target roles in Figure 1-8? Are there any bullet points that your peers interested in ML have but that you're missing? Don't worry yet—we'll create an action plan at the end of this chapter and throughout this book. The point here is to start self-reflecting and connecting your experiences to the ML jobs we talked about earlier. For now, are there any volunteering experiences, interests, or additional experiences that you have that are relevant? Write them down.

Skills summary

The skills summary is a place to list a bunch of programming languages and frameworks you have had exposure to. Beware: don't exaggerate too much; if you list a framework or library here that doesn't match up with what you've elaborated on in the bullet points, the technical interviewers might ask you to elaborate. Everything you've listed on your resume is fair game to ask about. Here's an example:

Skills summary

- Python
- TensorFlow, PyTorch
- NumPy/pandas, Polars
- C++
- And so on…

Interviewer's Perspective: Should You Include a Skills Section on Your Resume?

When I review resumes, I tend to skip this area and go straight to the work experience bullet points. However, this may vary depending on the reviewer; a skills section might be more relevant to a recruiter who's trying to match off of the job description, for example, and the more you have listed there, the more likely there will be overlap with a job description.

Volunteering

For this section, you can just use bullet points on one line instead of grouping them under an experience unless (1) your volunteering experience is very impactful and substantial, in which case I might just put it under the Experience section, or (2) you're *really* trying to pad out your resume. Here's an example:

Volunteering experience

- Volunteer, SIGIR Conference 2023, Taipei
- Volunteer, Toronto Machine Learning Summit, 2020, Toronto
- And so on…

Interests

Some people recommend including this section to show that you have some interests outside of work. In my opinion, the general rule applies that if you don't have space, you can drop these optional sections without consequence. On the other hand, you can keep it if your interests are something cool like chess grandmaster or equestrian cup title holder—whatever you're proud of. When I was a student, I padded this area with the following:

Interests

- Team Fortress 2 scrap trader, 2012–2015
- AISC (formerly Toronto Deep Learning Series) blog editor, 2019
- And so on…

Yes, I put video-game-related interests in my resume. Yes, I did trade scrap metal, an informal online currency[6] in Team Fortress 2, an online game. There's a whole economy around it. Yes, it was really because I had to pad the space and for no other reason. However, no one asked me about it.

Additional resume sections

You can choose to add other sections, which pretty much follow the same format as the Volunteering and Interests sections. I encourage you to do this if you have notable interests, volunteering, and whatnot that would make more sense to rename under their own sections. For example, once I started public speaking, I had enough entries to warrant a new section, replacing my Volunteering section on my resume:

Public speaking

- Keynote speaker, O'Reilly AI Superstream (MLOps)
- Keynote speaker, PyCon DE & PyData Berlin
- And so on…

Resume Resources

- "Resume Checklist" (*https://oreil.ly/F7XhB*) to make sure your resume looks polished (University of Waterloo)
- Action verbs for when you run out of ideas: "Action Verbs for Resume Writing" (University of Washington) (*https://oreil.ly/NsWMe*)
- Resume format and checklist (*https://oreil.ly/_koWG*) via CareerCup (North America focused)
- Resume templates on Overleaf (*https://oreil.ly/zcBf7*) (LaTeX markdown): The one I've used for the last five years is AltaCV (*https://oreil.ly/emhFz*) (two-

---

6 I'm wondering if my fellow economics enthusiasts will define virtual online materials as commodity money or not. In-game scrap metal items can be used to enhance game weapons, so there is a use for them.

column). I personalized the template by removing the graphics, leaving only text. A popular single-column template is Modern-Deedy (*https://oreil.ly/nyKWd*).

That's it for this section. As usual, be sure to check if there are any regional expectations for information you should include in your resume. I also have included a resume-related FAQ at the end of this chapter.

Tailoring Your Resume to Your Desired Role(s)

Now that you have your basic resume, let's look into how to tailor it for common ML job titles (see Figure 1-8). If the job title you're looking for isn't in Figure 1-8, you can map it to the ML lifecycle (Figure 1-5) and use the same tips for similar roles in the ML lifecycle. Recall that you don't have to tailor your resume for every job application, but even if you do it only for the most common job titles that you are interested in, you can increase your EPA on average.

If you refer back to the skills matrix (Table 1-3), you can probably see why tailoring your resume can be useful: if you have "programming tools" and "statistics" skills, you can possibly apply for both DS (data scientist) and MLE roles, but to highlight additional skills that differ between the two roles, changing some bullet points will help market your skills better. The ML skills matrix (Table 1-3) helps you narrow down job titles that fit your past experience better, but from then on, your job search is dependent on the actual job descriptions.

Once you start to look at job descriptions, you might sometimes see DS postings that involve skills mapped to the data analyst role ("product" data science), and sometimes the job posting could map more to the MLE role on the matrix.

Exercise 2-4

Head over to the job postings search engine of your choice! I personally like to start with LinkedIn since I'm familiar with the platform, but most jobs from bigger companies are cross-posted on all the major platforms anyway.

Start typing in a few job titles (you can use Figure 1-8 for the common ML job titles as inspiration). Click on ones that catch your eye and look at the job descriptions. Are there any keywords that match up with bullet points on your resume? After browsing some more, note any keywords, tools, or frameworks that show up repeatedly. Do you have that skill, or would it be worth learning so that your resume can match up more closely with those job descriptions?

In my own experience, my job title has been data scientist for all of my full-time roles, but I've always been focused on building and deploying ML models into a product or improving the ML product. Based on the matrix, I've done everything from MLE to applied scientist, and even some MLOps-related roles.

Let's now imagine that I'm browsing jobs online and you're looking over my shoulder. I'm going to search "Spotify machine learning" and start clicking into the results, beginning with the example in Figure 2-8.

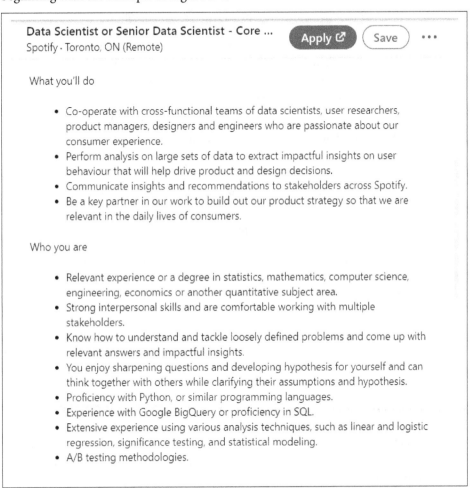

Figure 2-8. Screenshot of Spotify data scientist job posting via LinkedIn.

Job posting example 1: Data scientist

After reading this Data Scientist posting (Figure 2-8), I write down what I think is important:

- Cooperation with stakeholders, communication (mentioned multiple times and at the top of the bullet points)
- Perform data analysis, using BigQuery or SQL
- Some statistical modeling such as linear, logistic regression

Next, I'll look back at my resume experience—for example, the bullet points for a previous job where I made my first ML churn model—and map it to the data scientist posting. If you haven't finished up your resume yet, you can use the inventory list that you made for "Exercise 2-2" on page 39.

The most relevant out of the points from my first ML churn model (see "Take Inventory of Your Past Experience" on page 37) that I initially wrote down are:

- Performed exploratory data analysis (EDA) with SQL, Python
- Created simplified and cleaner visualization to use in presentation with Excel, PowerPoint
- Presented the results with PowerPoint

Based on the ML lifecycle, it feels like this role is more focused on reporting and data analysis (step D in Figure 1-5), so I should make sure I am interested in that part of the lifecycle before proceeding to actually tailoring my resume.

If I'm interested in applying for this data scientist role, I'll focus on the three points I listed from the job description and shorten or remove the other bullets. Recall the inventory list you created for "Exercise 2-2" on page 39; if you have other experiences more relevant to this job posting, swap them in. If your current resume is pretty relevant to this job posting, then you can keep it as is.

If you do remove some less relevant points, keep an eye out for the space remaining in your resume. How much you remove depends on how much space you have on your resume! I have more experience now so I err on the side of removing more, while early on I chose to pad more points and hardly ever removed points. It's fine to remove things as long as the core is there; if the interviewers are interested in how I train more complex ML models—a bullet point I removed since it wasn't on the job description—they can ask me in the interview.

Job posting example 2: Machine learning engineer

Let's continue to scroll through the search results for "Spotify machine learning" and look at another posting in Figure 2-9.

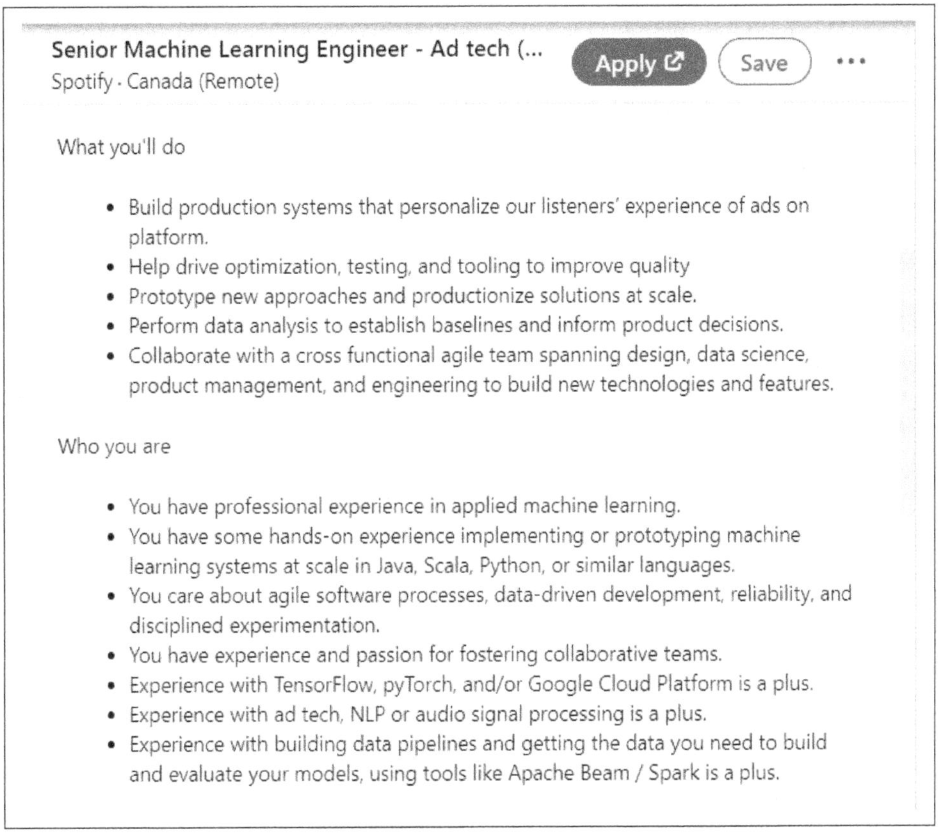
Senior Machine Learning Engineer - Ad tech (...
Apply
Save
Spotify · Canada (Remote)

What you'll do

- Build production systems that personalize our listeners' experience of ads on platform.
- Help drive optimization, testing, and tooling to improve quality
- Prototype new approaches and productionize solutions at scale.
- Perform data analysis to establish baselines and inform product decisions.
- Collaborate with a cross functional agile team spanning design, data science, product management, and engineering to build new technologies and features.

Who you are

- You have professional experience in applied machine learning.
- You have some hands-on experience implementing or prototyping machine learning systems at scale in Java, Scala, Python, or similar languages.
- You care about agile software processes, data-driven development, reliability, and disciplined experimentation.
- You have experience and passion for fostering collaborative teams.
- Experience with TensorFlow, pyTorch, and/or Google Cloud Platform is a plus.
- Experience with ad tech, NLP or audio signal processing is a plus.
- Experience with building data pipelines and getting the data you need to build and evaluate your models, using tools like Apache Beam / Spark is a plus.

Figure 2-9. Screenshot of Spotify machine learning engineer job posting via LinkedIn.

As with the first example, I read through the Machine Learning Engineer posting and write down what I think is important:

- Implementing ML in production
- Prototyping
- Testing and tooling, platform improvements
- Collaboration with cross-functional teams

Based on these points, it seems that this role is more focused on ML model training, with some parts on the ML infrastructure, which are illustrated by steps B and C.1 respectively in the machine learning lifecycle (Figure 1-5).

If I'm interested in applying for this machine learning engineer role, I'll focus on these relevant three bullet points and shorten or remove the other bullets. To do so, I'll look back to the list of seven points from "My first ML churn model" example and map it to the MLE posting. The most relevant points are:

- Trained model with SAS
- Ran model evaluation and analyzed results with SAS, SQL, Python
- Collaborated with ML engineer to put the model in production
- Cleaned data with SQL

The inventory you created for "Exercise 2-2" on page 39 can be reused for different types of roles without the need to rewrite anything. It's good to remember that communication and collaboration skills are also important to companies, and you'll notice these skills listed a lot in all types of job postings. Don't forget to include the points where you were collaborating with other teams or presenting your work to another organization in at least one of your resume bullet points. This is especially relevant for folks who think they don't have enough "ML experience"! Your experience analyzing data, as well as communicating it, is important and can strengthen your resume more than you might think.

I'd recommend making the technologies you used in your past role very clear in your job experience bullet points. You can list them inline or at the end of a bullet point, depending on the space you have and what is most concise. Otherwise, if you have space, feel free to include a skills section in your resume.

Final Resume Touch-ups

Zooming out a bit now that you've been head down crafting and refining your resume: the companies and teams you're applying to have posted this job for a reason. They have a gap on their team and want someone to fill that gap.

Therefore, your application and resume should focus on convincing the hiring committee that you are a candidate who can fill that gap and be part of their team. This includes:

- Real and relevant experience that you can apply to the job, including transferable skills: skills that aren't identical but can easily be transferred between domains.
- Soft skills—you can work well with people in the team and communicate with broader groups of people, such as product managers, and so on.
- Technical skills—you can make individual technical contributions.
- Evidence that you can onboard to an existing project or gain enough context to start something new.

These skills are succinctly described in the three pillars of ML roles that we explored in Chapter 1.

You can show many skills and experiences in your resume, but not all of them. For example, take a quick look at your resume: does it completely lack any examples of teamwork? Are there other points that could help show you're a person who can learn quickly (if you don't have as many relevant working experiences)?

If things look good so far, start applying, but if not, take some time to keep improving your resume.

Applying to Jobs

Now that you have tailored your resume, it's time to apply! Head to job boards (you can use the ones listed at the beginning of this chapter for inspiration). I think it's OK to start applying even if you're not sure if your skills and resume are *perfect* yet; if you apply for a few jobs and don't even get a recruiter callback, that means your resume or skills need to be improved more. You may even find that continuing to improve your resume and spending time on getting referrals are enough to improve your EPA and start getting calls. It's a learning process, and even if you don't start out perfect, the goal is to move toward getting callbacks, through the volume of applications you submit or through applications with higher effectiveness.

Vetting Job Postings

Hopefully, you've done the previous exercises and it's not your first time viewing the job descriptions of ML roles you're interested in. If you vet the jobs that you're applying for, you can increase the chances of getting interviews. In my experience, this step is best used in conjunction with tailoring your resume, because if you're not tailoring your resume, you might as well mass apply and hope you happen to apply for the jobs that match you the best. So how do you filter jobs?

Mapping Your Skills and Experience to the ML Skills Matrix

Remember the variety of ML roles that were introduced in Chapter 1? Let's cut through the noise so that you can focus on marketing your skills to the roles that best fit your experience.

Refer to the common ML job titles in Figure 1-8: which roles do you feel suit you best? If you are most interested in a job that you don't currently have the experience for, do you have a better idea of where to focus your learning to bridge that gap?[7]

In the skills matrix, Table 1-3, you can see right off the bat that the role of data analyst can have overlapping skills with the data scientist role, which in turn overlaps a lot with the role of the MLE. The good news is that with a few of these skills in your skills list, you can apply for one or more of these positions.

---

7 Resources and guides are covered later in this book.

And don't worry—recall that for entry-level roles, as long as you have one or two of the skills listed, you're good to go for applying to those jobs. It's also perfectly normal for new grads to have strong skills in one pillar of ML skills but not in all, which most employers understand and welcome. Mapping your skills to the matrix is only part of the process, though, because the reality is that this matrix has to be taken with a heavy dose of "it depends." That's why the next section of this chapter asks you to analyze a real job posting.

I've seen plenty of job seekers encounter this situation: "this job title is data scientist; why were the questions in the interview about data engineering (or insert something unexpected)?" Recall that an ML title depends on the company or organization plus which team the role is in plus where in the machine learning lifecycle the role is (refer back to Figure 1-3).

As an extreme example, I've been through a "data scientist" interview where they did not ask any statistics or machine learning theory questions nor any data-related questions. Instead, the interview consisted of a few rounds of LeetCode-style (coding quiz) programming questions.[8] I wondered how they could gauge whether I would be a good ML practitioner whose core work centers around data when the questions were fully copied from a generalist software engineer loop. In hindsight, it was probably because that role was not really responsible for training ML models at all.

Because of the often-ambiguous nature of job titles, it can be difficult as a candidate to decide what topics to prepare for. Sure, you can spend time reviewing ML theory as well as grinding some coding quizzes, but your time is stretched thin, and you could be preparing for something that won't even be asked.

I've seen candidates rejected from jobs, not because they weren't strong ML candidates, but rather because they were applying for the "wrong" roles. Confusingly, those roles had the same job titles as ones that the candidate would actually be successful at. The key is to develop the intuition for how to categorize a job title depending on the job description and find the best roles to apply for that suit your skills.

Some of these job titles show up in multiple sections, and that's OK! Well, it's not that OK when it causes confusion and rejections, but you'll be able to better vet and target them by the end of this chapter.

When I apply to jobs, I glance at the job title, but to ensure I'm applying to the right jobs for my skills, I do the following:

---

8 This type of interview is covered in Chapter 5.

- Look at the job description.
- Categorize the job responsibilities; where is it in the machine learning lifecycle (Figure 1-4)?
- Determine whether the job title and job description match up enough; for example, if the job title is machine learning engineer but the description makes it seem somewhat like a data engineering role (which my past experience isn't relevant to), I will pass on the role.

Exercise 2-5

Polish up your resume and apply to one job. The worst they can do is ignore your application. Try it!

Tracking Applications

It can be worth it to track applications so that it's easier to remember what jobs you have applied for. If you've passed the resume screening and at least reached the recruiter screening, tracking those applications can help you remember to follow up, in case you don't hear back during the time frame when they told you they'd let you know.

I used to track most of my applications, but to be honest, I now think you should only track applications where you've at least passed the resume screening. Especially if you mass applied to any job related to ML, there's no point in spending the additional time to track your applications, and not tracking them won't affect your pass rate. One scenario where you might find it useful to track your applications is if you personally plan to summarize or visualize your journey and stats later on.

I do think it's useful to keep track of who I've interviewed with, so I can reach out if I have more questions about the team or company. I could also reach out to them if I interview with the same company a few years later. Recall that networking is a long-term investment with long-term horizons!

As for tools to track applications and interviews, I think Google Sheets, Microsoft Excel, or another simple spreadsheet tool is more than adequate.

Table 2-2 is an example of how I tracked applications and interviews in Google Sheets (names are fictionalized).

Table 2-2. Spreadsheet example of tracking applications and interviews

Application date	Company	Job posting URL	Interview type	Interview date	Interviewers	Emails	Notes	Results
2023-08-02	ARI Corp	https://[url-to-job-description]	Hiring manager: behavioral and past project deep dive	2023-08-15	Xue-La (hiring manager)	*xue.la@domain.com*	Recruiter says this is the ad revenue ML team	Pending
2023-08-03	Taipaw AI	https://[url-to-job-description]	Recruiter screen	2023-08–5	Max (recruiter)	*max@domain.com*	Asked about PyTorch exp	Passed

After you've received some offers, you can then look back to see how many interviews you did. It's also nice to have a list of relevant interviewers and their emails in case you want to reach out to them a few years later. However, I've heard from some people that keeping track of their application-to-interview-to-offer ratio can make their mood go more down than up, so it depends on you.

Additional Job Application Materials, Credentials, and FAQ

I've walked through the resume guide, but there still are some additional components of job applications, such as project portfolios and online certifications. This section gives some best practices and FAQs.

Do You Need a Project Portfolio?

Project portfolios are basically project examples. As a student, I had a few side projects (aka personal projects). I put the code up on GitHub and also created some figures/visualizations. GitHub is a pretty common place to host projects, but some candidates publish their project portfolios as a website, such as a Heroku site.

Recall that the goal of your application and interviews is to convince the employer that you're a good candidate for the job: you have the skills or can easily be trained for the job. For junior, entry-level, and new-graduate candidates: if you don't yet have a lot of work experience but do have a project portfolio, it can help showcase your skills and increase the hiring manager's and hiring team's confidence in your abilities.

But if you have plenty of work experience already, there are marginal returns to having a project portfolio; in interviews, employers would rather discuss your past work, case studies, technical deep dives of past projects, and so forth. You may still benefit from having a project portfolio on GitHub because much of the code and many of the models that you developed in your past job experience may be proprietary, so you might not have code samples that you can share. In that case, showcasing a personal project in a GitHub repository or contributions to open source projects would be useful.

Interviewer's Perspective: Common Mistakes in Project Portfolios

Here are some common mistakes I've seen in candidates' project portfolios and how to avoid them:

Not having a README or overview about the project
   If you're on GitHub, follow the instructions (*https://oreil.ly/JXq8T*) to create one that renders.

Using cliché datasets such as MNIST or widely available tutorials
   Many other candidates likely have the exact same code examples, and interviewers can tell. Enhance common datasets with custom data that you gathered yourself or scrape your own.

Only dumping your code, without any explanation or inline documentation
   Add more code comments (*https://oreil.ly/kACdC*) to help your interviewer understand what they're looking at.

Having a confusing or highly nested folder structure
   Use your judgment to tidy things up; don't just dump a bunch of *.py* scripts.

The real consequences of these mistakes are that the recruiter or person filtering out candidate resumes wastes too much time trying to click through your GitHub or website to find your relevant code. They run out of time (less than one minute per resume) and simply pass on your resume.

For your portfolio to make a difference and boost your application, you should make it easy to navigate and understand at a glance. For that reason, I suggest putting important visualizations on the README and clearly marking which code files the reviewer should click on.

Do Online Certifications Help?

When I review resumes, I don't place too much importance on certifications if the candidate has past ML experience or ML projects that they did on their own time (side projects). If the candidate does not have prior relevant experience, then relevant projects and project portfolios make the biggest difference. I'd recommend you build that up in parallel with earning certifications.

Some certifications hold more weight than others—recall again that the goal is to set yourself apart from other job candidates—so courses that are seen as more comprehensive and practical could help. Examples include the Amazon Web Services (AWS), Google Cloud Platform (GCP), and Microsoft Azure Cloud certifications.

 If your entire resume consists of certifications that anyone could complete in a weekend, then your resume won't stand out.

Interviewing.io (*https://oreil.ly/KMxhk*) analyzed data from many job candidates and found that in its data sample, putting certifications on LinkedIn had a negative impact on the perceived quality of the candidate.[9] Their guess is that more qualified candidates would put work experience or relevant projects on their profiles and resumes while less qualified candidates who didn't have either would fill up their profiles with certifications.

Regardless, candidates have found success with certifications, especially if they come from a nontraditional educational background. Here's a crucial tip: watch out for diminishing returns. In economics, this means that once you've done several more units of something, you benefit less and less from each subsequent unit. In this case, if you've done five certifications, it doesn't make too much difference whether you complete three more or five more. Five certifications will look pretty much the same on a resume as eight or ten.

Interviewer's Perspective: Introductory Credential Mistakes

A mistake I see entry-level candidates make is taking the same 100-level/introductory courses again and again. For example, they will take the beginner courses on Coursera, then take another similar beginner course on Udacity, and then on edX. To an interviewer, this is almost the same as if you'd taken one single beginner course since the contents of the three courses overlap so much. It doesn't help you stand out against other candidates who have taken more advanced courses or have good portfolio projects.

So once the number of online certifications you've taken approaches three to five, you should try to diversify your experience:

---

9 Aline Lerner, "Why You Shouldn't List Certifications on LinkedIn," interviewing.io (*https://oreil.ly/KMxhk*), updated May 15, 2023, *https://oreil.ly/AQi3Q*.

- Make sure your certifications are from reputable sources; don't list them if they seem like they were completed in a weekend. If this removes everything in your current certification list, you should continue with the following two steps.
- Take certifications in more specialized fields of your interest, such as reinforcement learning or natural language processing (NLP).
- Start a side project and build a project portfolio on GitHub.

Table 2-3 summarizes the general decision criteria I suggest.

Table 2-3. Should you keep doing online courses and certifications?

Experience level	Benefit of online certifications
If you have no ML/data science resume line items...	Yes, do the online courses and assignments and put them on your resume.
If you have some (three to five) online courses under your belt and are not sure whether to take more...	Consider doing a side project, which is an even better resume line item and gives you a better return on investment (ROI) of your time. Self-assess if your programming and statistics skills are past a sufficient baseline.
If you have learned statistics and programming to a good baseline level and have some data science resume line items...	Pause here and check whether you have enough relevant bullet points from your work experiences or a good project portfolio. If not, start that ASAP! Start applying for jobs (or taking direct action toward your job goals) instead of getting stuck in a self-learning cycle, sometimes called "tutorial h*!!." Interviews are often a great way to find out what you can improve on, even if you don't get the job.

Should You Take a Master's Degree to Boost Your ML Resume?

The same criteria for deciding whether online certifications are useful for you apply to the question of graduate school: is the ROI enough? Master's degrees usually require more commitment, though, so you'll need to look at some of these additional considerations:

Monetary cost
Some master's degrees are quite costly.

Opportunity cost
If you're taking master's courses full time, would you have gone further in your career if you'd started working? You'd be giving up on work experience, work progression, and potential earnings.

ROI
Given the monetary and opportunity costs, is it worth it? When making big decisions like getting a master's degree, you should estimate that the degree will return more in the long run than in the short term.

If you're interested in a master's or higher degree only to boost your ML resume, then I recommend taking a course part time. Maybe your existing resume is enough, but you're just missing some good side projects or interview practice. However, if there are other factors that make it worthwhile, such as intellectual curiosity, then go for it!

To learn more, I recommend Eugene Yan's review (*https://oreil.ly/cSq_q*) of his experience doing the part-time online master of science in computer science (OMSCS) degree at Georgia Tech.

Now that I've covered project portfolios and credentials, here are some additional FAQs about resumes.

FAQ: How Many Pages Should My Resume Be?

I often hear the advice to keep tech resumes to one page. In general, I agree, and I personally keep my resume to one page. However, I can see this changing depending on your situation.

What are the expectations of your region?

I've interviewed many candidates from Europe who had two-page resumes, and they did fine going through the resume screening. In the United States and Canada, I tend to see candidates with one-page resumes. In tech in North America, it's not custom to include profile pictures on a resume, but I have seen that when looking over the resumes of candidates from Asia and Europe. If you are job seeking in other parts of the world, double-check with people in the industry or even online forums to see if there are expectations for resume length or information to include that I haven't listed here.

Coming from academia? Create an industry resume instead of a CV

When I was in grad school, there was a type of resume called a *CV* (curriculum vitae). You use a CV to apply for graduate programs, postdoctorate programs, teaching positions in academia, and the like.

A CV focuses more on your research publications and tends to be lengthier; it is rarely only one page long. Some CV formats I've seen use paragraphs more than the bullet-point format I see in industry. If you already have a CV, you can repurpose your research responsibilities into bullet points, condense them, and rework them as a more common industry format when applying for industry jobs.[10]

---

10 By *industry jobs*, I'm not referring to *research* positions in industry such as at Google DeepMind.

Of course, it's probably fine if you just submit a CV directly as your resume, and I've seen candidates successfully get interviews without modifying their academic CVs, but investing a small amount of time could increase your EPA when applying to industry jobs.

Interviewer's Perspective: Resume Real Estate

When I'm reading a resume, it's not about the length but rather the quality of the presented information. The first page and the top and center of the first page are what the interviewer will see first. You should put your most impressive and relevant experiences there. If you have other experiences you'd like to include, you can use the less important resume "real estate." The question you should be answering is: if the person is screening a stack of 50 resumes, and they have only 5–10 seconds per resume, how can I make sure they see my most relevant experiences in those first 5–10 seconds?"

FAQ: Should I Format My Resume for ATS (Applicant Tracking Systems)?

As I mentioned in Chapter 1, I don't think there's enough evidence that automatic filtering will reject your resume if you happen to have two columns or one column, or you use a certain font, or you use PDF versus Microsoft Word documents, and so on. Regardless, in this book, I'm assuming that automatic ATS rejections may be possible. Personally, I've used two-column PDF resumes made with LaTeX for my entire career so far and haven't had any issues at all, even with online job sites that automatically parse my resume into text.

But if you think the formatting of your resume is the only thing keeping you from getting interviews, you *might* have bigger things to worry about.[11] First, let's use the points from this chapter to see what else, apart from ATS filtering, might have kept your resume from being noticed:

- Did you include the most important and ML/data-relevant information in the sections where a resume reviewer can quickly see it?

- Do you have much relevant ML/data-relevant information on your resume? Have you made sure your resume includes keywords that overlap with those in the job descriptions? Are the bullet points on your resume clear? Are there typos

---

11 I've seen tips online to copy and paste the entire job description onto your resume, make the font small, turn the font white so that it's invisible, and export the PDF so that ATS can "pass" your resume. I haven't seen anyone prove they've gotten many more ML interview invitations from tricks like these yet.

or obvious errors on your resume? Use a resume checklist (*https://oreil.ly/bfUw_*) (listed earlier in the resume resources) to double-check.

- Have you been trying referrals, tailoring your resume, or taking other actions that increase your EPA?

That said, it is true that online forms will parse your resumes for text strings, so don't send in a *.png* file or use avant-garde formatting and fonts (unless you're applying for a niche design role, something that is beyond the scope of this book). Use a simple template linked in "Resume Resources" on page 43 or even from Google Docs and export it to a PDF. KISS (keep it simple, stupid) applies here. In summary, follow the instructions of the online application portal[12] and craft your resume using the best practices mentioned in this chapter.

Next Steps

You've learned how to identify the ML roles best suited for you, and you've created a resume that's relevant and tailored to the type of ML job you're aiming for.

Browsing Job Postings

My recommendation is to browse through some more job postings. When I browse for job postings, I learn a lot from simply reading job descriptions. For example, the types of "data scientist" roles I'm interested in could be very different from the "data scientist" roles that interest another job seeker. Recall the example where a "data scientist" in one company could be responsible for data analysis rather than training ML models.

For the jobs with descriptions that do interest me, I note the requirements that they have in common. Optionally, I try to create two to three tailored resumes that I can send out en masse to roles that require similar skills. The reason I have two to three versions is because one is for job descriptions that seem to be looking for people who have more software skills, and another is for job descriptions for startups where I might emphasize my startup experience.

Identifying the Gaps Between Your Current Skills and Target Roles

The next step is to take an honest look at your current skills and the resume you've constructed for the ML role(s) you're aiming for. When you were reading through ML job descriptions, in what ways did you think you could potentially strengthen your resume? What are keywords that showed up when you browsed job postings in

---

12 Kerri Anne Renzulli, "75% of Resumes Are Never Read by a Human—Here's How to Make Sure Your Resume Beats the Bots," CNBC, updated March 14, 2019, *https://oreil.ly/XwLWw*.

"Exercise 2-4" on page 44 where you think you could learn more and add to your resume?

Exercise 2-6

Here's a version of the ML skills matrix (Table 1-3) but with blank spaces where you can evaluate your skills. Are you interested in model training but don't have much knowledge in ML theory, statistics, or relevant programming tools? Are there other skills that you should boost in order to fit your target ML job? Fill in Table 2-4, aided by the checklists that follow. In the table, rate your own skill levels: 1 being low and 3 being high.

Table 2-4. ML and data skills self-assessment

Skills	Skill level self-assessment (Float between 1 and 3)
Data visualization, communication	
Data exploration, cleaning, intuition	
Machine learning theory, statistics	
Programming tools (Python, SQL, etc.)	
Software infrastructure (Docker, Kubernetes, CI/CD, etc.)	

To help guide your assessment, here is a list of questions to ask yourself:

Data visualization, communication—0.5 points per checkmark:

- You have built dashboards and visualizations.
- You are able to choose effective graph types, such as bar versus line charts, depending on the type of visualization you are building.
- You have presented data insights to nontechnical team members and stakeholders.
- You are able to structure a presentation so that the information for the data is clear to an audience outside the data team.
- You are able to work with product teams to identify what is a good experiment.
- You are able to think deeply about user experience and how ML relates to the user experience.

Data exploration, cleaning, intuition—0.5 points per checkmark:

- You have explored raw data.
- You have dealt with imbalanced datasets before.
- You have optimized a complex and slow query before.

- You are able to understand from behind the scenes how data is flowing from the source to various layers.

- You can use different techniques depending on whether the data is an analytical use case or a transactional use case.

- You have done data modeling before and are able to ingest and transform raw data into the form defined by the schema.

Machine learning theory, statistics—0.5 points per checkmark:

- You know about various ML algorithms and what types of projects to use them on.

- You know how the main algorithms in your field work, beyond just importing and using them in code.

- You are familiar with hypothesis testing and significance.

- You are aware of ML model evaluation methods.

- You have done troubleshooting on ML model issues before.

- You have (at some point) understood matrix algebra and multivariable calculus and how that related to a few ML algorithms, or at least regression.

Programming tools (Python, SQL, etc.)—0.75 points per checkmark:

- You have trained ML models with Python-based tools or other languages or frameworks.

- You have experience building scripts or apps in Python or other programming languages or frameworks.

- You are familiar with SQL queries and methods such as window functions.

- You have used Python libraries such as pandas or NumPy to wrangle data.

Software infrastructure (Docker, Kubernetes, CI/CD, etc.)—0.75 points per checkmark:

- You have done DevOps-related work before.

- You have dealt with fixing slow runtimes.

- You have deployed an ML model before, via a web app or other method.

- You have worked with automation via tools such as Jenkins, Kubernetes, or Docker.

Compare your scores to those in the ML skills matrix (Table 1-3) to see where your skills roughly are.

Note that this list is nonexhaustive and, depending on the job description, you may see more skills not listed here. Remember, you don't have to get top marks in all sections since this depends on which area in the ML lifecycle that you're interested in. However, this assessment should give you a good starting point. You should aim to get higher marks in the sections you're interested in, or learn and prepare so that you have higher marks.

Summary

This chapter focused on the ML job application step. This happens before you get interviews and is the key to getting interviews. You saw where to find jobs online and some ways to increase your chances of getting interviews via networking and referrals. You also read through some resume best practices, and hopefully, you have created an initial version of your resume. If you have it and feel ready, I encourage you to start applying for ML jobs even if you feel that your skills or your resume aren't 100% perfect.

Next, in the following chapters I'll go through the various types of interviews, spanning technical and behavioral interviews. First up are ML algorithms and theory, which are part of the technical interview.

## CHAPTER 3

Technical Interview: Machine Learning Algorithms

In Chapter 1, you learned about the various steps you will go through as part of your ML interviews. In Chapter 2, you looked at how to tie your experiences to roles of interest as well as how to craft a relevant resume. The goal of the previous chapters was to get you invited to interviews. In this chapter, I'll focus on ML algorithms. As you recall, the interview process is illustrated in Figure 1-9, and the ML algorithms interview is only one portion of the technical interviews; the rest, such as ML training and evaluation, coding, and so on, will be covered in subsequent chapters.

Overview of the Machine Learning Algorithms Technical Interview

You're likely to be asked ML algorithm technical questions in an interview if you're applying for any of the following jobs:

- Data scientist who builds ML models
- Machine learning engineer
- Applied scientist
- And similar roles

Recall that within the common ML job titles (Figure 1-8), there are some jobs that have the responsibility of training ML models in the ML lifecycle. This chapter focuses on assessing candidates for those skills; if the job you're aiming for focuses less on training ML models, you might get a simplified version of this type of interview, or it might be skipped completely.

This interview is meant to assess your understanding of ML algorithms, especially on the theoretical side. As to how you implement the algorithms with code, I cover that in the model deployment questions in Chapter 6 and the coding/programming technical interview in Chapter 5. The goal for you as an interviewee is for the interviewers to confirm that you understand the underlying concepts behind ML algorithms. Roles do exist where all you have to know is how to import the library with Python, but for more advanced projects, an underlying understanding can help you customize various ML approaches and better debug and troubleshoot models. As covered in Chapter 1, in the three pillars of ML roles, this is the pillar of ML algorithm and data intuition, which showcases your ability to adapt (refer to Figure 1-6). This skill is especially important in companies that have complex ML use cases and custom-made solutions, where you might modify or combine various off-the-shelf methods or create something from scratch.

 I try to mention as many common algorithms as space allows, but there are many more techniques under the sun. Be sure to check out the linked resources to extend your learning and interview preparation!

It is also important to note that, in addition to understanding the ML algorithms' inner workings and underlying statistical methods, you need to successfully communicate that understanding to the interviewer. Yes, I know that communication skills have been brought up many times in this book, but they are what help set you apart as a successful candidate.

As a rule of thumb, it's important to be able to explain algorithms and ML concepts at two levels: on a simple "explain like I'm five years old" level and at a deeper, technical level, one more appropriate for a college course. A second rule of thumb is to be prepared to answer follow-up questions to these ML algorithm interview questions. This is so the interviewer knows that you didn't just memorize and then regurgitate the answer, but that you can apply it to various real-life scenarios on the job.

In this chapter, I break down technical questions on the following topics so you can easily refer to a specific question if your interview focuses on that topic:

- Statistical techniques
- Supervised, unsupervised, and reinforcement learning
- Natural language processing (NLP)
- Recommender systems
- Reinforcement learning
- Computer vision

In technical interviews that are very structured, such as the Amazon data science initial phone screen, they will ask you clearly scoped questions, such as asking for a definition of a particular algorithm. After you answer, they will generally move on without additional follow-up questions. There are companies that mix structured questions with a free-form discussion, where the interviewer might dig deeper into your answer, and the conversation might branch out from there into your past experiences.

Statistical and Foundational Techniques

Statistical techniques are used in every data role, and these techniques are the foundations for ML projects. Hence, in ML interviews, you will most likely have questions that cover this topic.[1] Statistical techniques help build baseline models to compare more costly models and algorithms against or help discover if there is enough meaningful data in the first place to build ML models.

For the purposes of this book, I will be placing the foundational regression techniques in this section, as well as various techniques for training and improving ML models. In short, these are (1) foundational techniques and (2) methods used during model training, such as training splits, regularization, and so on. These concepts are foundational knowledge for any type of ML algorithms that will be mentioned later as well as foundations for ML interview questions.

This section covers the basics of statistical techniques for those who are unsure whether they have sufficient background knowledge in this area. Feel free to skip the subsections if you already have expertise in any of these areas. Regardless of your expertise, I've highlighted specific advice for ML interviews in the tip boxes to help you apply your knowledge of each ML area and excel in your interviews.

Resources for Learning About Statistical and Foundational Techniques

To further supplement your knowledge on statistical and foundational techniques beyond the summaries I've provided in this book, I recommend the following resources:

- *The Elements of Statistical Learning* (*https://oreil.ly/oZ5si*) by Trevor Hastie et al.

- *An Introduction to Statistical Learning with Applications in Python* (*https://oreil.ly/bhhoq*) by Gareth James et al.

---

1 Depending on the types of responsibilities the job has in the ML lifecycle, this portion might be skipped—for example, for "applied machine learning engineer" or "software engineer, machine learning," roles, especially at Google. Double-check with your recruiter or hiring manager when in doubt!

- Courses on Coursera by DeepLearning.AI and Andrew Ng; this resource is also useful for all following subtopics of ML (I won't repeatedly link their courses— since they sometimes change and update—in the following sections).

- Introduction to Machine Learning Interviews (*https://oreil.ly/p1NEd*) by Chip Huyen has additional questions for overall ML interviews which can be referenced for most sections in this chapter.

Refer back to this section for reference material when preparing for interviews.

Now, let's jump in.

Summarizing Independent and Dependent Variables

Here's an overview of one of the foundations of ML algorithms—variables—and a simple example of fitting a model.

Let's say that you have a dataset about apples, with the *weight* and *height* of each apple. You also have a list of *past sales prices* of each apple. With the list of apple weights, heights, and past sales prices, you want to guess the sales price of *new* apples, before they are sold. For the sake of this example, ignore big grocery chains automatically calculating a price, but let's say you're selling as a hobby to friends and family, or maybe you're running a farm that a grandparent left you. So you are making use of the weight and height of each single new apple to predict its price. Weight and height are fixed observations at that point in time (an apple can't be both 100 grams and 150 grams at the same time).

Now, to connect all these concepts, let's add in some terminology. *Variables* refer to everything that is being taken into account in your model of how apple prices are calculated. So the variables in this case include weight, height, and price. Within these variables, you know the weight and height of each new apple, and they are fixed at that point in time. So the weight and height are *independent* variables. Then, you have another variable, price, that you'd like to predict for new apples prior to knowing the correct answer before selling them. The predicted price *depends* on the height and weight of the new apple. For example, heavier and taller apples sell for more money. Thus, price is a *dependent* variable (shown in Table 3-1).

Table 3-1. Examples of independent and dependent variables

Independent variables	Dependent variable
Apple weight	Price
Apple height	
Apple color	
Apple variety	

Terminology That May Arise During Your Interview

The concepts of independent and dependent variables are tried and true, but the terminology might not be. In different fields, you may have come across the terms listed in Table 3-2, although they may differ from industry to industry or from textbook to textbook. During your interview, make sure you and the interviewer aren't crossing wires due to terminology, and double-check with your interviewer if you sense that you're using a different term to refer to the same thing. Knowing the most common terms can help you use them appropriately in your interviews in various fields.

Table 3-2. Synonyms of independent and dependent variables

Synonyms of "independent variable"	Synonyms of "dependent variable"
Regressor	Regressand
Explanatory variable	Response variable
Predictor variable	Outcome variable
Input variable	Output variable
Feature	Target
(Common notation) x	(Common notation) y

Defining Models

Models are a way of using past data points to describe "the way the world works," or, in other words, a way of finding patterns and connections with past information. The apples example from the previous section uses a *model* that describes the way pricing works. The model is something that knows the "truth"—even if it's not the full truth but rather our best attempt to approximate the truth. Thus, the model can be used to predict our best approximation of future data points. This applies for all "models" in ML models. Recommender-system models seek to predict what a user will like or click on when visiting a website. Convolutional neural networks (CNNs) for image recognition "learn" a model of what various pixels represent: is this cluster and layout of pixels a cat or a dog?

Just as for independent and dependent variables, it is important to have a shared definition for "model" to prevent miscommunication during an interview, such as confusing algorithms with models.[2] The model is the outcome of having run and fit an ML algorithm.

---

2 Jason Brownlee, "Difference Between Algorithm and Model in Machine Learning," *Machine Learning Mastery* (blog), August 19, 2020, *https://oreil.ly/TrduX*.

Summarizing Linear Regression

I wanted to make sure I included regression models. I'm glad that I learned the detailed ins and outs of linear and logistic regression, even calculating them by hand (a requirement for the second-year statistics course I was taking as part of an economics major at university). This knowledge has compounded and helped me understand the new ML algorithms I've encountered as well as how to apply them in practice. All of my learning stemmed from understanding these entry-level concepts, so I highly recommend not shying away from learning the mathematics of regression models. Again, feel free to skip this section if you already have expertise in this area.

Let's use the apple example from an earlier section in a graph. For simplicity and to squeeze it onto a two-dimensional graph, let's use just one independent variable, *weight*, to predict the dependent variable, *price*. Each dot on the graph in Figure 3-1 represents a data point from past sales, so you already know the sale prices for them. For example, the dot with a callout on the graph weighs 80 grams (its intersect on the x-axis) and sold for $1 (its intersect on the y-axis). Note that this is a simple example; most usage of linear regression will have multiple independent variables ("multivariable") and if visualized, will be a line in an *N*-dimensional space, where *N* = number of variables + 1 (when there is one output variable). In addition, this example has one dependent variable; when there are multiple dependent/output variables, the regression task is referred to as being *multivariate*. Note that *multivariate* is separate from the "multivariable" concept mentioned earlier.

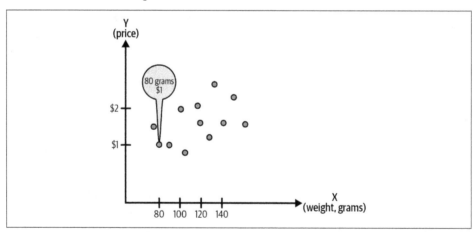

Figure 3-1. Data points to be used for linear regression.

The next step in linear regression is fitting the titular "line" to the data points. Behind the scenes, software tools like Python, Stata, IBM SPSS, SAS, MATLAB, and the like will calculate a "line of best fit." According to the definition of a *model* given previously in this section, this line is the *model*, which is the best *approximation* of the *truth* with the data points that you have. Starting with an initial line, the software will calculate the *residual*: the y-axis distance between a data point and the line, as illustrated in Figure 3-2. Colloquially, the *residual* is also referred to as the *residual error*.

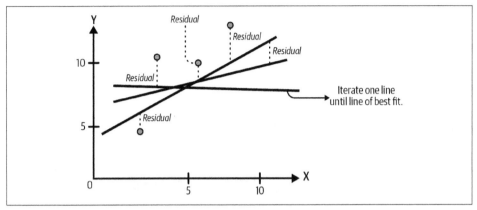

Figure 3-2. Fitting the line of best fit in linear regression; the line is iterated on until the residuals are as small as possible.

All the residuals are squared so that predictions above and the line don't cancel each other out due to having opposite signs (positive, negative). The goal is that the sum of the residuals is as small as possible since if you have a line that is drastically far away from the data points, that means the line isn't fitting well to as many data points as possible and as correctly as possible. Mathematically, a common technique to tell how well the line is fitting is the process called *least squares*. Achieving least squares means finding the line that results in the smallest sum of squared residuals, which in turn means you have the "line of best fit": the line is fitting the data points with least distance from the data points overall, as shown in Figure 3-3.

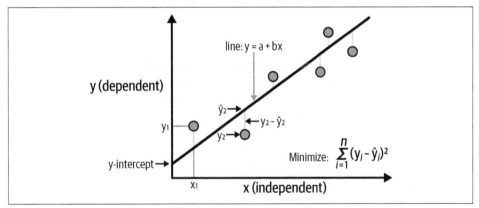

Figure 3-3. Least squares and terminology; y represents observed data points, and ŷ (y-hat) represents the predicted/estimated values.

The end result is a line that has the smallest sum of least squares to the data points, as illustrated in Figure 3-4.

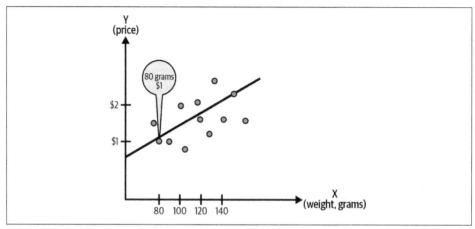

Figure 3-4. The resulting line of best fit with least squares from the data in Figure 3-1.

Going forward, you can use this "line of best fit" as a model to predict new apple prices! You can plug the apple weight into the line (in equation form) to get a numerical value for the predicted price. This is one of the most basic ways of calculating a model from data points, but it has the same pattern as more in-depth ML models and algorithms that are covered in the next chapter. Namely, you'll initialize a line (you don't know if this is the best model yet) and calculate the residuals, or how well it fits. Next, you'll change the line by tilting it a little—mathematically, this is called *updating coefficients* or *weights*—and calculate the residuals again, as illustrated in Figure 3-2.

This updating process is called *training*, which is where the commonly used phrase "training/to train an ML model" comes from. If the sum of the squared residuals is getting smaller, then you are on the right track. When you can't make the squared residuals any smaller, you've achieved least squares, and that's how you can say the line is your best approximation with this dataset (as illustrated in Figure 3-4). It's like that game where there's an item hidden in the room, and as you walk around the room trying to find it, your friend says "hot" if you're getting closer and "cold" when you're walking farther away. You want to walk toward hotter and hotter areas in the room, until you reach the final position.

In Chapter 4, I'll walk through ways to evaluate models via error terms such as mean squared error (MSE), root mean square error (RMSE), and more, which are very similar concepts to residuals. The main difference here is that residuals are the difference between past observation data and model estimations while errors are the difference between model estimations and actual data previously unseen by the model. In other words, errors are the differences after applying the model to previously unseen data in order to evaluate model performance.

Defining Training and Test Set Splits

To sum up, when using supervised[3] machine learning such as the simple linear regression example in the previous section, you'll generally start with a dataset and want the ML algorithm to learn a model of how things work. You then will use the model to calculate the values of dependent variables, such as predicting how much apples will sell for before they are actually sold. In other words, you have a dataset of past data points and, of course, no future data points. When the ML model is being trained, it's learning to "fit" the data that you currently have. There are some issues that could arise with model training when the model is used in the real world. For one, there will always be outliers or changing events in the real world.

One example is in financial predictions with ML: the market could swing suddenly to a bear (downturn) market, and the model we've trained with financial data in a bull (upswing) market will produce horrible and wildly inaccurate predictions. Another example is that the dataset you have isn't representative enough of the behaviors of the real world. In the apples example from the previous section, you assume that with the weight and height data of the apples, you can predict the sell price of new apples. But what if the data you have on hand isn't enough, and apple variants like Fuji or Honeycrisp (one of my favorites) sell for more? You didn't have each apple's variant name tracked in your dataset, so then your model may be incorrect once you put it to the test.

But for now, you have only the current dataset. To make the most of it, you need to keep some of the data you have for testing purposes. What this means is that you can break out 80% of the apple data points to use for model training and then save 20% of the apple data points to run the trained model predictions on. The 80% the model is trained on is called the *training set* (sometimes referred to as the *train set*), and the 20% of data that is unseen by the model during the training phase is called the *test set*. This mimics the real-world scenario of running the model to predict new data points; the test set serves that purpose. In many cases, you might even split the data into three chunks: 80% as the training dataset, 10% as the validation (holdout) dataset, and another 10% as the test dataset (Figure 3-5).

The validation set allows you to monitor the model's performance during the training process without "formally" evaluating it, and it enables you to diagnose weak spots of the model and tune its parameters. The test set, as previously mentioned, was unseen by the model during the training process and thus is used to formally evaluate the model performance, mimicking a real-world environment as much as possible. Of course, having a test and validation set isn't infallible, which brings us to more robust techniques and the concepts of model overfitting and underfitting.

---

3 Details are in "Supervised, Unsupervised, and Reinforcement Learning" on page 76.

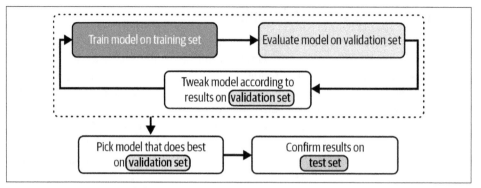

Figure 3-5. Training, validation, and test set splits.

 For interview questions on training and test sets, make sure you can name common ways to augment the simpler splits, such as using cross-validation:[4] splitting up data into smaller chunks and rotating through them as training sets.

Defining Model Underfitting and Overfitting

There are many reasons a model may not perform well on real-world data (or even the validation or test set). A common starting point is addressing overfitting or underfitting. *Underfitting* is when the model isn't fitting well. This might mean that the model isn't able to capture the relationship between the dataset's independent variables (e.g., weight, height, etc.) and the dependent variables (e.g., price). Consequently, some ways to reduce underfitting are related to helping the model learn more nuances or patterns during the training process.

For example, adding more variables, or model features, such as apple variant or age of the apple, could help the model learn more patterns from the training data and potentially reduce underfitting. A second way to reduce underfitting is to increase the number of iterations the model trains for before training is stopped.[5]

Overfitting is when a model fits the training data too closely and very specifically, perhaps finding patterns that happen to be in the training set but not elsewhere. A simplified example is that the training data just so happens to have a lot of apples that

---

4 "Cross-Validation: Evaluating Estimator Performance," in *Scikit-learn: Machine Learning in Python User Guide*, accessed October 24, 2023, *https://oreil.ly/Spja4*.

5 "What Is Underfitting?" IBM, accessed October 21, 2023, *https://oreil.ly/SSihF*.

are disproportionately expensive despite their weight (e.g., Sekai Ichi apples[6]). The model learned from that data and overfit to it, therefore making incorrect predictions that are overpriced for cheaper apple variants. Simply put, the model is overmemorizing the training data and unable to generalize to new data points. There are many techniques to make the model generalize better, such as adding more training data, data augmentation, or regularization.[7] I'll cover the details of regularization next.

Summarizing Regularization

Regularization is a technique used to reduce overfitting of ML models. Generally, regularization will create a damper on model weights/coefficient. By this point, you likely know what I'm going to do—which is to bring up the apples again! Apples are my favorite fruit, which is probably why I use the example so often. So let's say the model has learned to weigh "weight of apple" more heavily (accidental pun, but model "weights" is legitimate terminology); then the weight of the apple is mathematically increasing the results of the ML model's prediction of the price by a relatively high positive value. If you can dampen the amount by which the weight of the apple increases the model's predictions of the price, via regularization, that can make the model generalize more and take other variables into account more evenly.

The Variance Bias Trade-Off

The variance bias trade-off is a common topic in ML interviews. When applying ML model improvement techniques such as regularization, it is important to consider the trade-off between fixing for bias versus variance. *Bias* refers to the overall inaccuracy of the model and can often be caused by an oversimplified (underfit) model.

Variance comes from overfitting, when the model has learned too specifically from the training set. One way to remember why this is called "variance" is that the term refers to the variability of the model: the model is overfit to specific points or traits, so the model is very sensitive to different data points, causing fluctuation and variability.

Regularization might cause a model to reduce its variance but might inadvertently increase bias, so that's a reason to be cautious and test various model-improvement techniques.

---

6 Sekai Ichi apples could sell for between $20 and $25 each (source: Silver Creek Nursery (*https://oreil.ly/U_54R*)).

7 "What Is Overfitting?" IBM, accessed October 21, 2023. *https://oreil.ly/p9V_u*.

Sample Interview Questions on Foundational Techniques

Now that I've covered various statistical and ML techniques at a higher level, let's look at some sample questions. Here, I will dive into the details of common interview questions that stem from the concepts covered in this section. These details may not have been previously addressed, so my hope is that these sample questions also serve to explain the new concepts.

Interview question 3-1: What is L1 versus L2 regularization?

Example answer

L1 regularization, also known as *lasso regularization*,[8] is a type of regularization that shrinks model parameters toward zero. *L2 regularization* (also known as *ridge regularization*) adds a penalty term to the objective function that is proportional to the square of the coefficients of the model. This penalty term shrinks the coefficients toward zero, but unlike L1 (lasso) regularization, it does not make any of the coefficients exactly equal to zero.

L2 regularization can help reduce overfitting and improve the stability of the model by keeping coefficients from becoming too large. Both L1 and L2 regularization are commonly used to prevent overfitting and improve the generalization of ML models.

Interview questions on model overfitting and underfitting may lead to follow-up questions. For example, if you bring up L1 and L2 regularization, the interviewer might ask, "What other types of regularization could work?" In that case, you could bring up *elastic net*, which is a combination of L1 and L2 techniques. Or for the overfitting case, ensemble techniques can also help (refer to "Interview question 3-3: Explain boosting and bagging and what they can help with." on page 76).

Interview question 3-2: How do you deal with the challenges that come with an imbalanced dataset?

Example answer

Imbalanced datasets in ML refer to datasets in which some classes or categories outweigh others.[9] Techniques to deal with imbalanced datasets include data augmentation, oversampling, undersampling, ensemble methods, and so on:

---

8 "Lasso and Elastic Net," MathWorks, accessed October 21, 2023, *https://oreil.ly/yOCEe*.

9 "Imbalanced Data," Machine Learning, Google for Developers, accessed October 21, 2023, *https://oreil.ly/sKP4h*.

Data augmentation

Data augmentation involves generating more examples for the ML model to train on, such as rotating images so that the dataset includes images of humans turned upside down as well as the normal upright image orientation. Without data augmentation, the model might not be able to correctly recognize images of humans who are laying sideways or doing headstands since the data is imbalanced toward humans in an upright pose.

Oversampling

Oversampling is a technique to increase the number of data points of a minority class via synthetic generation. As an example, SMOTE (synthetic minority oversampling technique)[10] uses the feature vectors of the minority classes to generate synthetic data points that are located between real data points and their k-nearest neighbors. This could synthetically increase the size of the minority class(es) and improve the performance of the ML model trained on a dataset with oversampling treatment.

Undersampling

Undersampling does the opposite: it reduces examples from the majority class to balance the number of data points of the majority class and minority class(es). Oversampling is generally preferred in practice since undersampling may cause useful data to be discarded, which is exacerbated when the dataset is already small.

Ensemble methods

Ensemble methods can also be used to increase model performance when dealing with an imbalanced dataset.[11] Each model in the ensemble can be trained on a different subset of the data and can help learn the nuances of each class better.

Interviewer's Perspective: Check the Scope of the Interview Question

When answering ML interview questions, take a second to confirm the scope of the question. In other words, if the question is asking only for a definition of logistic regression, don't go on a tangent about various other techniques. If the question is open-ended, you can confirm whether the interviewer is asking for something specific.

---

10 Nitesh V. Chawla, Kevin W. Bowyer, Lawrence O. Hall, and W. Philip Kegelmeyer, "SMOTE: Synthetic Minority Over-Sampling Technique," *Journal of Artificial Intelligence Research* 16 (2002): 321–57, doi:10.1613/jair.953.

11 Chip Huyen, "Training Data," Ch. 4 in *Designing Machine Learning Systems* (*https://oreil.ly/bsqEg*) (O'Reilly).

Interview question 3-3: Explain boosting and bagging and what they can help with.

Example answer

Bagging and boosting are ensemble techniques used to improve the performance of ML models:

Bagging

Bagging trains multiple models on different subsets of the training data and combines their predictions to make a final prediction.

Boosting

Boosting trains a series of models where each model tries to correct the mistakes made by the previous model. The final prediction is made by all the models. Ensemble techniques can help with a variety of issues encountered during ML training. For example, they can help with imbalanced data[12] and reduce overfitting.[13]

See Chapter 4 for more in-depth questions concerning model evaluation.

Supervised, Unsupervised, and Reinforcement Learning

In ML roles, knowing when and what to pick from each family of techniques—including supervised, unsupervised, or reinforcement learning—is an essential skill. In my previous jobs, I've used supervised learning to prevent fraud and customer churn, but at other times, I used unsupervised learning like anomaly detection for the same problem, depending on the data and situation. Sometimes (more often, as you grow more senior in your ML career), you might even create an ML pipeline with both supervised and unsupervised learning. In your reinforcement learning pipeline, you might use supervised learning in a previous step to label features. Understanding the underlying mechanics can help you adapt to new situations when using different techniques might be more effective than sticking to what is convenient.

Therefore, in interviews there are often questions about supervised versus unsupervised learning. Reinforcement learning (RL) is considered a somewhat advanced topic and may not be touched on in many interviews. However, I've been asked about it in a nontrivial number of interviews because of the growth of RL use for industry applications such as in conjunction with recommender systems—although my past

---

12 Chip Huyen, "Model Development and Offline Evaluation," Ch. 6 in *Designing Machine Learning Systems*.

13 "What Is Overfitting?" IBM, accessed October 21, 2023. *https://oreil.ly/p9V_u*.

work experience in RL may have prompted the interviewers to ask me about it. As I mentioned in Chapter 2, if something's on your resume, it's fair game to discuss in the interview! For a more comprehensive overview of RL, see "Reinforcement Learning Algorithms" on page 101.

 Regardless of what types of ML roles you're interviewing for, knowledge about supervised and unsupervised learning is a must. Brush up on reinforcement learning concepts afterward, in terms of priority.

This section covers the basics of labeled data, supervised learning, unsupervised learning, semi- and self-supervised learning, and reinforcement learning, those who are unsure whether they have the background knowledge in this area. Feel free to skip the subsections if you already have expertise in any of these areas. Regardless of your expertise, I've highlighted specific advice for ML interviews in the tip boxes to help you apply your knowledge of each ML area and excel in your interviews.

Resources for Learning About Supervised and Unsupervised Learning

To further supplement your knowledge on supervised and unsupervised ML techniques, beyond the summaries I've provided in this book, I recommend the following resource:

- *The Elements of Statistical Learning* (*https://oreil.ly/wR-ar*) by Trevor Hastie, Robert Tibshirani, and Jerome Friedman

Refer back to this section for reference material when preparing for interviews.

Defining Labeled Data

Returning to our apple dataset from "Summarizing Independent and Dependent Variables," you have the data points for how much apples sold for in the past. The price is also the dependent variable in "Summarizing Linear Regression." The fact that you do have labels for the dataset[14] means that the ML tasks you were doing previously were with *labeled* data. An example of *unlabeled* data is when you have the prices and weights of the apples but not the apple variants, yet you try to deduce commonalities within different variants of apples. Because you don't initially have the

---

14 As a reminder, the labels for this apple dataset are the past apple prices—in other words, the "correct" or expected outcomes of the past, in order for us to check how accurate the trained model is.

correct or expected "label"—in this case, the apple variant—you would be using unlabeled data and conducting unsupervised learning.

Summarizing Supervised Learning

Building on the concept of labeled and unlabeled data, let's move on to supervised learning. *Supervised learning* is the first type of machine learning as defined by its use of labeled data, illustrated in Figure 3-6. Supervised learning uses correct or expected outcomes of the past to predict the dependent variables for new or future data points. The example of using apple weight, variant, and so on to predict sales prices for new apples is supervised learning. Supervised learning can be broken down into two main categories: regression and classification.

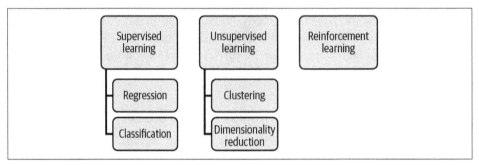

Figure 3-6. Overview of machine learning families (simplified for understanding).

In *regression* tasks, the dependent/output variable is a continuous value. For example, predicting stock prices, housing prices, or weather (temperature) produces continuous values. *Classification* is a type of supervised learning in which the dependent/output variable is categorical—that is, it is put into a category, such as "it's a dog" or "it's a cat." Classification examples include detecting whether something is or isn't spam, using image recognition such as tagging animal types in a picture, and so on.

It is possible to mix categorical data with continuous data via techniques such as *one-hot encoding*. For example, if we're trying to classify if there is a dog or a cat in an image, an image that has a dog will be encoded with 1 for the "dog" category and 0 for the "cat" category. Think of it like a Boolean (True/False) representation of the data for each category. Then you can mix these numerical encodings (0 or 1) with datasets with continuous values.

Defining Unsupervised Learning

Unsupervised learning is training a model with unlabeled data: when you do not have the "labels" available (the labels being the correct or expected values that you are looking for). You'd likely use unsupervised learning to find patterns, commonalities, or anomalies in the dataset without prior knowledge in the ML model of correct or expected result labels.

Common usage of unsupervised learning includes clustering and dimensionality reduction (see Figure 3-6). Many generative models are unsupervised, such as variational autoencoder (VAE), which is used with applications like Stable Diffusion for image generation.

Clustering is an ML task that groups similar data points together into clusters, as illustrated in Figure 3-7, which allows you to see any emerging patterns. While you won't be able to deduce any labels that you don't have, you can still find outliers or clusters of interest to further investigate. Unsupervised learning can be used for customer segmentation because you can hypothesize that customers in the same clusters might have similar preferences or behaviors. You can use unsupervised learning for anomaly and outlier detection since you can find abnormal patterns in the data without prior knowledge of what an "anomaly" looks like.

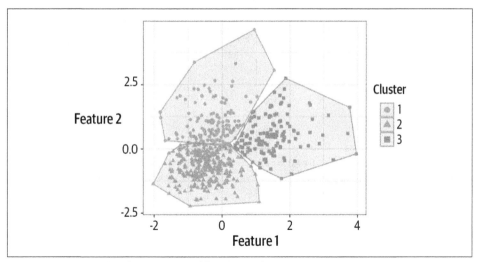

Figure 3-7. Example of unsupervised learning: clustering.

Dimensionality reduction is a common technique used to reduce the number of redundant input variables in training data. Reducing the number of features/input variables can help to reduce overfitting since models that learn from too many variables might also learn from the "noise" from those variables.

Summarizing Semisupervised and Self-Supervised Learning

Additional variations as extensions of supervised and unsupervised learning have become more popular in the industry, especially because of limitations on fully labeling large amounts of data. You might not encounter these concepts much during interviews, but you should be aware of them. If the team you're interviewing with uses these techniques, it will be good to be prepared to discuss them.

Semisupervised learning uses a small amount of labeled data (usually manually labeled) to train a separate ML model specifically meant to help with machine labeling previously unlabeled data. The initial labeled dataset is then combined with the machine-generated labels with highest confidence to create a larger labeled dataset, as illustrated in Figure 3-8.

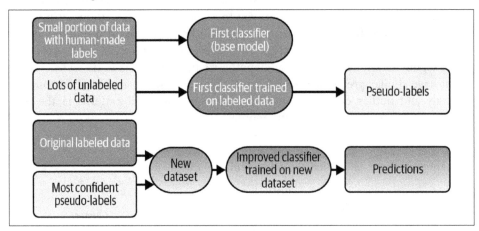

Figure 3-8. Semisupervised learning overview.

Self-supervised learning[15] relies on the dataset itself to learn latent representations, without labels. For example, in an image, if certain parts are removed, can we predict or generate those missing parts? Common usage of self-supervised learning includes filling in missing parts of images, audio, video,[16] text, and so on.

 Semisupervised and self-supervised learning can be brought up in interview answers to help with a lack of labeled data or cases where it's not necessary to label all the data.

---

15 See Randall Balestriero et al., *A Cookbook of Self-Supervised Learning*, June 28, 2023, *https://oreil.ly/M20OU*, and the accompanying blog post "The Self-Supervised Learning Cookbook," *Meta AI* (blog), April 25, 2023, *https://oreil.ly/XT6wX*.

16 To learn more, see Andrew Zisserman, "Self-Supervised Learning" (presentation, Google DeepMind), *https://oreil.ly/wGQ98*.

Summarizing Reinforcement Learning

The third major type of machine learning based on the dataset or the usage of labels is *reinforcement learning* (RL). In it's simplest form, RL doesn't necessarily require a prior dataset, although generally in industry, I'd still prefer to have some existing dataset or existing model so I can test the RL algorithms offline (not live) before deploying the RL agent into the real world or into the hands of customers.

RL relies on an "agent," which is not the same as the concept of an ML "model" that I introduced earlier, although they do have similarities in that they both improve and learn through iterations. RL learns through trial and error. The agent only needs to react to each new data point as it comes in, and the agent eventually learns enough from experience to figure out an optimal way of predicting the best action to carry out next.

A common RL example is a robot learning to navigate a maze that has rewards, traps, and an exit (for an example, see Figure 3-14 later in this chapter). The first time the robot moves through the maze, it has no knowledge of where the gold, traps, and exit are. But as it encounters those things in the environment, it also acquires knowledge, or data points, about the past, similar to constructing its own dataset via trial and error. After the robot has navigated the maze enough times, it learns the fastest and safest path to the exit. But based on how you design the RL agent, it can also optimize for various goals, such as collecting the most gold instead of reaching the exit as fast as possible.

There are various types of RL, some of which resemble supervised learning, but I will leave the in-depth discussion of those for the section "Reinforcement Learning Algorithms" on page 101. RL is commonly used in gaming, robotics, and self-driving cars, but RL can also be used for a growing number of applications that previously used supervised learning, such as a system that recommends videos on YouTube.

Sample Interview Questions on Supervised and Unsupervised Learning

Now that I've covered supervised, unsupervised, and reinforcement learning at a higher level, let's look at some common interview questions that stem from these concepts.

This section specifically covers interview questions on supervised and unsupervised learning; since RL has its own section, "Reinforcement Learning Algorithms" on page 101, the questions on RL can be found there.

Interview question 3-4: What are common algorithms in supervised learning?

Example answer

The *regression* family of algorithms includes linear regression and logistic regression, among other algorithms such as generalized linear models (GLMs) and various time-series regression models such as autoregressive integrated moving average (ARIMA).

The *decision tree* family of algorithms can be used for both classification and regression tasks within supervised learning; these include XGBoost, LightGBM, CatBoost, and so on. Decision trees can be combined in random forest algorithms, which ensemble (combine) a multitude of decision trees. Like decision trees, random forests can be used for both classification and regression tasks under supervised learning.

Neural networks can be used for supervised learning tasks as well as unsupervised learning. In terms of supervised learning, these include many tasks in this section, such as image classification, object detection, speech recognition, and natural language processing (NLP).

Other algorithms include naive Bayes,[17] which is a supervised classification algorithm that uses Bayes' theorem.[18] Applications of Bayes' theorem in ML include Bayesian neural networks,[19] which predict a distribution of results (for example, a normal model might predict the price is $100, but the Bayesian model will predict the price is $100 with a standard deviation of 5).

Interview question 3-5: What are some common algorithms used in unsupervised learning? How do they work?

Example answer

Unsupervised learning is commonly used for clustering, anomaly detection, and dimensionality reduction. I'll group the algorithms by those categories. *Clustering* is often done with algorithms such as k-means clustering and density-based clustering (DBSCAN algorithm). *K-means clustering* groups the data into k clusters, and the algorithm iteratively labels each data point with the cluster's centroid. The cluster centroid is then updated, and the algorithm continues until the cluster assignments have reached a stable state and no longer shift or change. *DBSCAN* is a popular algorithm that groups together data points that are close to one another (high density) and also separates those clusters from one another

---

17 Jake VanderPlas, *Python Data Science Handbook* (*https://oreil.ly/kyA6E*) (O'Reilly, 2016).

18 "An Intuitive (and Short) Explanation of Bayes' Theorem," Better Explained, accessed October 23, 2023, *https://oreil.ly/I7ika*.

19 "Bayesian Neural Network," Machine Learning Glossary, accessed October 23, 2023, *https://oreil.ly/BotI7*.

depending on their distance. Because unsupervised learning algorithms can handle large class imbalances, there are common unsupervised learning algorithms that address anomaly detections.

There are many algorithms that can be used for dimensionality reduction. *Principal component analysis* (PCA) can "flatten" datasets into a lower-dimensional space. This is useful for data preprocessing since it can reduce the number of redundant features that are used while keeping the variance in the data so that enough signals and patterns are preserved in the data.

Autoencoders are a type of unsupervised learning with a broad range of applications, notably in NLP—but not limited to NLP. They can be used to encode a compressed representation of input text, which is also a form of dimensionality reduction, and then decode the compressed representation for the generation of the next chunk of text data. This is useful for text completion and text summarization tasks. As a subset of unsupervised learning, self-supervised learning is also a case where autoencoders can be used. Examples include self-supervised learning to fill in missing parts of images or fix audio and video.[20]

Interview question 3-6: What are the differences between supervised and unsupervised learning?

Example answer

The major difference between the two types of machine learning is related to the training data that is used. Supervised learning uses labeled data while unsupervised learning uses unlabeled data. *Labeled data* refers to the correct output or result from the ML model already being inside the training dataset.

Supervised and unsupervised learning also differ in terms of the ML model outputs. In supervised learning, the ML model aims to predict what the label would be. Unsupervised learning doesn't predict specific label(s) but rather tries to find latent patterns and groupings within the dataset, which can be used to cluster new data points.

In terms of evaluation, the two types of ML are assessed differently. Supervised learning is evaluated by comparing its outputs with the correct output (with the test/holdout/validation datasets). In unsupervised learning, the model is evaluated based on how well it groups or captures patterns within the data, via metrics such as the *Jaccard score* or *silhouette index* for clustering and receiver operating characteristic curves (ROC)/area under the curve (AUC) metrics for positive rate comparisons for anomaly detection.[21]

---

20 Andrew Zisserman, "Self-Supervised Learning" (presentation, Google DeepMind), *https://oreil.ly/o32MY*.

21 ML model evaluation is covered in more detail in Chapter 4.

Finally, supervised learning and unsupervised learning are generally used for different types of tasks. Supervised learning is often used for classification (predicting the correct category) or regression (predicting the correct value) tasks while unsupervised learning is often used for clustering, anomaly detection, and dimensionality reduction tasks.

Interview question 3-7: What are scenarios where you would use supervised learning but not unsupervised learning, and vice versa? Please illustrate with some real-world examples.

Example answer

Unsupervised learning and supervised learning differ in the usage of results or labels. Hence, unsupervised learning is most suitable for cases where labeled data is not available or when the task isn't to predict a "correct" output, but rather to find patterns or anomalies in the data.

As a real-world example, supervised learning can be used for classification and object detection, such as in image recognition tasks. In the training dataset I'll have the correct objects labeled, and the algorithms will then know if they're learning to detect objects correctly based on comparing their predictions with the ground truth. In other words, if the algorithm isn't correctly boxing faces in images, I'd know since I'll have each image (with the faces correctly boxed) to compare to. Other scenarios for supervised learning could include predicting the price of a rare trading card based on its features, such as its age, its series name, and the condition of the card. Given that I have a dataset with fraudulent data already correctly labeled, fraud detection could also be an application of supervised learning. If I didn't already have labeled data about fraudulent behavior, I might opt to use unsupervised learning instead, via detecting anomalous behaviors.

In a real interview, you might not have to come up with so many examples, but as a reference answer, I'm including a few. It's even better if you can come up with an example that's a common concern for the industry of the company where you're interviewing. For example, time-series examples are often relevant to finance and fintech industries, and fraud detection is relevant to online sales platforms, banking, and finance.

Sometimes unsupervised learning is more suitable than supervised learning. For general warning signs of abnormal behavior, anomaly detection can be used to find an anomalous login location for a user's online bank account. Clustering is an unsupervised learning task, and a real-world application could be to group customers into segments based on their features (e.g., behavior, preferences), something that businesses might use to identify how they can tailor products to users in a cluster or to target marketing campaigns. If I investigate a cluster and it shows that young professionals have similar behaviors via the clustering algorithm, then we might know that we can give them similar promotional materials in the company's next digital ad campaign.

Interview question 3-8: What is a common issue that you might run into while implementing supervised learning, and how would you address it?

Example answer

One common problem that can affect supervised learning is the lack of labeled data. For example, when I want to classify specific cartoon and anime characters in images with ML, I don't have labeled data available on the internet to download and use. There are open source datasets such as CIFAR,[22] which are labeled for general objects and items, but when it comes to more specific use cases, I would have to acquire and label images myself (for personal usage).

I had to address the issue of not having enough labeled data; in this case, hand labeling a few examples worked as a starting point. However, there still weren't *enough* labeled examples, which resulted in an imbalanced dataset. To artificially increase the amount of labeled data, I used data augmentation, creating synthetic data and variations on existing data to make the ML model more robust. An example of data augmentation in image recognition is to randomly flip or rotate images. To illustrate why this can increase samples, if I flip one upright anime character looking to the right, it becomes two data points for the model to learn from: one looking right and one looking left. Rotation can also help: can the ML algorithm correctly identify anime characters who are leaning sideways or who are even upside down, doing a headstand?

Interviewer's Perspective

Another tip is to tie techniques that you've used to your past experience (so you can answer the interviewer's follow-up questions more easily) or to scenarios that you know would be relevant to the employer's industry, as mentioned before.

---

22 Alex Krizhevsky, "The CIFAR-10 Dataset," Canadian Institute for Advanced Research, accessed October 23, 2023, *https://oreil.ly/x1g7o*.

Natural Language Processing Algorithms

NLP has gained traction in recent years, with the notable example of OpenAI's ChatGPT. There are a lot of interview questions that build off the foundational techniques of transformers, and subsequently the BERT and GPT families of models, so I will cover those concepts in this section.

NLP is often applied in chatbots and sentiment analysis (for example, to see if the general attitude toward a product or company is positive or negative, based on Reddit or Twitter posts) as well as to generate written content. If you are interviewing for a company or team that is working on NLP, you will definitely be asked to demonstrate your understanding of these concepts in depth. Even if you're not interviewing for an NLP team specifically, I'd still recommend having a general understanding of NLP applications, which will make you a more well-rounded candidate and ML professional. Not to mention, NLP techniques are no longer used to generate written content only; they are also being combined with computer vision, text-to-image models to generate images, video, audio, and so on. Even time-series prediction and recommender systems have started picking up NLP techniques. You'll benefit from learning the basics of NLP because of how generalizable the techniques are.

This section covers the basics of NLP techniques for those who are unsure whether they have the background knowledge in this area. Feel free to skip the subsections if you already have expertise in any of these areas. Regardless of your expertise, I've highlighted specific advice for ML interviews in the tip boxes to help you apply your knowledge of each ML area and excel in your interviews.

Resources for Learning About NLP

To further supplement your knowledge of NLP techniques beyond the summaries I've provided in this book, I recommend the following resources:

- *Generative Deep Learning* (*https://oreil.ly/6BBxv*) by David Foster (O'Reilly)
- *Natural Language Processing with Transformers* (*https://oreil.ly/3Jw0x*) by Lewis Tunstall, Leandro von Werra, and Thomas Wolf (O'Reilly)
- The Practical Guides for Large Language Models (*https://oreil.ly/SeYwE*) on GitHub
- *Practical Natural Language Processing* (*https://oreil.ly/bp_6b*) by Sowmya Vajjala, Bodhisattwa Majumder, Anuj Gupta, and Harshit Surana (O'Reilly)

Refer back to this section for reference material when preparing for interviews.

Summarizing NLP Underlying Concepts

Let's break down the components that power NLP. First, you have a dataset, often called a *text corpus*.[23] A text corpus can consist of many types of text, such as news, online forums, or anything with a lot of authentic and meaningful text that isn't gibberish. Next, with this dataset you'll need to preprocess the data much like you would for other ML jobs. Some common techniques that are quizzed about in interviews are tokenization, bag of words, or TF-IDF (term frequency–inverse document frequency).

Tokenization is the process of breaking down the text into individual words, phrases, or useful semantic units.[24] For example, depending on the situation, the word "preprocess" could be left as its own token or separated into "pre" and "process." "Aren't" could be left as its own token but could also be separated into "are," and "n't."

Once the dataset has been preprocessed, language modeling can be formulated to predict the next sequence of items, which could be the next word (as illustrated in Figure 3-9), the next sentence, the next paragraph, missing words, and so on.

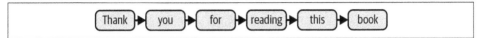

Figure 3-9. Next word or phrase prediction, as seen in autocomplete (https://oreil.ly/ MoMsz) on phones or email.[25]

Bag of words (BoW) is a way to map a sentence or phrase by mapping the words in it to a vector. The vector can consist of the words and other info, such as how many times the word has appeared (1 if once, 2 if twice, and so on). An example *.json* representation for the sentence "Syd likes to drink bubble tea and chamomile tea" would be:

```
{
    "Syd": 1, "likes": 1, "to": 1, "drink": 1, "bubble": 1, "tea": 2,
    "and": 1, "chamomile": 1

}
```

Note that the word "tea" appears twice, and thus the count is 2.

---

23 "Text Corpus," Wikipedia, updated September 17, 2023, *https://oreil.ly/v2IbE*.

24 Christopher D. Manning, Prabhakar Raghavan, and Hinrich Schütze, "Tokenization," in *An Introduction to Information Retrieval* (Cambridge University Press, 2022), *https://oreil.ly/0opkO*.

25 Yonghui Wu, "Smart Compose: Using Neural Networks to Help Write Emails." *Google Research* (blog), May 16, 2018, *https://oreil.ly/gqnBt*.

TF-IDF uses the frequency of the appearance of words in a passage or document to determine how relevant those words are.

Although it shares many foundational concepts with other types of ML, NLP comes with unique challenges. In cases where supervised learning is used, such as downstream fine-tuning, the data is hard to label. For example, if you are using supervised fine-tuning for sentiment analysis to quickly predict if a user review is positive or negative, it can be ambiguous at times. Another challenge is that there's a large amount of variability, such as slang and regional syntax differences, which can also lead to data sparsity, where exact combinations of words might rarely appear in the text corpus but are still valid.

Common use cases of NLP include sentiment analysis, chatbots, text classification (e.g., spam versus not spam), text generation, text summarization, text-to-image generation, and many more.

BoW and TF-IDF are useful underlying techniques that I've recently heard mentioned in interviews.

Summarizing Long Short-Term Memory Networks

Long short-term memory (LSTM) networks are a type of recurrent neural network designed to handle long sequences of data, which is useful in NLP applications. Like attention units in transformers, long-term dependencies and context of prior text are important for NLP to be effective. However, LSTMs have some limitations, such as when dealing with very long sequences of text—that is, understanding the context of text that came much earlier in a page or paragraph. To that end, transformers (covered in the next section) are able to handle long-term dependencies better.

LSTMs can be used for feature engineering and time series as well. I don't include more explanation here because of space constraints, but I encourage you to read more. Christopher Olah's blog Understanding LSTM Networks (*https://oreil.ly/C-jwG*) offers a good series of illustrations for understanding how LSTMs are used.

Summarizing Transformer Models

The transformer model was introduced by Google in 2017,[26] which has enabled a larger scope of language models in recent years. Transformers are effective at NLP modeling because of their improvements in handling context and meaning over longer text strings compared to existing architectures like convolutional neural networks (CNNs) and recurrent neural networks (RNNs).[27] Transformers are also better suited to finding patterns within the dataset, as opposed to requiring large, labeled datasets like CNNs and RNNs do. Hence, there is a lower barrier to entry for what datasets are available. With transformers, large, free-form text corpora from the internet became available for use, without the need for costly labeling beforehand.

Attention units within the transformer network are part of transformers' effectiveness and can find both short- and long-distance relationships between words, which helps the model correctly label the context. Take, for example, the sentences "Max went to the record store. Later, *he* bought a Jay Chou album." Self-attention units can correctly identify that "*he*" is referring to "Max." Combined with BERT's encoder architecture and multihead attention mechanisms, this has resulted in significant improvements in the performance and capabilities of NLP tasks.

Summarizing BERT Models

Developed by Google, BERT (Bidirectional Encoder Representations from Transformers) models have been used to process queries on the Google search engine since 2019.[28] As hinted at in its full name, BERT makes use of the transformer neutral network discussed earlier. BERT is pretrained, meaning the initial training step done by Google generates the model that users can access[29] via "self-supervised" learning on a large corpus of text, such as Wikipedia and other text datasets. There are two tasks BERT is trained on during pretraining: masked language modeling (MLM) and next sentence prediction (NSP).

Masked language modeling refers to randomly "masking," or blocking/removing, several tokens in a sentence and letting the model learn to correctly predict those tokens—for example, "Lisa is singing a [MASK]," where [MASK] signifies the token for BERT to predict. This is illustrated in Figure 3-10. If BERT can predict that "song" or "melody" or other words have a higher probability of being correct, then

---

26 Ashish Vaswani et al., "Attention Is All You Need" (paper presented at the meeting of the Advances in Neural Information Processing Systems, 2017), *https://arxiv.org/abs/1706.03762*.

27 Rick Merritt, "What Is a Transformer Model?" *Nvidia* (blog), March 25, 2022, *https://oreil.ly/As2W6*.

28 Pandu Nayak, "Understanding Searches Better than Ever Before," *The Keyword* (blog), Google, October 25, 2019, *https://oreil.ly/xONdR*.

29 See "Pre-trained Models," BERT, on GitHub, *https://oreil.ly/XkaY2*.

the model training is going well. If it's predicting words or tokens like "dog," then it is not being accurate at that point during model training.

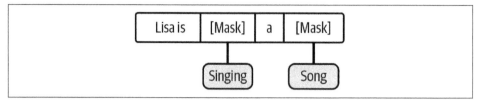

Figure 3-10. Illustration of masked language modeling.

Next sentence prediction is the second task that BERT is trained on. The goal is to accurately predict the next sentence in a text sequence. Since this training process can provide feedback to the model without external labeling, it is not "supervised" learning per se, but it is described as "self-supervised" since the feedback comes from the text corpus itself.

After model pretraining, users can then download the model or use an API[30] to "fine-tune" the model to their own use cases. This improves on the user's copy of the BERT model and requires supervised learning. For example, the user may wish to use BERT for sentiment analysis; in that case, the user would need to provide examples and labels of text that have a positive sentiment, negative sentiment, or ambiguous sentiment (if the user wishes). If you want to use BERT to generate text with a specific tone—for example, a movie supervillain—you'd need to provide BERT-specific examples as part of fine-tuning. BERT saves the user a lot of time on tasks like these since it already has a general understanding of the target language (English, among pretrained models of other languages that have been created by various developers[31]).

 Fine-tuning can be used for many other ML models, not just BERT. For example, you can fine-tune models such as GPT-3.5 (*https://oreil.ly/5IMBU*) (at the time of writing). However, I include fine-tuning under BERT since I have seen many interviews ask about fine-tuning in the context of BERT.

---

30 "Getting Started with the Built-in BERT Algorithm," AI Platform Training: Documentation, Google Cloud, updated October 20, 2023, *https://oreil.ly/HeJax*.

31 See "BERT Multilingual Base Model (Cased)" on Hugging Face, *https://oreil.ly/tyO6D*.

Summarizing GPT Models

The GPT (Generative Pretrained Transformer) family of NLP models is known for powering the OpenAI tool, ChatGPT. The GPT family of models includes GPT-1, GPT-2, GPT-3, and GPT-4 at the time of writing.[32] They are trained on large corpora of text,[33] such as BookCorpus, WebText (Reddit), English Wikipedia, and more.

The GPT family leverages transformers and is pretrained on predicting the next word. Like other major NLP models, it can be fine-tuned[34] downstream to update the pretrained model's parameters to parameters targeted toward more specific tasks, such as text generation. Notably, GPT-3 (with GPT-3.5 and GPT-4 powering ChatGPT at the time of writing) also uses RL via user feedback to improve its model predictions. RL is covered in more detail in "Reinforcement Learning Algorithms" on page 101.

Apart from GPT, several other large language models (LLMs), such as PaLM2 (which powers Google Bard), Llama/Llama 2 (*https://oreil.ly/MkMeN*) (Meta AI), and more[35] are trained on similar techniques.

Going Further

NLP has been growing at a fast pace, with many well-known LLMs being released in recent years (as illustrated in Figure 3-11). I encourage candidates interested in the field to learn more about these models and techniques. I remember exploring Word2vec[36] and GloVe[37] at work, and now there are so many other ways to develop NLP applications. Many foundational methods such as those two and models like BERT are still commonly used, and hiring managers I know still ask about them, so don't neglect the foundations either!

---

32 GPT-4 came out after I had written the first draft of this chapter, so I had to add it! By the time this book reaches your hands, I wonder what else will have been released.

33 "Generative Pre-trained Transformer," Wikipedia, updated October 23, 2023, *https://oreil.ly/Emp_M*.

34 "Fine-tuning," OpenAI Documentation, accessed October 23, 2023, *https://oreil.ly/B19eG*.

35 This field is moving fast; by the time this book comes out, I wonder if these models will have been superseded.

36 "Word2vec," Wikipedia, updated September 5, 2023, *https://oreil.ly/JyqBW*.

37 Jeffrey Pennington, Richard Socher, and Christopher D. Manning, "GloVe: Global Vectors for Word Representation," Stanford University, August 2014, *https://oreil.ly/LdCcH*.

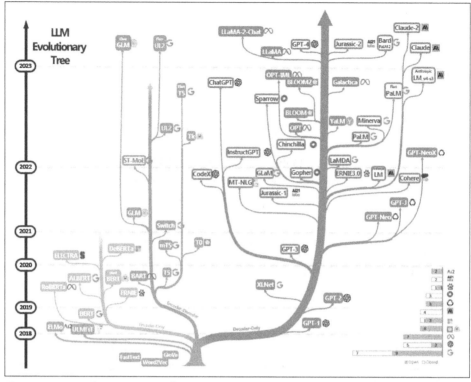

Figure 3-11. Evolutionary tree illustration of large language models; used with permission from "The Practical Guides for Large Language Models" (https://oreil.ly/eVJEK).

Sample Interview Questions on NLP

Now that I've covered some foundational techniques used in NLP, it's time to look at some interview questions. The NLP space and applications in generative AI have been moving very quickly, so we'll see how things change! However, from speaking to hiring managers in my network, I know that all of them still expect knowledge on foundational topics and data preprocessing techniques for NLP use cases.

Interview question 3-9: How would you leverage pretrained models like BERT for specific downstream tasks such as sentiment analysis, chatbots, or named entity recognition?

Example answer

> BERT and other NLP models that have been pretrained can be fine-tuned. A large source of pretrained NLP models is the Hugging Face model repository. Pretrained models may include user-uploaded fine-tuned models of original models by Google, OpenAI, and so on, but users can also download models fine-tuned on tasks like sentiment analysis.

If I wanted to fine-tune one of the original models myself, I'd need to provide a labeled dataset for the NLP model. For example, for sentiment analysis, that would include examples of both positive and negative sentiment text; for chatbots, I might provide labeled data with the correct corresponding answer to a help desk question; and for named entity recognition, I'd provide examples of the named entities that I'd expect the NLP model to correctly output.

Interview question 3-10: How do you clean/process a raw text corpus for training an NLP model? Can you name one or two techniques and the reasons behind them?

Example answer

When starting from a raw corpus, a quick first step is to use regex (regular expression) techniques to clean up unwanted characters. Some downstream tasks don't rely much on punctuation, but tasks like sentiment analysis could benefit from keeping punctuation; we can see how "!" could be useful for sentiment analysis. Next, we can use tokenization to break the text down into meaningful units, which often happen to be words; for example, "Susan is writing a sentence" becomes the five tokens: "Susan, is, writing, a, sentence."

Stemming and lemmatization both aim to reduce a word to its base form so that tense variations and derivations can still point to the same root word. *Stemming* is a rough heuristic that removes the ends of words (such as cars → car; history → histori and historical → histori).[38] Stemming is a cruder technique than *lemmatization*, which makes use of the dictionary forms of a base word; for example, in lemmatization, "studying," "studies," and "study" will all be lemmatized as "study." This is useful for the NLP model to recognize that these words mean the same at their root.

Interview question 3-11: What are some common challenges of NLP models, and how would you address them?

Example answer

Possible challenges with NLP, even with robust pretrained models, could be homonyms/synonyms, sarcasm, or domain-specific language such as that of financial or legal documents and the like. All of these can be improved upon with better downstream fine-tuning with more data that targets the specific case. For example, you can provide more examples of the usage of synonyms so that the NLP model can pick out more signals on when to use which word.

---

38 Christopher D. Manning, Prabhakar Raghavan, and Hinrich Schütze, "Stemming and Lemmatization," in *Introduction to Information Retrieval* (Cambridge University Press, 2008), *https://oreil.ly/JsXCj*.

There are also inherent biases in many cases; pretraining corpora that are commonly used for LLM training, such as Wikipedia, have a disproportionate number of male volunteer editors. Reddit, being a forum with a large text dataset, is also commonly used as a base for a training dataset and has a disproportionate number of male users.

Language Models and Fairness

Laura Weidinger et. al (Google DeepMind and collaborators) have published a paper on ethical and social risks of harm from language models that discusses perpetuation of stereotypes, unfair discrimination, and so on within language models.[39]

It's important to read through considerations like these; especially in interviews covering language models or data acquisition (see Meta's system design interview in Chapter 6), candidates being knowledgeable and thoughtful about potential risks (including biases) is important to succeeding at interviews.

Interview question 3-12: What is the difference between BERT-cased and BERT-uncased? What are the advantages and disadvantages of using one over the other?

Example answer

BERT-uncased has a tokenizer that will lowercase text input, so regardless of passing in cased (including uppercase) or all lowercase (uncased) text, it will be the same for BERT-uncased. *BERT-cased*, however, has a separate entry for the same words with different cases; for example, "The" will be different from "the" in BERT-cased. Thus, BERT-cased has the ability to distinguish between different semantics based on case. In applications where the case information doesn't matter much, then BERT-uncased may be suitable. However, for situations where cased information is important, such as where proper nouns are valuable for the NLP task, BERT-cased will be preferred.

 You can see a trend in these questions: regardless of the NLP application (even if it's generative AI!) knowing how to adapt to situations is essential. Preprocessing will be different if proper nouns are useful (don't lowercase everything), and while sometimes you might keep the punctuation (such as in sentiment analysis), sometimes you don't. Deeply understanding NLP techniques can help you respond much better in interviews than if you only memorize and regurgitate.

---

39 Weidinger et al., *Ethical and Social Risks of Harm from Language Models*, Google DeepMind, December 8, 2021, *https://oreil.ly/-ZFL7*.

Recommender System Algorithms

Recommender systems (RecSys) are everywhere in our digital lives and are responsible for personalization of the web pages and apps you visit, such as Netflix, YouTube, Spotify, any social media site, and much more. One way to tell if a site has personalization is by comparing the order of items or products shown on its front page or search results when two different people are logged in. For example, what is shown on your YouTube front page is likely not the same as the front page of a sibling or friend.

A recommender system recommends items or products that it thinks you might enjoy, interact with, or purchase based on your past behavior. For example, Netflix uses information on what shows and movies you've watched before as signals in its recommender systems to suggest new shows and movies for you.

 Since so many tech products use recommender systems, this is a common "default" category that interviewers at big tech companies will ask about.

This section covers the basics of recommender systems techniques for those who are unsure whether they have the background knowledge in this area. Feel free to skip the subsections if you already have expertise in any of these areas. Regardless of your expertise, I've highlighted specific advice for ML interviews in the tip boxes to help you apply your knowledge of each ML area and excel in your interviews.

Resources for Learning About RecSys Algorithms

To further supplement your knowledge on recommender techniques beyond the summaries I've provided in this book, I recommend the following resources:

- *Practical Recommender Systems* (*https://oreil.ly/mNis7*) by Kim Falk (Manning)
- Use cases and papers (*https://oreil.ly/cmW6s*) via Eugene Yan's curated applied ML repository

Refer back to this section for reference material when preparing for interviews.

Summarizing Collaborative Filtering

Collaborative filtering is a common technique in recommender systems. The term comes from using data on preferences of many users and/or items (collaborative) to make recommendations for a singular user (filtering). This is based on an assumption that individuals with similar past preferences can share preferences for new, unseen products; hence, the algorithm will recommend new items liked by similar users.

There are two main types of collaborative filtering techniques: user based and item based. *User-based* collaborative filtering identifies users with similar interests and preferences and then recommends products or items to each of those similar users that they haven't seen before. "Similar" users are calculated by ML algorithms, such as matrix factorization, which will be covered later in this chapter. *Item-based* collaborative filtering identifies items that are similar to one another based on their user ratings or user interaction. Items are then recommended by the collaborative filtering algorithm if a user has previously enjoyed similar items.

Summarizing Explicit and Implicit Ratings

In user-based and item-based collaborative filtering, you generally need to know users' ratings and preferences. If a user has left a good rating and review, then you can *explicitly* know that they enjoy a product. But users simply don't have enough time to provide explicit, detailed feedback on everything—think about the times you've left a review; you likely didn't do so for every single item you've used in the past. However, you can still calculate *implicit* feedback, such as the time spent on a YouTube video: if someone watches to the end, it could mean the viewer liked it more than a video they closed after two seconds. Using implicit feedback within a recommender system can help alleviate some common biases as well; people are more likely to leave an explicit review if they either loved or hated the product (and you know people are more vocal if something went wrong).

In Chapter 4, I'll discuss model training and data preprocessing. For recommender systems applications, making sense of the available explicit and implicit ratings during exploratory data analysis, model training, data preprocessing, featuring engineering, evaluation, and monitoring is important to discuss in interviews.

Summarizing Content-Based Recommender Systems

Another common type of recommender system is the content-based system. In a *content-based* recommender system, you need detailed information about the products themselves. This information could include traits of text descriptions (book blurbs, movie genres and descriptions), images (product screenshots), audio/video (trailers, product videos), and so on to create an understanding of which items are similar to one another. In contrast, the user- and item-based collaborative filtering described earlier relies on user preferences of items or products but not the traits of the items themselves.

An example content-based movie recommender system could recommend movies based on the genre, director, or actors of movies that the user has previously watched and enjoyed, as measured by explicit and implicit feedback. Hence, a content-based recommender systems can be formulated as a ranking or classification problem, and algorithms like tree-based models are suitable.

User-Based/Item-Based Versus Content-Based Recommender Systems

There are some pros and cons to using user-based/item-based or content-based recommender systems. User-based systems don't perform as well with new users; this is commonly referred to as the "cold-start" problem since there isn't enough data on the users' preferences because they may not have bought or rated any products yet. Content-based recommender systems might need less user-behavior data since they do not rely on other users' preferences or ratings, which makes them suitable for newer users or niche items with less user feedback overall. But content-based systems might be limited to recommending items similar to what the user has interacted with before; therefore, new items are not introduced to the user, limiting the diversity of the products or items that the user might have enjoyed had they been recommended those products.

Knowing the trade-offs between user-based, item-based, and content-based recommender systems can help you in interviews as well as on the job. In reality, explicit feedback can be hard to come by, and implicit feedback might not be perfect. Knowing how to mix and match all the data and RecSys algorithms at your disposal will help you stand out by a lot.

Summarizing Matrix Factorization

Matrix factorization is a technique used in collaborative filtering. First, a matrix is constructed with users as the rows and items as the columns, with the ratings or preferences of a user on an item as the cell values. This is called the *user-item matrix*, as illustrated in Figure 3-12. Since not all users interact with all items, the original matrix will be very sparse. For example, a user might have interacted with only a handful of items, but the online platform has thousands or millions of products. The goal of matrix factorization is to predict those empty values in the matrix—that is, how much a user would rate the items they haven't interacted with before—and recommend those that you estimate that the user would enjoy.

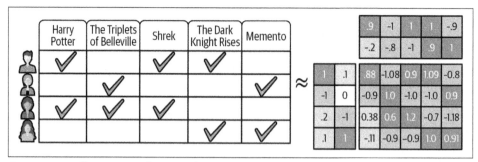

Figure 3-12. Illustration of matrix factorization; source: Google (https://oreil.ly/F7Tzg).

A classic algorithm is singular value decomposition (SVD); however, I have never seen it used outside of practice datasets because of its expensive computational requirements.[40] For industry applications, if as an ML practitioner you choose to use matrix factorization, the chosen algorithm needs to be able to handle very sparse and large matrices since many online platforms have a large number of products and users. Algorithms such as ALS help address this issue since they use approximation via least squares (covered in "Summarizing Linear Regression" on page 68) to calculate their best guesses for the missing matrix values (how much a user might enjoy an item) instead of the complex matrix manipulations that traditional SVD uses.

Sample Interview Questions on Recommender Systems

Now that I've covered the basics of recommender systems, let's go through some example interview questions.

Interview question 3-13: What's the difference between content-based recommender systems and collaborative filtering recommender systems? When would you use one over the other?

Example answer

> Content-based recommender systems require knowledge of categorization or traits of the products being recommended to determine product similarity. Collaborative filtering relies on user behavior and user preferences to recommend products that users with similar tastes enjoyed and thus can be more ignorant about the products themselves.
>
> Hence, content-based recommenders work well when there are not many users or items to construct the user-item matrix for collaborative filtering. In other words, content-based recommenders can still make recommendations when

---

40 For those who are curious, the time complexity of SVD (*https://oreil.ly/z4_x0*) of an *m* x *n* matrix, where $m > n$: $O(m^2 \times n + n^3)$. In practice, it might depend on the implementation, as this MathWorks discussion (*https://oreil.ly/GFa4z*) mentions.

---

there is the "cold-start" problem, as long as there is information on the features of the items/products and some information on the traits or preferences of the users, without requiring more data on user behavior and interactions like collaborative filtering does.

On the other hand, collaborative filtering is suited for scenarios in which a lot of data on user behavior is available. At times, it can be hard to gather sufficient, meaningful features that describe the products, which makes content-based recommender systems ineffective. In these cases, collaborative filtering can be more suitable.

 Anecdotally, I once worked on a project where a collaborative filtering algorithm (ALS) worked better for users who had used the web platform for a while but poorly for new users. Using content-based filtering with XGBoost worked better for new users, and we deployed different models depending on what type of user they were. Of course, this is only one example, and it may differ for your case.

Interview question 3-14: What are some common problems encountered in recommender systems, and how would you resolve them?

Example answer

The cold-start problem: this is when there aren't a lot of past data points available for an ML model to train on. Therefore, the model won't be able to learn enough patterns from the past to accurately predict the correct results for new data points. In recommender systems, content-based systems can be used, which require less user-behavior data but do still require sufficient product-feature data. This can help with the cold-start problem and still provide recommendations to newer website users.

Recommender systems can also encounter challenges with data quality, a problem that isn't exclusive to recommender systems. This can include errors in the source data—for example, due to a bug while ingesting the data. This issue can be addressed by analyzing where the source data has issues and then fixing it with the teams that handle data quality (at times, data engineers or platform engineers, or the MLEs and data scientists themselves). However, identifying that there is a data quality issue is important in the first place, and some preventative measures include using data quality monitoring tools like Great Expectations to alert the team when there are shifts in the data distribution or many missing values, for example.

When there are many missing values in an ML dataset, this is called *sparsity*. For example, users who sign up for a web platform with a questionnaire that asks for user preferences might not input several signup fields correctly or might skip them altogether. As an example, when someone signs up for a new Reddit account, there is a prompt that shows them common subreddits (subforums) that they may be interested in, but the user can skip this step. This is by design to make the web signup as frictionless as possible, but scenarios like this could cause data sparsity when you are trying to build a feature set for a RecSys. Possible solutions include imputation (e.g., filling in missing values with the mean or using a tree-based method to fill in the data), using collaborative filtering or matrix factorization techniques, feature engineering, and more.

Interview question 3-15: What is the difference between explicit and implicit feedback in recommender systems? What are the trade-offs with using each type, respectively?

Example answer

Explicit feedback includes user ratings or reviews while implicit feedback has to be derived from available user behavior, such as the time spent on a web page or clickstream behavior. The benefits of explicit feedback include a clearly quantified rating to use in machine learning as well as clarity when compared to implicit feedback. However, explicit feedback can be harder to gather since not all users will leave a review after every interaction (most don't).

Thus, measuring the user's engagement or enjoyment via implicit feedback, such as video watch time or time spent reading on a website, might be used. Of course, this can lead to imperfect measures: is the user spending a long time on the webpage because they enjoyed the content or because they were confused about the text on it? Overall, it is important to consider the trade-offs, but in practice, you can often combine both feedback signals in your ML models.

Interview question 3-16: How would you address imbalanced data in recommender systems?

Example answer

This is a common problem facing ML scenarios: there are a few classes or categories that have many more observations or data points than others, and there are many classes/categories that have so few observations that they form a long tail.[41]

To handle this issue, oversampling techniques may be helpful in simpler cases, such as creating more data points of categories that have fewer observations. However, when there are many classes/categories of observations, simple oversampling techniques won't be able to alleviate this issue. Additional techniques such as feature engineering and ensemble methods can be used instead, or in conjunction with oversampling. An example of ensemble methods could be creating a separate recommender for popular items versus low-engagement items.

---

41 Sometimes, this problem is referred to as the "long-tail" problem (*https://oreil.ly/Zd1Yp*) in RecSys.

In companies like Amazon and Spotify, combining RecSys with other families such as reinforcement learning helps ensure that long-tail products, artists, or items are shown to users at least some of the time.[42]

 To loop back to the beginning of this section, recommender systems are a common default ML topic to ask about since many tech companies' ML use cases can be formulated as a ranking or recommendation problem. In big tech, I've seen an increase of combining NLP techniques or RL with RecSys, so be sure to check out the papers in "Resources for Learning About RecSys Algorithms" on page 95 for existing examples of well-known RecSys-focused products, such as social media (e.g., Facebook, Instagram), entertainment (e.g., Netflix, Spotify, YouTube), online shopping (e.g., Amazon), and more.

Reinforcement Learning Algorithms

In "Supervised, Unsupervised, and Reinforcement Learning" on page 76 I briefly introduced reinforcement learning (RL) algorithms. To recap, RL relies on learning through "trial and error," and in the simplest of cases, it doesn't need a preexisting dataset or known labels. RL will gather knowledge through a live environment, such as a robot navigating a maze multiple times, learning where the gold, traps, and exits are.

Reinforcement learning has many applications in industry, such as autonomous vehicles, gaming,[43] as part of large-scale recommender systems, improvements of LLMs (RLHF[44] was a big part of improving ChatGPT (*https://oreil.ly/qoWME*)), and more. Hence, an understanding of RL is required for interviewing for teams that use RL.

 As mentioned earlier, RL is a somewhat more advanced family of techniques to use in production. So for new-graduate roles, you should focus on gaining a broader knowledge of ML first. Once you have that, knowing RL can help you stand out as a job candidate (based on my anecdotal experience).

---

42 Rishabh Mehrotra, "Personalizing Explainable Recommendations with Multi-Objective Contextual Bandits" (video presentation for MLconf, YouTube, March 29, 2019), *https://oreil.ly/v587X*; Brent Rabowsky and Liam Morrison, "What's New in Recommender Systems," AWS for M&E (blog), Amazon Web Services, *https://oreil.ly/Z0Qq2*.

43 I've spoken to someone at Ubisoft whose team trained RL agents to help optimize and test their games. Here are more examples from Ubisoft (*https://oreil.ly/1RP1h*).

44 Chip Huyen, "RLHF: Reinforcement Learning from Human Feedback" (blog), May 2, 2023, *https://oreil.ly/xE7tR*.

This section covers the basics of RL techniques for those who are unsure whether they have the background knowledge in this area. Feel free to skip the subsections if you already have expertise in any of these areas. Regardless of your expertise, I've highlighted specific advice for ML interviews in the tip boxes to help you apply your knowledge of each ML area and excel in your interviews.

Resources for Learning About RL Algorithms

To further supplement your knowledge of RL techniques beyond the summaries I've provided in this book, I recommend the following resources:

- *Reinforcement Learning: An Introduction* (*https://oreil.ly/AN7y9*) by Richard S. Sutton and Andrew G. Barto
- Use cases and papers (*https://oreil.ly/Nr5eg*) via Eugene Yan's curated applied ML repository

Refer back to this section for reference material when preparing for interviews.

Summarizing Reinforcement Learning Agents

In RL, an *agent* is an autonomous entity that interacts with an environment with certain goals or objectives and learns to make optimal decisions through trial and error. An example is a self-driving car that doesn't drive well but, while learning in a test environment, over time, learns which behaviors are good (following speed limits and road signs) and which are bad (such as bumping into trees and running red lights).

While the *model* is the focus of most ML algorithms mentioned in the previous sections, in RL the *agent* is being updated as the agent interacts with the environment. This does not mean there are no "models" in RL, but models are often used as supporting components that can be mixed and matched within the entire RL workflow.

To illustrate RL, I'll continue with the example of a self-driving car, simplified for understanding. Creating this basic RL agent requires the following building blocks: state, action, reward, and policy.

 There are many types of reinforcement learning, so the way the policy, state, action, or rewards interact in each type of algorithm may differ, and they may be mixed and matched with other concepts. Pay attention to which concepts you are being asked about in the interview.

The RL agent is attempting to learn the best policy for how to react to the environment in order to drive safely. When the agent is initialized, it doesn't know the policy

---

to choose the best action in a given scenario yet, so you just let it drive around in the environment. The building blocks for this specific scenario are:

State

> The *state* that the agent encounters is a representation of the environment, or the state of the environment. This could include updating information about the car's surroundings; tracking if there is an object to the left, right, front, or behind the car; and special tags for drivable roads and traffic lights and their status.

Action

> The *actions* that the agent can choose in this example are: turn left, turn right, go forward, and brake. Note: this scenario is simplified to discrete actions, but complex scenarios might include how many degrees to turn the steering wheel. All the actions that the agent can carry out are collectively referred to as the *action set*, and the agent aims to carry out the best action at each decision point.

Reward

> Each time the agent makes an action, given a state of the environment, the agent then gains feedback on how much benefit was gained or lost—this is called *reward* in RL. For example, during the state when there is a red light in front of the self-driving car RL agent, and the RL agent makes the action to brake, that can be rewarded with a positive reward. If the RL agent had chosen to go forward and run the red light, it would have gotten a penalty: a reward with a negative value, also referred to as a *negative reward*. The agent will remember that for the next time. The rewards are usually defined externally, and the agent doesn't know about them beforehand, only learning about them during trial and error. Note that the wording "action made *given* a state" is deliberate; the same action in different states might yield different rewards. For example, turning right and crashing when there is a lamppost to the right and turning right when there is a right-turn lane will yield a negative and a positive reward, respectively. Hence, the *state* is essential to the decision and the learning of the RL agent, not just the *actions* and *rewards*.

Policy

> The *policy* is how the agent chooses the action. In most cases, it will choose the action that is known to yield the highest reward, but this simple policy causes the agent to stop exploring new scenarios and often yields strange behavior. For example, the agent might have learned early on that turning right at a red light doesn't have a negative reward (allowed under traffic law in many places in North America). The agent might *exploit* the fact, always turning right at a red light, instead of trying something new and stopping at a red light instead.

So the policy can be defined as choosing the action given that state that is known to yield the highest reward, given that it balances additional factors such as *exploitation* of known rewards and *exploration* of the environment to learn new state-action-reward combinations. Commonly used policies include the epsilon-greedy policy,[45] where the agent explores more in the beginning of the training process and then exploits more after it's experienced more states, actions, and rewards. In some types of RL, its policy is a parametrized model that is then updated; I'll cover that more in the later section about policy-based RL.

In summary, the agent uses the policy to choose an optimal action at a given state, after which it looks at the reward from the action and then updates the policy to improve for future states and actions, as illustrated in Figure 3-13.

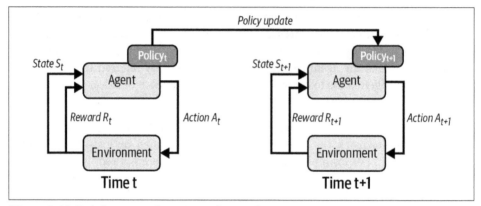

Figure 3-13. Reinforcement learning policy update.

 In interviews, I've experienced more follow-up questions and drill-downs on why the reward is set up in such a way—for example, "Why did you choose to include a click-through as a positive reward but not the video watch time?"

Summarizing Q-Learning

I'll continue to build on the concepts of state, action, reward, and policy as foundations for the following sections. The RL agent generally wants to maximize the highest rewards from choosing an action at a given state. However, without further nuances in the rewards, this can lead to short-term thinking, as you've seen when the agent only *exploits* and doesn't *explore*. One way of addressing short-term thinking in RL is through adding more sophistication in the design of the reward beyond the immediate action. Thus, the long-term *expected* reward, which includes not only the reward from the immediate action but also possible rewards that are available to the agent in the future, is important.

---

45 "Epsilon Greedy Policy," Machine Learning Glossary: Reinforcement Learning, accessed October 23, 2023, *https://oreil.ly/ZYbkN*.

The expected total reward is calculated as part of the RL process as a weighted sum of the expected values of the future rewards that are available given the current step. I'll illustrate this with the example of a robot that needs to find the way out of a maze, as illustrated in Figure 3-14:

- In this maze, bombs are bad while gold/money is good.
- The exit is at the upper-right side of the maze, and there is a dead end in the middle of the maze, which the robot has learned about during previous exploration.
- If the robot chooses to go toward the middle, then it has a higher probability of going to the dead end and a lesser probability of going to the exit, which is captured in the sum of expected values of future reward.
- Hence, all things held constant, the total expected reward (aka the expected cumulative reward) from heading to the upper-right will be higher than the total expected reward from heading toward the middle. Of course, the robot needs to have explored those places already; before it has, it will still calculate the expected reward, but it might not be as accurate.

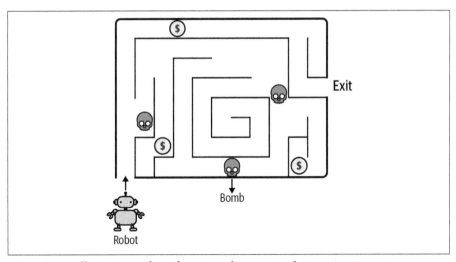

Figure 3-14. Illustration of reinforcement learning: robot navigating a maze.

Now let's connect the concept of expected cumulative reward to the *Q-value*, which is the expected cumulative reward for taking an action in a particular state. The *Q-function* is a related concept; it takes the inputs of the state-action pairs and outputs the Q-values. The policy determines the action that the RL agent should take in a given state. To tie everything together, the optimal policy in Q-learning comes from selecting the action with the highest Q-value in each state. After each step, the policy is evaluated and the Q-values are updated using an optimization method called the

Bellman equation.[46] The process is repeated until the policy converges and selects the same action at a given state.

It is also possible to use Q-learning without policy iteration, instead using the simpler epsilon-greedy policy, which was mentioned in the previous section. This simpler format is often more practical in situations where the policy is less likely to converge or is expensive to learn or when the state and/or action space is very large.

Summarizing Model-Based Versus Model-Free Reinforcement Learning

Because Q-learning doesn't use a model to try to model the world—or in other words, the *relationship* between the states and the actions—it is a *model-free RL* technique. Model-free RL like Q-learning requires the representation of the state and the action, but then it only needs to observe the rewards to continue improving its Q-values and policy (if using policy iteration).

 Common model-free RL algorithms include Q-learning, SARSA (state-action-reward-state-action),[47] and proximal policy optimization (PPO).[48]

In model-based RL, the agent learns a model of the environment, which includes the way the various possible states are related to one another, called *state transitions*. The agent uses this model to make decisions about the best action(s) to take in a given state. Therefore, model-based RL requires explicit knowledge of the environment. Examples include dynamic programming and Monte Carlo tree search (MCTS).[49]

46 "Bellman Equation," Machine Learning Glossary: Reinforcement Learning, accessed October 23, 2023, *https://oreil.ly/KP8kh*.

47 "SARSA Agents," MathWorks, accessed October 23, 2023, *https://oreil.ly/KP8kh*.

48 Yuewen Sun, Xin Yuan, Wenzhang Liu, and Changyin Sin, "Model-Based Reinforcement Learning via Proximal Policy Optimization," *2019 Chinese Automation Conference (CAC)*, 2019, pp. 4736–40, doi:10.1109/CAC48633.2019.8996875 (*https://oreil.ly/M-POc*).

49 Michael Janner, "Model-Based Reinforcement Learning: Theory and Practice," *Berkeley Artificial Intelligence Research*, December 12, 2019, *https://oreil.ly/ZuF22*.

Summarizing Value-Based Versus Policy-Based Reinforcement Learning

Value-based RL is built on estimating the expected cumulative reward (aka the "value") of being in a certain state and choosing to take a certain action, such as in Q-learning,[50] SARSA,[51] and deep Q-networks (DQNs). The focus of these algorithms is on being able to predict the expected cumulative reward.

On the other hand, *policy-based* RL learns the policy, the method or pattern that the agent uses to choose actions in a given state. Policy-based RL has a parametrized policy function that can be optimized with gradient ascent methods as it learns the mapping between states and actions. Gradient ascent is used because policy-based RL aims to maximize the expected cumulative reward, as opposed to gradient descent, which is used to minimize errors. Common policy-based algorithms include policy gradient algorithms such as REINFORCE and actor-critic methods (the "actor" learns a policy, and the "critic" learns the value). You can see an illustration of the various types of RL in Figure 3-15.

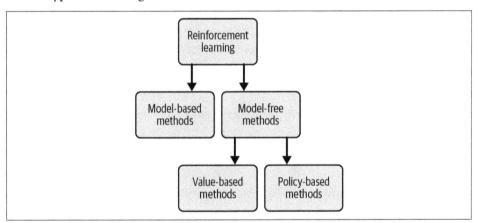

Figure 3-15. Overview of reinforcement learning methods; source: "Introduction to Reinforcement Learning" by J. Zico Kolter (https://oreil.ly/d0sua).

---

50 J. Zico Kolter, "Introduction to Reinforcement Learning" (presentation, 28th International Conference on Automated Planning and Scheduling, Delft, The Netherlands, June 24–29, 2018), *https://oreil.ly/b_5nO*.

51 "SARSA Agents," MathWorks, accessed October 2, 2023, *https://oreil.ly/iZOG3*.

Summarizing On-Policy Versus Off-Policy Reinforcement Learning

On-policy RL updates its policy based on the data points collected while following the current iteration of the policy. Note that not all policy-based RL is necessarily on-policy.[52] Let's say that an RL algorithm takes an action (a1) with the current policy (p1), and with the observations from that action, it updates that policy with gradient ascent, notated as (p2): the latest learned policy. If the agent continues the next action (a2) with the new policy (p2), then it is considered on-policy. Policy iteration methods like SARSA[53] are on-policy RL. In other words, if the agent's behavior policy is its target policy[54] (the policy being updated), then that is on-policy RL.

An *off-policy* RL algorithm updates its policies based on data points or experiences collected from a different policy or a mixture of policies. This includes Q-learning and DQNs. Coincidentally, these are value-based RL algorithms. To prevent confusion, think of on-policy versus off-policy as pertaining to whether the agent is using the newest policy that is being updated while policy-based versus value-based refers to the types of algorithms used to derive the optimal behavior.

There are many additional algorithms to explore, such as temporal difference (TD), A3C (Asynchronous Advantage Actor-Critic), and PPO; if you're interested in learning more, I encourage you to take a look at the reinforcement learning textbook by Richard Sutton and Andrew Barto, available for free online (*https://oreil.ly/MCgBK*) and also included in the resources at the beginning of this section.

Sample Interview Questions on Reinforcement Learning

Now that you're familiar with introductory RL concepts, let's look at some example interview questions.

Interview question 3-17: Explain the DQN (deep Q-network) algorithm in reinforcement learning.

Example answer

DQN is an extension of Q-learning; DQN uses neural networks to approximate the Q-values, which represent the expected future reward from taking an action in a given state (the same definition as Q-learning). In DQN, you have two networks: a target network and the Q-network. The target network is responsible

---

52 Tingwu Wang, "Learning Reinforcement Learning by Learning REINFORCE" (presentation, University of Toronto Machine Learning Group), *https://oreil.ly/Fgmck*.

53 David L. Poole and Alan K. Mackworth, "On-Policy Learning," in *Artificial Intelligence*, 2nd ed. (Cambridge University Press, 2017), *https://oreil.ly/KmgMu*.

54 Tingwu Wang, "Learning Reinforcement Learning by Learning REINFORCE" (presentation, University of Toronto Machine Learning Group), *https://oreil.ly/Fgmck*.

for predicting the best Q-value out of all actions that can be taken from a given state (the target Q-value). The Q-network takes the current state and action and predicts the Q-value for a particular action (the predicted Q-value). To improve the Q-network, the difference between the predicted Q-value, the target Q-value, and the observed reward is used as a loss function for the Q-network.

The weights of the neural network are updated based on the difference between the predicted Q-learning and the actual Q-value obtained through experience. The reason for using the target network is to ensure that the training results are more stable since with reinforcement learning and updating the Q-network with each step, the variance of each action can be quite large. After sufficient steps, the target network is updated with the new weights of the Q-network, and training continues.

Interview question 3-18: As a follow-up question, could you explain the main modifications that DQN added on top of regular Q-learning?

Example answer

One of the main new advances that DQN uses is experience replay. Experience replay is a component before the Q-network and target networks that uses a simple epsilon-greedy method to take an action in the current state in the real environment and get a reward. It saves these actions, states, and rewards as experiences for the networks to use as training data. The reason for using experience replay is the sequential nature of reinforcement learning; the training dataset for the networks should have the sequence of rewards and new states that result from each action in the previous state.

Interview question 3-19: Explain exploration and exploitation in reinforcement learning with an example. What are the trade-offs of these two concepts? What are some ways you would balance exploration and exploitation?

Example answer

I'll use the example of an RL agent that is part of a simple self-driving car. During its exploration, it first finds that turning right at a red light isn't penalized (going by rules in North America). The agent may continue to exploit this knowledge instead of trying something new and learning to stop at the red light, causing undesired behavior: never stopping at a red light. Therefore, it is important to encourage exploration as well so that the agent tries out new behaviors. As the agent has explored more iterations of the environment, then it is safer to continue to increase the exploitation parameter because at that point it may be more important for the agent to perform well and become an accurate self-driving car with the experience it has gathered so far. By allowing more exploration early on and then reducing exploration and increasing exploitation later, via techniques such as the epsilon-greedy policy, I can balance exploration and exploitation.

In summary, to balance exploration and exploitation, I'd use an epsilon-greedy policy[55] so that the RL agent can explore more of the environment. As the agent interacts and learns more from the environment, the epsilon value is reduced, which makes the agent start to increase exploitation. Eventually, once the agent has explored sufficiently, it can exploit the good decisions it's seen in the past and reduce exploration.

Interview question 3-20: In the following scenario, you've found that the reinforcement learning algorithm keeps recommending an item that is incorrectly labeled as 10% of its sale price. What might have caused this, and what would you investigate, assuming that the data is all correct?

Example answer

In the case that there is a reward function in our RL agent, I would investigate the reward/reward function and see if it's rewarding perverse behavior of the RL agent. It could be that the agent is exploiting ways to increase users' click-through rate artificially, for example, by recommending items that are highly discounted. The artificial increase in click-through rate in this case leads to a positive reward for the RL agent. If the reward takes into account the cost of the discounts in the reward function, then the agent will be less likely to only optimize click-through rate at the cost of losing money on the product.

Interview question 3-21: Explain model-based or model-free reinforcement learning. What are some examples of each, and when would you choose one over the other?

Example answer

Model-free RL is often preferred when a model of the environment is difficult to estimate or where the environment is constantly changing. This is because model-based algorithms try to build an accurate model of the full environment they are operating in. The "model" includes the transition probabilities from one state to another. Note: the use of the word "model" here does not mean other components of RL are not ML models. Specifically, "model-based" RL refers to the model of the environment, which is not exclusive to having other ML models in the workflow.

Model-based RL is more feasible when you have a reasonable ground-truth representation of the entire environment, such as in a game environment like Atari or chess. These environments can be simulated many times, with (usually) deterministic results, so that the model that describes the environment and its state transition probabilities can be learned or built. In most real-world cases, it is less feasible to fully describe the environment, although with deep learning and

---

55 "Epsilon Greedy Policy," Machine Learning Glossary: Reinforcement Learning, accessed October 23, 2023, *https://oreil.ly/jHrup*.

a very, very large number of features that describe the environment, such as advanced sensors on a self-driving car, it might be possible. Generally in cases where the environment is not known, though, model-free RL can be used.

Computer Vision Algorithms

Computer vision is a common ML application that includes image classification, image recognition, and so on. Examples include applying computer vision to medical images, such as X-rays, to classify whether a patient has a certain disease, or checking waveform images to classify certain sounds. Self-driving cars represent a complex use of various computer vision techniques.

Some computer vision applications can be used across multiple industries. For example, optical character recognition (OCR) can be used to read checks for a bank's online check-deposit system, detect logos in social media posts, or identify products in advertising images.[56] Regardless of the industry, ML practitioners leveraging computer vision ML benefit from domain knowledge, especially for high-impact applications in health care or autonomous vehicles, for example.

 Interview questions about computer vision can rely heavily on domain knowledge, so beyond this book and resources on technical know-how, I encourage you to read about computer vision applications specific to your target field.

This section covers the basics of computer vision techniques for those who are unsure whether they have the background knowledge in this area. Feel free to skip the subsections if you already have expertise in any of these areas. Regardless of your expertise, I've highlighted specific advice for ML interviews in the tip boxes to help you apply your knowledge of each ML area and excel in your interviews.

Resources for Learning About Computer Vision

To further supplement your knowledge on computer vision techniques beyond the summaries I've provided in this book, I recommend the following resources:

- Image Classification with TensorFlow (*https://oreil.ly/K-0F7*) (tutorial)
- *Practical Machine Learning for Computer Vision* (*https://oreil.ly/kQ7r5*) by Valliappa Lakshmanan, Martin Görner, and Ryan Gillard (O'Reilly)

---

56 "What Is OCR (Optical Character Recognition)?" Amazon Web Services, accessed October 24, 2023, *https://oreil.ly/0ms_Z*.

- PyTorch: Training a Classifier (*https://oreil.ly/_Hy_U*) (tutorial)

Refer back to this section for reference material when preparing for interviews.

Summarizing Common Image Datasets

Because of their visual and relatively easy-to-understand nature, image datasets are commonly used as beginner tutorials for deep learning. For example, I remember using the dogs and cats dataset in a Coursera course on CNNs, along with hundreds of thousands of other learners. Using ML on images has captured the imagination of ML enthusiasts and is popular for self-learning and portfolio projects. In research, many of the same datasets have propelled major advances in ML. You might recall in Chapter 1 I mentioned that the ImageNet dataset and challenge led to a development and explosion of accuracy in deep learning models that hadn't been seen before.

Here are some common public datasets that are used in computer vision:

- ImageNet (*https://oreil.ly/yQHl1/*)
- CIFAR-100 (*https://oreil.ly/regHX*)
- MNIST (*https://oreil.ly/4Yf5C*) and related datasets, such as Fashion-MNIST (*https://oreil.ly/OeMdK*)
- COCO (*https://oreil.ly/FsK3V*) (Common Objects in Context)
- LVIS (*https://oreil.ly/2h6JQ*) (annotated COCO)

I encourage you to give them a try. If it's your first time, you can try the following Colab notebooks:

- Image Classification—Colaboratory tutorial (TensorFlow) (*https://oreil.ly/XnUJz*)
- Transfer Learning for Computer Vision tutorial (PyTorch) (*https://oreil.ly/AgB50*)

Once you've familiarized yourself with the basics, I encourage you to come up with a project yourself. You can find more image datasets here or even collect your own:

- Machine Learning Datasets—Image Classification (*https://oreil.ly/b_uhg*) on *paperswithcode.com*
- Know Your Data Catalog (*https://oreil.ly/Z2YS4*) by Google
- Kaggle (*https://oreil.ly/Fy-9E*) datasets

Many online tutorials start with a simple image dataset such as classifying cats and dogs, the Iris dataset (*https://oreil.ly/4Bhjc*), MNIST, and so on. As such, they should be used for learning purposes, not for portfolio purposes. Candidates will find it hard to stand out with projects that only use these most common datasets[57] since we interviewers have seen thousands of applicants (not an exaggeration) with these projects. Try to find more unique datasets if you're building a portfolio project.

Summarizing Convolutional Neural Networks (CNNs)

As discussed previously, examples of computer vision tasks include object detection, facial recognition, and medical classification. The data commonly used in computer vision algorithms are images, and often they are implemented with the CNN architecture, as illustrated in Figure 3-16. CNNs are particularly effective for tasks like image recognition because they can intake the information encoding from images, where images are represented as matrices (input feature maps). The inputs are then "convoluted" via various convolutional layers in the network—a process that extracts information from the images' matrix representation and creates new features that capture more nuanced information about the image. Convolution also allows information in the image to be flattened and compressed, which is effective for computation.

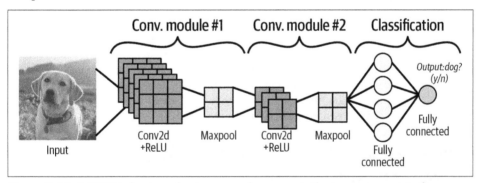

Figure 3-16. A CNN takes in a dog image and represents the image in matrix form, then two convolutional modules extract useful features, which are fed into the last two fully connected layers that predict if the image is a dog or not; based on an image from "ML Practicum: Image Classification" (https://oreil.ly/I3yeL), Google.

---

57 Unless you have some truly creative twist, but even so, you might have better ROI using a less-clichéd dataset.

Summarizing Transfer Learning

For computer vision tasks, you can find many pretrained models online. These pretrained models have already been tweaked and tuned on general tasks, such as image-classification tasks. It is time-consuming and resource heavy to train these models from scratch, so in practice, transfer learning is a common technique.

Transfer learning leverages a pretrained model and modifies the last layers' task to focus on the smaller task at hand. For example, the pretrained model might have been trained to classify one thousand items. At work, you have to classify only desktop computers and laptops for an inventory-tracking task. You can download the pretrained model, use its architecture and weights apart from the final layer, and train only the final layer(s) so that it can specialize in those two objects.

The result is a model that already has a general understanding of classifying images as well as the specialized tasks you've fine-tuned the model to do. This process is called *transfer learning*.

Here are some tutorials:

- Transfer Learning and Fine-Tuning (TensorFlow) (*https://oreil.ly/qVisB*)
- Transfer Learning for Computer Vision (PyTorch) (*https://oreil.ly/zO3Af*)

 In interviews, it is helpful to be aware of transfer learning. In many situations, it's useful to identify pretrained models to use and build on top of for the specific task at hand. In industry, it's rare for the first option to be training a whole new neural network, due to the costs. If you only mention training a model from scratch for computer vision, that might show that you haven't thought about or been exposed to practical situations enough.

Summarizing Generative Adversarial Networks

"Deepfakes" (fake images generated by deep learning) have been in the news for creating fake images of politicians and celebrities. Deepfakes are an example of how results of generative AI have already started to get very realistic. They are commonly generated by networks referred to as *generative adversarial networks* (GANs).

The architecture of GANs[58] focuses on two models: a generator and a discriminator. The *generator* learns and improves to generate good outputs. The *discriminator*

---

58 "Overview of GAN Structure," Machine Learning, Google for Developers, July 18, 2022, *https://oreil.ly/EfpSR*.

learns and improves in order to evaluate whether the outputs that the generator created are real or fake.

For example, the process training to generate images of Labrador retrievers (or Labs, for short) is as follows (see Figure 3-17):

- Training begins. The generator is bad at generating objects that look like Labs, while the discriminator is bad at distinguishing the images that the generator created from real pictures of Labs.

- As the generator is trained more, it learns to create images that look slightly more like Labs. As the discriminator is trained more, it's better able to distinguish the generator's fake Labs from the real ones. The goal of the generator is to create Labs that look real enough for the discriminator to mistake them for real Lab pictures from the real world.

- Finally, the generator gets so good at generating Lab images that the discriminator can no longer tell them apart.

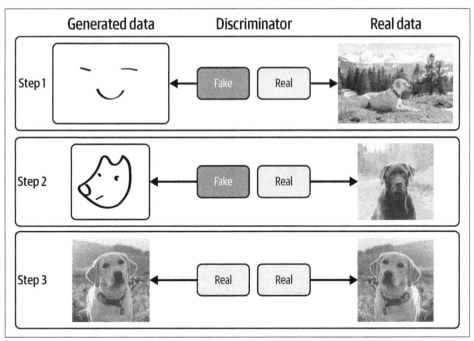

Figure 3-17. Illustration of GAN training. Note that the GAN can generate passable images not in the training dataset that are good enough to fool the discriminator. (In this illustration we just have a flipped image for simplicity, but the real network can generate images even more different from the real training data.)

Diffusion models are now common for image-generation tasks. I won't go into details in this book, but you can read the original paper[59] if you're interested.

Summarizing Additional Computer Vision Use Cases

In addition to classification and image generation, there are many more use cases for computer vision, such as super resolution, semantic segmentation, and object detection. I will go through a few common industry use cases here, but as mentioned before, I highly recommend you read about examples relevant to the company or industry you're interviewing for, to further enhance your answers during interviews.

Super resolution summary

Super resolution is the task of taking a low-resolution image and creating a high-resolution version of it. This task is also called *upscaling*. Common use cases are to upscale historical images, photos, films, and so on. In the health industry, this task can be used to increase the resolution of older medical equipment so that better diagnoses can be made if it's difficult to upgrade the equipment.

GANs and diffusion models are commonly used for this task. For more examples, here are some resources:

- "High Fidelity Image Generation Using Diffusion Models" (*https://oreil.ly/5b_5Y*), by Jonathan Ho (Google Research Blog)
- "SUPERVEGAN: Super Resolution Video Enhancement Gan for Perceptually Improving Low Bitrate Streams" (*https://oreil.ly/nw0e2*), by Silviu S. Andrei et al. (Amazon Science)

Object detection summary

Object detection is a task used to recognize and localize objects in an image. It is more advanced than image classification, which classifies the entire image; *localizing* tells us *where* in the image the object of interest is located. As an extension, by applying object detection to individual frames in a video, you can conduct object tracking and follow a subject's or object's location in a video feed, and even across multiple camera angles. Object detection and object tracking with ML can be used in sports matches to track a ball, for example.

Relevant algorithms to object detection include:

---

59 Jascha Sohl-Dickstein et al., "Deep Unsupervised Learning Using Nonequilibrium Thermodynamics" (2015), *https://oreil.ly/0Zp8Q*.

- YOLO (*https://oreil.ly/2RAW5*) (You Only Look Once) and its newer versions by Chien-Yao Wang et al.
- "Pix2Seq: A New Language Interface for Object Detection" (*https://oreil.ly/n14_h*), by Ting Chen and David Fleet (Google Research Blog)

Semantic image segmentation summary

Semantic image segmentation is the task of assigning a semantic label, such as "computer," "phone," "person," or "dog," to every pixel in an image. Examples include isolating categories in images, such as isolating humans in the foreground from buildings in the background. One common example is portrait mode in smartphone cameras. Read more about semantic segmentation applications in the Google Pixel mobile phone camera's portrait mode[60] as an example.

You can learn more with these resources:

- "Semantic Image Segmentation with DeepLab in TensorFlow" (*https://oreil.ly/qDr94*), by Liang-Chieh Chen and Yukun Zhu (Google Research Blog)
- "Comparison of Object Detection and Semantic Segmentation" (*https://oreil.ly/UmZhc*) from *Practical Machine Learning for Computer Vision* by Valliappa Lakshmanan, Martin Görner, and Ryan Gillard (O'Reilly)

Here are some more industry examples (note that they usually combine multiple techniques):

- Amazon consistently experiments and researches computer vision to help customers shop online, for example, helping them find relevant products by describing variations of existing products.[61] For instance, a customer could be searching for dresses and see one they like. However, the style is not available in the color they prefer. They can find dresses similar to the current product by typing, "I want a similar one, but change black to pink."
- Meta AI (*https://oreil.ly/yf9xL*) often seeks to leverage computer vision to improve automation on its social media platforms. For example, it has improved the automatically generated text descriptions of images for people with visual

---

60 Marc Levoy and Yael Pritch, "Portrait Mode on the Pixel 2 and Pixel 2 XL Smartphones," *Google Research* (blog), October 17, 2017, *https://oreil.ly/VdtgX*.

61 Larry Hardesty, "How Computer Vision Will Help Amazon Customers Shop Online," *Amazon Science* (blog), June 5, 2020, *https://oreil.ly/xGyam*.

impairments,[62] provided better automatic categorization of Facebook Market-place items, content moderation, and so on.

- Netflix uses computer vision to experiment with and improve thumbnails for content, and other use cases, using its wealth of video, audio, and image data.[63]

Sample Interview Questions on Image Recognition

Now that I've walked through an overview of computer vision, common datasets, algorithms, and use cases, here are some example interview questions.

Interview question 3-22: What are some common techniques of preprocessing in image-recognition tasks?

Example answer

Common preprocessing techniques in image-recognition tasks include data nor-malization, data augmentation, and image standardization. Data normalization converts the numerical representation of the pixels in an image to a predefined range—for example, (0, 1) or (-1, 1). This is so the algorithms being applied to different layers can follow the same range. Data augmentation can help reduce overfitting on the training dataset. For example, if the training data coinciden-tally only includes cats that are facing to the right, then the CNN might not learn that cats facing to the left are also cats. Using various data augmentation tech-niques such as flipping, rotating, cropping, and so on, we can add more represen-tations of the same object into the dataset and help the CNN learn to generalize the detection of objects. Image standardization makes the dataset easier to work with by ensuring that images have heights and widths that are close to one another. During this preprocessing step, images are resized so that they are within a certain range of widths and heights.

Interview question 3-23: How might you handle class imbalance in image-recognition tasks?

Example answer

There are several methods we can use to handle class imbalance in image-recognition tasks. A "class" in this case means a category or label; for example, an image may contain a "cat" or a "dog". One way to handle class imbalance is to merge very similar categories, such as "orange" and "tangerine". Of course, we'd have to determine the trade-off between the labels that are being merged. If the

---

62 "How Facebook Is Using AI to Improve Photo Descriptions for People Who Are Blind or Visually Impaired," *AI at Meta* (blog), January 19, 2021, *https://oreil.ly/_3YYj*.

63 "Ava: The Art and Science of Image Discovery at Netflix," *Netflix Technology Blog*, Medium, February 7, 2018, *https://oreil.ly/3S9NZ*.

---

image-recognition model is responsible for labeling citrus fruits, then we should try another approach or merge other types of labels.

A second option is resampling, which generates synthetic data or duplicates data points in the minority class. There are built-in tools in TensorFlow and PyTorch to do this for image-recognition tasks. Another method to handle class imbalance is to adjust the CNN's loss function to weigh mistakes on minority or rare categories more than mistakes on common classes and labels. This is to help avoid underfitting on rare categories due to class imbalance.

Interview question 3-24: How would you handle overfitting in image-recognition tasks?

Example answer

Adding a dropout layer (a type of regularization) within the CNN will set random neurons' activations to 0; this prevents the layer from overexploiting a certain feature. Another method is early stopping, where training stops when there isn't meaningful reduction of the loss (which the CNN is aiming to minimize). Reducing layer complexity can also reduce overfitting because when the CNN layers are too complex, it may find more patterns in the images than are meaningful. For example, many images of singers involve them standing on a stage and holding a microphone, and the model might learn that the presence of a microphone in the image means the presence of a singer. Another technique for handling overfitting in image recognition is data augmentation, which can help add more diversity into the training dataset and reduce overfitting.

Interview question 3-25: How would you improve and optimize the architecture for a CNN used for image recognition?

Example answer

If the existing network isn't working well, for example, if it is underfitting and not classifying objects well, I might consider adding more layers of specific types—for example, adding a convolutional layer or rearranging the order of various layers. This is also how researchers optimize various algorithm architectures, such as creating variations of layers on ResNet.

Summary

Congratulations on making it through some dense topics! First, you went through a summary of statistical techniques commonly mentioned in interviews, including common techniques for ML, like regularization, and topics such as overfitting and underfitting. We walked through supervised learning, unsupervised learning, and reinforcement learning. Then you dove into the various core ML areas: natural language processing, recommender systems, reinforcement learning, and computer vision.

In this chapter, you were given some example interview questions as well as resources for each topic, which you can refer to when you're preparing.

Now that you've gotten an overview of the machine learning algorithms portion of technical interviews, let's look at the training process of ML models and model evaluation.

## CHAPTER 4

Technical Interview: Model Training and Evaluation

In this chapter, we will cover the ML model training process and related interview questions. To many practitioners, the model training is the most exciting part, and I agree—it's very satisfying to see the model become more and more accurate throughout the process. However, to begin ML model training, hyperparameter tuning, and running experiments with various algorithms, you'll need to have data. Machine learning at its core is letting algorithms find patterns in data and then making predictions and decisions based on those patterns. Having useful data is the foundation of ML, and as the industry adage says, "Garbage in, garbage out." That is, if the ML models are training on useless data, then the resulting model and inferences will also be useless.

I'll start with an overview of data processing and cleaning, which transforms raw data into a format that is useful for (and compatible with) ML algorithms. Next, I'll go through algorithm selection, such as trade-offs between ML algorithms in different scenarios, and how to generally select the best one for a given problem.

After that, I'll cover model training and the process of optimizing the model's performance. This can be an ambiguous and challenging process, and there are some best practices you'll learn, such as hyperparameter tuning and experiment tracking, which can prevent the best results from being lost and ensure that they are reproducible. On that note, I'll also go over how to know when an ML algorithm is *good*, in a practical sense. This involves model evaluation and comparisons against some baseline models or baseline heuristics. Model evaluation can also help you determine the efficacy of the model on new, unseen data and discover whether the model might overfit, underfit, or otherwise underperform in the real world.

I try to mention as many common ML interview techniques as space allows, but there are many more under the sun. Be sure to check out the linked resources to extend your learning and interview preparation!

Throughout this chapter, I'll give practical tips and examples to help you succeed in your ML interviews. By the end of this chapter, you should have a solid understanding of the data cleaning, preprocessing, model training, and evaluation process and be able to discuss them well in your own interviews.

Defining a Machine Learning Problem

In this section, I provide a high-level overview of defining an ML problem, including why and how this shows up in interview questions.

Consider the following scenario: you, the candidate, are walking through an ML project you've built. The goal is to predict if a user will click on a promotional email for a particular singer's concerts.[1] Your interviewer thinks for a few seconds after your overview, then says, "It sounds like you can use the time that a user listens to artist A to determine who gets sent promotional emails for that artist. For example, if they listen to artist A for more than five hours a week, then send an email if artist A has a concert in the listener's area. Given that there are simpler approaches that don't use machine learning and achieve the same thing as your model, *why did you choose ML?*"

You freeze because you hadn't thought of this question. It seemed like a fun, self-directed project at the time, and you just wanted to learn. You can't quite understand what the interviewer is probing at with their question. What do you do?

It's important to understand beforehand how you can answer these questions well. Here are some possible angles:

- Did you think about using a heuristic-based (i.e., rules-based) baseline first? In applicable situations, you can also use an as-simple-as-possible model, such as a logistic regression model, as a baseline. Then, the goal of your ML model would be to perform better than the baseline.

- In real-world situations, new ML initiatives often aren't launched or approved unless there's clear business value to justify the engineering time and effort. For example, if the costs of implementing an ML system to recommend concerts from scratch don't outweigh the expected earnings, then it's easier to use

---

1 Let's assume that for this project, there exists some public dataset that is well suited for this problem.

heuristics. Projected savings on complexities, manual work, or time is also a reason to use ML over heuristics.

Don't worry though—the interviewer isn't slighting your project but rather asking, "Why ML?" This is very common in the professional ML world. Asking "why ML?" *doesn't* mean "you really shouldn't have used ML." It's just the beginning of a discussion, one that ML professionals have often in their day-to-day lives. The way you respond to this question, especially for new grads, can be a good signal of whether you can transition well to working in ML in industry.

Here's what you could say that would work in this scenario:

- Be honest: "To be honest, I just wanted to learn some new modeling techniques with a side project, and since I'm a heavy user of Spotify, I wanted to see how I could emulate its email feature with ML."
- If you're talking about a work project: "In reality, I found that heuristics worked, but only for the most average users. For example, heavy users require a longer listening time to determine their favorite artists. Additionally, once we included other data like *likes* and *add to playlists* to the heuristics, we noticed a higher response to the promotional email. Thus, the heuristics became too complicated and hard to scale. That's why we started using ML instead, so it could find patterns in a larger number of features."

 Being honest is fine. As a new grad, I once prefaced one of my side project walkthroughs with, "This is a classifier for Ariana Grande images. I just wanted to do this project for fun, and there's no real reason it had to be Ariana Grande. Here's how I did it…" But I still managed to be taken seriously by interviewers, by justifying the project as an opportunity to use convolutional neural networks.

If you're doing your own side project and expect to use it for answering interview questions, consider what heuristic methods could achieve the goal you want. Later, you can use them as a simple baseline to see if the ML method is better. This will help you stand out from other candidates. I'll cover model selection and model evaluation later in this chapter.

Data Preprocessing and Feature Engineering

In this section, I'll summarize common data preprocessing and feature engineering techniques and scenarios as well as common ML interview questions that cover this step in the ML lifecycle. For simplicity, I'll assume that data is available for the ML interview questions, even if that is a common challenge in real-life scenarios. I'll start with an introduction to data acquisition,[2] exploratory data analysis (EDA), and feature engineering.

 All data and ML roles will use data preprocessing and EDA. Some of the techniques in this chapter are specifically for ML but are still useful for data analysts or data engineers.

Introduction to Data Acquisition

Acquiring data, commonly referred to as *data acquisition* in the context of ML, can involve the following options:

- Work access, usually proprietary data
- Public datasets, such as from Kaggle, census bureaus (*https://oreil.ly/_BFu5*), and the like
- Web scraping (beware of some sites' terms and conditions)
- Academic access, such as being part of a research lab at your university

---

2 Keep in mind any licensing, copyright, and privacy issues.

- Purchasing data from vendors:
  - Some vendors also help annotate and label data, such as Figure Eight (*https://oreil.ly/LAH7w*) and Scale AI (*https://scale.com*).
  - Your workplace or academic institution will usually help cover the costs, as the prices are typically too high to be worth it for individual side projects.
- Creating synthetic data through simulations
- Creating your own raw data, such as taking your own photos, crowdsourcing data, or using art/designs that you create yourself

---

End-to-End Knowledge of the ML Lifecycle Is Preferred

Companies expect to help onboard and train you, and they don't expect candidates to be perfect. However, having knowledge about data acquisition will strongly benefit your interview answers. Between a candidate who will take less time to train and one who will take more time, guess which one gets preference for a job offer?

Introduction to Exploratory Data Analysis

Now that you have acquired the data, it's time to analyze it. Your primary aim with EDA is to see if the data is sufficient as a starting point or if you need more. Thus, aim to get a high-level overview of the distribution of the data and find any flaws and quirks. Flaws and quirks may include too many missing values, skewed data distributions, or duplicates. EDA also covers general traits of each feature, looking at the means, distributions, and so on. If you find flaws, there are ways you can resolve the issues later during data cleaning and feature engineering; what is important during EDA is simply to be *aware* of potential issues.

For ML and data practitioners, it is important to have *some* domain knowledge. In my side projects on video-game pricing, I was well aware of industry dynamics and customer behaviors, being an avid gamer myself. At work, I need to learn about each domain to build useful ML models; for example, customers in telecom have different behaviors than those in fintech.

My common approach is to run ydata-profiling (*https://oreil.ly/S3XXt*), formerly known as pandas-profiling, and start drilling down from the generated report (an example report is shown in Figure 4-1). Note that this is merely a starting point, and using domain knowledge to suss out patterns or abnormalities will be important. What might be an issue for some industries and models might be expected in others. For example, in the case of a RecSys problem, it is more common to have sparser data than in a time-series dataset. Simply looking at generated stats isn't enough. Also, some domains have algorithms that take care of common issues for that domain, and those issues are thus less cause for alarm.

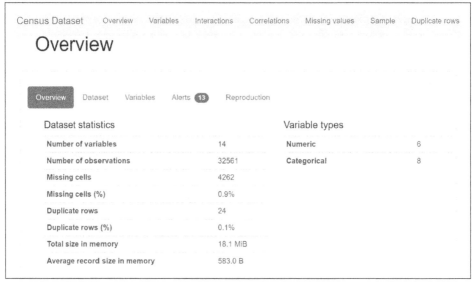

Figure 4-1. Screenshot of ydata-profiling; source: ydata-profiling documentation (https://oreil.ly/jOE08).

More details on EDA are out of scope for this book, but I recommend reading *Making Sense of Data* (*https://oreil.ly/zFoDd*) by Glenn J. Myatt and Wayne P. Johnson (Wiley) for more information.

After some iterations, let's say that you've completed the EDA, coming to a decision point: the data seems sound enough (for now) to continue, or you might need to acquire more data or another dataset first; rinse and repeat.

 When interviewers ask what you'd do when you begin with an ML problem, they are expecting to hear you mention EDA at some point early in the process, after you've acquired some data source(s). It's important to show that you're able to look critically at the data and even find flaws, not just take in a precleaned dataset.

Introduction to Feature Engineering

After exploration of the data, iterating until there is a good starting point for model training, it's time for feature engineering. In ML, features refer to inputs to ML models. The goal is to make modifications to the dataset to ensure compatibility with the

ML models, but also to handle any observed flaws or incompleteness in the data, such as missing values. The topics I discuss here include handling missing data, handling duplicate data, standardizing data, and preprocessing data.

 Some of the techniques overlap with what is commonly referred to as "data cleaning," which can happen in more stages of the ML lifecycle than feature engineering, but is useful to introduce here.

Handling missing data with imputation

There are common imputation techniques for handling missing data that you should be able to mention in an interview, along with their pros and cons. These include filling in with the mean or median value and using a tree-based model.

Table 4-1 lists some things to keep in mind when filling in missing values.

Table 4-1. Pros and cons of common imputation techniques

Technique	Pros	Cons
Mean/median/mode	Simple to implement	Might not account for outliers compared to tree-based methods Not as suitable for categorical variables
Tree-based models	Can capture more underlying patterns Suitable for both numerical and categorical variables	Adds a level of complexity during data preprocessing Model needs to be retrained if the underlying distribution of data changes

Beware of Data Leakage When Imputing Missing Values

Let's say you're planning to fill in the missing values for an ecommerce purchase dataset. You're planning to impute the missing values in the age column in this dataset with the mean value; this makes sense, for example, if you are assuming that the missing values come from the same distribution as the observations where you have the customer's age. (When making assumptions like this in ML, be sure to note them down in a central place; they will help you debug the model if the predictions go wrong down the road.)

However, if you use the mean of all the available data before splitting it into training, validation, and test sets, then it inevitably captures traits of the test set. Hence, the ML model will be trained on imputed data that contains latent information about the test set, which sometimes causes the accuracy to increase for no reason other than the way the data was imputed. This is called *data leakage*. If you want to use imputation, then be sure to split the training, validation, and test sets first, and impute missing values in the training set with the summary statistics of the training set only. If you don't mention this in the interview or explain it correctly, that's a pretty obvious oversight in your ML model, unless you can defend your reasoning.

Handling duplicate data

There are just about an infinite number of ways that observations can be duplicated by accident, so this is one of the issues to discover when conducting EDA:

- Data ingestion jobs might run twice due to error.
- While doing some complicated joins, some rows could have been unintentionally duplicated and then not discovered.
- Some edge cases can cause the data source to provide duplicated data.

… and so on.

If you encounter duplicated data, you can use SQL or Python to deduplicate the data, and make sure the records are represented in a format that's easier for you to access and use later down the road.

Standardizing data

After you handle missing and duplicate data, the data should be standardized. This includes handling outliers, scaling features, and ensuring that data types and formats are consistent:

Handle outliers
Techniques for handling outliers include removing extreme outliers from the dataset, replacing them with less extreme values (known as *winsorizing*) and logarithmic scale transforms. I'd caution against removing outliers since doing so really depends on domain knowledge; in some domains, there are more severe consequences; for example, removing horse-carriage image data from a self-driving car training dataset just because they aren't a common type of vehicle might cause the model to not recognize horse-carriages in the real world. Hence, carefully evaluate the impacts before deciding on a particular technique.

Scale features
For datasets with multiple features with numerical values, larger values might be misconstrued by ML algorithms to have more impact. For example, one column is price, which ranges from $50 to $5,000, while another feature is the amount of time an ad shows up, which ranges from 0 to 10 times. The two features are in different units, but both are numerical, so it is possible that the price column will be represented as having a higher magnitude of impact. Some models, such as gradient-descent-based models, are more sensitive to the scale of features. Hence, it's better to scale the features so that they range from [-1, 1] or [0, 1].

Be careful when scaling features. It is useful to combine different techniques or to use what you found while conducting EDA. For example, a feature might have extreme outliers, such as most of them being in the range [0, 100], except one observation of 1000. Without checking, you might scale the feature values based on the min of 0 and max of 1000. This may cause the information contained in the features to be compressed.

Data type consistency

I was once working on an ML model and got results that weren't what I expected, and it took me a while to debug. Finally, I identified the issue: a numerical column was formatted as a string! Surveying your final data types to ensure that they will make sense once fed into your ML model will be useful before you go through the rest of the process; consider it a part of quality assurance (QA).

An interviewer may ask follow-up questions about how exactly you have handled outliers, feature scale, or datatype consistency, so be sure to brush up on the rationale and trade-offs of each approach.

Data preprocessing

Preprocessing data will allow for features to make sense to the ML model in the context of the type of algorithm you're using. Preprocessing for structured data can include one-hot encoding, label encoding, binning, feature selection, and so on.

Unstructured data is "information that is not arranged according to a preset data model or schema, and therefore cannot be stored in a traditional relational database or RDBMS (relational database management system). Text and multimedia are two common types of unstructured content."[3] When you encounter unstructured data, the preprocessing may be different (potentially even transforming the data to become structured). For illustration purposes, I focus on examples of preprocessing structured data in this chapter.

One-hot encoding of categorical data.   You may want to represent categorical data as numerical data. Each category becomes a feature, with 0 or 1 representing the state of that feature in each observation. For example, imagine a simple weather dataset where it's only possible to have sunny or cloudy weather. You would have the following:

---

3 "Unstructured Data," MongoDB, accessed October 24, 2023, *https://oreil.ly/3DqzA*.

March 1
- Weather: Sunny
- Temperature (Celsius): 27

March 2
- Weather: Sunny
- Temperature (Celsius): 25

March 3
- Weather: Cloudy
- Temperature (Celsius): 20

But the "Weather" feature can be one-hot encoded to have features with all the possible weather states:

March 1
- Sunny: 1
- Cloudy: 0

March 2
- Sunny: 1
- Cloudy: 0

March 3
- Sunny: 0
- Cloudy: 1

One-hot encoding is often used because numbers are easier for ML algorithms to understand; some algorithms don't take in categorical values, but this has improved over the years, where some implementations can take categorical values into account and transform them behind the scenes.

One downside of one-hot encoding is that for features originally with high cardinality (there are lots of unique values in that feature), one-hot encoding can cause the feature count to increase drastically, which can be computationally more expensive.

Sometimes, lack of domain knowledge or understanding of business logic might cause issues in data preprocessing. An example is defining churned users as those who canceled a product within the last seven days, but the product or business logic actually counts churned users as those who left within the last 60 days. (If for some reason, the business logic doesn't work well for ML, we can then discuss a middle ground.)

Label encoding. Label encoding maps the categories to numbers but keeps them in the same feature. For example, types of weather can be mapped to unique numbers, as illustrated in Figure 4-2.

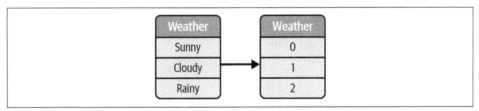

Figure 4-2. Label encoding illustration.

One of the downsides of label encoding is that some ML algorithms can conflate the scale and values to mean a higher magnitude of impact. To use our previous example, Weather can be label encoded: Sunny becomes 0, and Cloudy becomes 1. But to ML, this could conflate cloudy as a higher magnitude since 1 is greater than 0.

Thankfully, in many ML algorithms you can use built-in classes (e.g., scikit-learn's LabelEncoder (*https://oreil.ly/Wm_7r*) class) so that the algorithm will know behind the scenes that this is just a categorization and not necessarily indicative of magnitude.

Of course, if you forget to let the algorithm know that label-encoded features are, in fact, label encoded, then the ML algorithm will likely treat that feature like a normal numerical feature. You can see how this can cause issues if you didn't address this during interview questions.

Binning for numerical values. Binning can reduce the amount of cardinality and help models generalize more. For example, if the dataset has a price of $100, it might not generalize the first time it sees $95, even if in the particular application, $95 is similar to $100. As an illustration, you can define the bin edges as [15, 25, 35, 45, 55, 65, 75, 85, 99], which will create similar price ranges like "$15–$25," "$25–$35," "$35–$45," and so on.

A downside of binning is that it introduces hard edges into the meanings of the bins, such that an observation of $46 would be seen as completely different from the bin "$35–$45," even though it might still be similar.

Feature selection. Sometimes, your dataset will have features that are highly correlated—that is, there is *collinearity* between features. As an extreme example, you might have height in centimeters but also height in meters, which essentially capture the same information. There may be other features that capture a high proportion of the same information as well, and removing them might reduce accidentally overfitting or improve model speed because the model doesn't need to handle as many features. Dimensionality reduction is a common technique for feature selection; it reduces the dimensionality of the data while retaining the most important information.

You might also use feature importance tables, such as those provided in XGBoost or CatBoost, and prune the features with the lowest importance—that is, the lowest contribution to the model.

Sample Interview Questions on Data Preprocessing and Feature Engineering

Now that I've covered some basics of data preprocessing and feature engineering, let's go through some example interview questions.

Interview question 4-1: What's the difference between feature engineering and feature selection?

Example answer

Feature engineering is about creating or transforming features from raw data. This is done to better represent the data and make the data more suitable for ML compared to its raw format. Common techniques include handling missing data, standardizing data formats, and so on.

Feature selection is about narrowing down relevant ML features to simplify the model and prevent overfitting. Common techniques include PCA (principal component analysis) or using tree-based models' feature importance to see which features contribute more useful signals.

Interview question 4-2: How do you prevent data leakage issues while conducting data preprocessing?

Example answer

Being cautious with training, validation, and test data splits is one of the most common ways to prevent data leakage. However, things aren't always so simple. For example, in the case when data imputation is done with the mean value of all observations in the feature, that means the mean value contains information about all observations, not just the training split. In that case, make sure to conduct data imputation with only information about the training split, on the training split. Other examples of data leakage could include time-series splits; we should be careful that we don't accidentally shuffle and split the time series incorrectly (e.g., using tomorrow to predict today instead of the other way around).

Interview question 4-3: How do you handle a skewed data distribution during feature engineering, assuming that the minority data class is required for the machine learning problem?

Example answer

Sampling techniques,[4] such as oversampling the minority data classes, could help during preprocessing and feature engineering (for example, using techniques like SMOTE). It's important to note that for oversampling, any duplicate or synthetic instances should be generated only from the training data to avoid data leakage with the validation or test set.

The Model Training Process

Now that you have data ready for ML, it's time to move on to the next step: model training. This process includes the steps of defining the ML task, selecting the most suitable ML algorithms for the task, and actually training the model. In this section, I will also provide common interview questions and tips that will help you succeed.

The Iteration Process in Model Training

At the outset of an ML project, you likely thought about what you wanted the general result to be, such as "getting the highest accuracy possible on a Kaggle competition" or "using this data to predict video game sales prices." You might have also started researching some algorithms that are good at the task, such as time-series predictions. Determining what that final ML task will be is (often) an iterative process in which you may go back and forth between steps before you land on something, as illustrated in Figure 4-3.

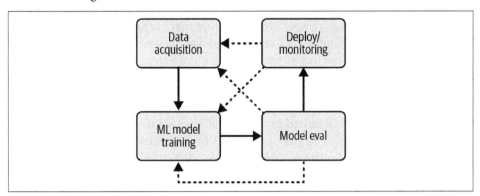

Figure 4-3. Example iteration process during ML training.

---

4 Sampling techniques are discussed in Chapter 3.

For example, let's take a look at all the steps in a project to predict video game sales:

1. Define the ML task, model selection. You might start with an idea: use time-series data with ARIMA (AutoRegressive Integrated Moving Average), because the problem seems simple—price prediction often uses time-series data.

2. Data acquisition. You might acquire a dataset with time-series data—that is, it only has the time, such as a date or timestamp, and the price. The future price is the output of the model predictions, and the historical prices are the inputs.

   However, you may run into a situation where using ARIMA doesn't seem to be working out, and you troubleshoot by analyzing the source data more closely. It turns out that you're combining data of the games from large companies (also known as "AAA" games) with smaller games from independent studios (also known as "indie" games). AAA games often have large budgets for marketing and promotion, so on average, they sell more than indie games.

3. Define the ML task (again). The next step is to reevaluate the ML task. After some thought, you decide to still predict the time series, thus keeping the ML task the same.

4. Data acquisition (again). This time, though, you already know what you may need to do differently so that the results will be better. Thus, you acquire more data: whether a game is AAA or indie. You might even end up hand labeling it.

5. Model selection (again). Now you realize the model needs to change since ARIMA doesn't take categorical variables such as the labels "Indie" and "AAA." Thus, you look online and find other algorithms (*https://oreil.ly/ApYUa*) that can mix categorical variables with numerical variables, and you try one of those.

6. Continue to iterate the previous steps until good enough. You might rinse and repeat if that still doesn't work well, acquiring more types of features, trying different models, or doing feature engineering like one-hot encoding. The ML task could change along the way as well: instead of predicting the exact sales numbers, you might opt to predict the bins, such as (high, mid, low) sales, with high sales being above 50,000 units or something you've defined through EDA.

If you've done a project from end to end, you know the iterative nature of the steps described in this section. You may notice that in this example, you can clearly see what led you to go back to data acquisition and what then led you to go back to defining the ML task. There's always a reason, even if the reason is just to see if the new approach works better than your current approach. This gives you a lot of interesting information to provide in response to your interviewer's questions.

Interviewers will want to make sure of the following:

- You are knowledgeable about common ML tasks in their field.
- You are knowledgeable about common algorithms related to said tasks.
- You know how to evaluate those models.

Interviewer's Perspective: Explain Why

If an interviewer asks you what model you chose or what technique you used for any step in model training, I strongly recommend mentioning *why* you chose it as well. You don't need to include the minute details if the interviewer didn't ask you to walk through the entire project, but including the *why* will make your answer much more convincing.

Defining the ML Task

In the previous section, you saw how the steps from data acquisition to model training are often iterative and that explaining the rationale for each of your iterations will help in your interview answers.

To select the ML model, you need to define the ML task. To figure this out, you can ask yourself what algorithm to use and what task(s) is associated with the algorithm. For example, is it classification or regression?

There is no prescriptive method to tell you the correct algorithms, but generally you'd want to know:

- Do you have enough data?
- Are you predicting a quantity/numerical value or a category/categorical value?
- Do you have labeled data (i.e., you know the ground truth labels)? This could determine if supervised learning or unsupervised learning is better for the task.

Tasks could include regression, classification, anomaly detection, recommender systems, reinforcement learning, natural language processing, generative AI, and so on, all of which you read about in Chapter 3. A simplified overview of selecting the ML task is illustrated in Figure 4-4. Knowing the goal and the data that you have available (or plan to acquire) can help you initially select tasks. For example, different types of ML tasks are better suited depending on the labeled data that is available or if the target variable is continuous or categorical.

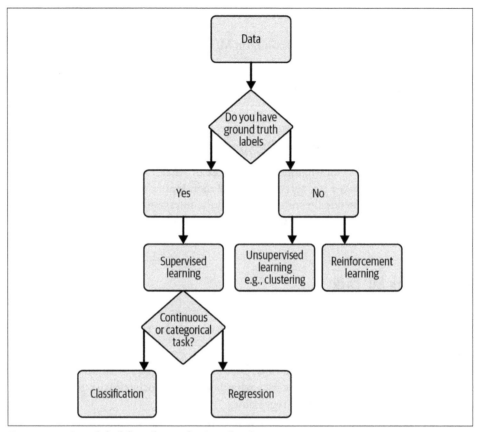

Figure 4-4. Simplified flowchart of ML task selection.

Overview of Model Selection

Now that you have an idea of the ML task, let's move on to model selection. Remember that this is an iterative process, so you might not decide this in one go. However, you do need to select a model (or a few) as a starting point. In interviews, you will be asked about why you selected such and such algorithm(s) or model(s), and just going off gut feeling won't be enough for a successful answer. As you saw in Figure 4-4, you already have a place to start from based on the ML task(s) that you defined. So let's dig deeper into some common algorithms and libraries (mostly in Python) that you can use to implement the task.

I want to make a quick clarification on terminology: when you are selecting an algorithm initially, that isn't technically *model selection* until you test it out and compare the performance of the resulting model. This term is often used interchangeably since you inevitably want to make the final decision based on actual model performance. As Jason Brownlee puts it in *Machine Learning Mastery*: "Model selection is a process that can be applied both across different types of models (e.g., logistic regression, SVM, KNN, etc.) and across models of the same type configured with different model hyperparameters (e.g., different kernels in an SVM)."[5]

Interview Tip: Simple Algorithms and Models as a Baseline

As mentioned in "Defining a Machine Learning Problem" on page 122 it's good to have a simple heuristic to compare your ML model with. If a few if statements or logistic regression can outperform a more complex model that you've selected, then you need to continue to improve your model before it will be viable.

Here are some algorithms and libraries that can be used as simple starting points for each task. Note that many libraries are versatile and can be used for multiple purposes (e.g., decision trees can be used for both classification and regression), but I list some simplified examples for understanding:

Classification
Algorithms include decision trees (*https://oreil.ly/EKZWI*), random forest (*https://oreil.ly/IkQXJ*), and the like. Example Python libraries to start with include scikit-learn (*https://oreil.ly/f2Frn*), CatBoost (*https://catboost.ai*), and LightGBM (*https://oreil.ly/_cFT3*).

Regression
Algorithms include logistic regression (*https://oreil.ly/EaQdP*), decision trees, and the like. Example Python libraries to start with are scikit-learn and statsmodels (*https://oreil.ly/ASFkP*).

Clustering (unsupervised learning)
Algorithms include k-means clustering (*https://oreil.ly/VSTOe*), DBSCAN (*https://oreil.ly/Dd1i0*), and the like. An example Python library to start with is scikit-learn.

Time-series prediction
Algorithms include ARIMA (*https://oreil.ly/EmD-0*), LSTM (*https://oreil.ly/Ym7mh*), and the like. Example Python libraries to start with include statsmodels, Prophet (*https://oreil.ly/xOtUh*), Keras/TensorFlow (*https://oreil.ly/_4vBj*), and so on.

---

5 Jason Brownlee, "A Gentle Introduction to Model Selection for Machine Learning," *Machine Learning Mastery* (blog), September 26, 2019, *https://oreil.ly/2ylZa*.

Recommender systems

Algorithms include matrix factorization techniques such as collaborative filtering. Example libraries and tools to start with include Spark's MLlib (*https://oreil.ly/tOH7V*) or Amazon Personalize (*https://oreil.ly/jmzwo*) on AWS.

Reinforcement learning

Algorithms include multiarmed bandit, Q-learning, and policy gradient. Example libraries to start with include Vowpal Wabbit (*https://oreil.ly/QgSWp*), TorchRL (*https://oreil.ly/O7V_d*) (PyTorch), and TensorFlow-RL.

Computer vision

Deep learning techniques are common starting points for computer vision tasks. OpenCV (*https://opencv.org*) is an important computer vision library that also supports some ML models. Popular deep learning frameworks include TensorFlow, Keras, PyTorch, and Caffe.

Natural language processing

All the deep learning frameworks mentioned before can also be used for NLP. In addition, it's common to try out transformer-based methods or find something on Hugging Face. Nowadays, using the OpenAI API and GPT models is also common. LangChain (*https://oreil.ly/t-AJ4*) is a fast-growing library for NLP workflows. There is also Google's recently launched Bard (*https://oreil.ly/1OjhJ*).

If the task is from one of the well-known ML families, then there are also well-known algorithms specific to that task. As always, the heuristics I provide are only a common starting point, and you might end up trying other versatile techniques, such as tree-based models or ensembling.

Overview of Model Training

Now that you've gone through the steps of defining the ML task and selecting an algorithm, you will start the process of model training, which includes hyperparameter tuning and optimizer or loss function tuning, if applicable. The goal of this step is to see the model get better and better by changing the parameters of the model itself. Sometimes, this won't work out, and you'll need to go back to the earlier stages to improve the model via the input data. This section focuses on tuning the model itself but not the data.

In interviews, it is more interesting to the employer to hear how you increased your model performance, rather than just that you got a high-performing model. In some cases, even having a low-performing model in the end can still demonstrate your suitability for the role if you were very thoughtful about your ML training process even when other factors were out of your control, such as data acquisition. In other cases, having a high-accuracy model doesn't matter to the interviewer so much if you haven't deployed it; it's common to see models perform well in the training phase and offline evaluation but then do poorly in production or live scenarios.

Hyperparameter tuning

Hyperparameter tuning is where you select the optimal hyperparameters for the model via manual tweaks, grid search, or even AutoML. Hyperparameters include traits or architecture of the model itself, such as learning rate, batch size, the number of hidden layers in a neural network, and so on. Each specific model might have its own parameters, such as changepoint and seasonality prior scale (*https://oreil.ly/ 6ydRg*) in Prophet. The goal of hyperparameter tuning is, for example, to see if the learning rate is higher or if the model will converge faster and perform better.

It is important to have a good system to keep track of hyperparameter-tuning experiments so that the experiments can be reproducible. Imagine the pain if you saw a model run that yielded great results, but because the edits were made directly to the script, you lost the exact changes and weren't able to reproduce the good results! Tracking will be discussed more in "Experiment tracking" on page 140.

ML loss functions

Loss functions in ML measure the difference between the model's predicted outputs and the ground truth. A goal of the model is to minimize the loss function since by doing so, the model is making the most accurate predictions based on your definition of accuracy in the model. Examples of ML loss functions include mean squared error (MSE) and mean absolute error (MAE).

ML optimizers

Optimizers are how the ML model's parameters are adjusted to minimize the loss function. Sometimes, there are options to change the optimizer; for example, PyTorch has 13 common optimizers (*https://oreil.ly/b9o1l*) to select from. Adam and Adagrad are popular optimizers, and it's likely the model's hyperparameters themselves are tuned to improve performance. This could be an additional lever to pull, depending on the structure of your model and any hypothesized reasons why your current optimizer isn't working out.

Interview Tip: Speak Fluently About Models Relevant to the ML Specialization

If you're interviewing for an ML job that requires NLP knowledge, take the time to do a small project to brush up your skills if you don't have prior work or research experience in the field. Being knowledgeable about common algorithms, libraries, loss functions, and the like helps you fluently speak the language of ML with your interviewer.

Experiment tracking

While conducting hyperparameter tuning, you'll need to keep track of the performance of each iteration of the model. You won't be able to figure out which set of parameters performs better if you don't have the records of past parameters to compare to.

A company you interview with might have tools for ML experiment tracking. Generally, it doesn't matter if you have experience with the specific tool the company is using as long as you are aware of experiment tracking. I've tracked experiments with Microsoft Excel before, and so have many other practitioners. It is becoming more common, though, to use a centralized experiment-tracking platform. Examples include MLflow (*https://oreil.ly/RNpng*), TensorBoard (*https://oreil.ly/tt-ur*), Weights & Biases (*https://oreil.ly/gIW5j*), and Keras Tuner (*https://oreil.ly/Xt1k-*). There are many more, such as Kubeflow (*https://oreil.ly/tTNa4*), DVC (*https://oreil.ly/OPFQ_*), Comet ML (*https://oreil.ly/cig1c*), and so on. For the interview, it is highly unlikely that it matters which exact ones you have experience in, as long as you are aware that you should be tracking the results somehow in a centralized location.

Additional resource for model training

Google has a Google Machine Learning Education site (*https://oreil.ly/BthDc*) (free at the time of writing) for those who are interested in a more detailed overview; start with the Machine Learning Crash Course (*https://oreil.ly/5rJ1q*) (focused on ML and TensorFlow and runnable on Google Colab).

Sample Interview Questions on Model Selection and Training

Now that we've reviewed common considerations during model training, let's look at some example interview questions.

Interview question 4-4: In what scenario would you use a reinforcement learning algorithm rather than, say, a tree-based method?

Example answer

RL algorithms are useful when it's important to learn from trial and error and the sequence of actions is important. RL is also useful when the outcome can be delayed but we want the RL agent to be continuously improving. Examples include game playing, robotics, recommender systems, and so on.

In contrast, tree-based methods, such as decision trees or random forests, are useful when the problem is static and nonsequential. In other words, it's not as useful to account for delayed rewards or sequential decision making, and a static dataset (at the time of training) is sufficient.

Interview question 4-5: What are some common mistakes made during model training, and how would you avoid them?

Example answer

Overfitting is a common problem, when the resulting model captures overly complex information in the training data and doesn't generalize well to new observations. Regularization techniques[6] can be used to prevent overfitting.

Not tuning common hyperparameters could cause models to not perform well since the default hyperparameters might (often) not work directly out of the box to be the best solution.

Overengineering the problem could also cause issues during model training; sometimes it's best to try out a simple baseline model before jumping right into very complex models or combinations of models.

Interview question 4-6: In what scenario might ensemble models be useful?

Example answer

When working with imbalanced datasets, where one class significantly outnumbers the others, ensemble methods can help improve the accuracy of results on minority data classes. By using ensemble models and combining multiple models, we can avoid and reduce model bias toward the majority data class.

Model Evaluation

Now that you're training your model, it's time to evaluate it and determine if you should continue iterating on it or conclude that it's good enough. As an aside, often the business metric will and should be decided before starting the ML modeling. *Business metrics* include increasing click-through rate, improving the conversion rate of customers, or achieving higher satisfaction as measured by customer surveys. These metrics are not the same as the ML model metrics mentioned in this section; rather, they are used to see if the model performs well on the test dataset after being trained on the training dataset and evaluated with the evaluation dataset.

Interviewers are looking for knowledge on common ways to evaluate models in the field. For example, time-series interview questions might expect you to know about mean absolute error (MAE), root mean square error (RMSE), and similar evaluation metrics, which were part of one of my interviews for a role in fintech. You'll likely also discuss trade-offs between false positives and false negatives, a big part of what I encountered when I interviewed for my job in security machine learning. Other

---

6 Mentioned in Chapter 3.

common expectations are knowing the variance bias trade-off and how to measure it, or accuracy versus precision and recall.

Summary of Common ML Evaluation Metrics

Here are some common metrics used for evaluating ML models. The metrics you'll choose depend on the ML task.

Note that I won't define all the terms in this book at the risk of it turning into a statistics textbook, but I will define and illustrate the most common ones. Additional resources are included if you want to understand the rest of the metrics in depth.

Classification metrics

Classification metrics are used to measure the performance of classification models. As a shorthand, note that TP = true positive, TN = true negative, FP = false positive, and FN = false negative, as illustrated in Figure 4-5. Here are some other terms and values to know:

- Precision = TP / (TP + FP) (as illustrated in Figure 4-6)
- Recall = TP / (TP + FN) (as illustrated in Figure 4-6)
- Accuracy = (TP + TN) / (TP + TN + FP + FN)

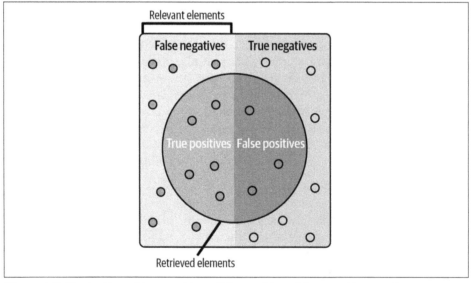

Figure 4-5. Illustration of true positives, false positives, false negatives, and true negatives; source: Walber (https://oreil.ly/1oyCp), CC BY-SA 4.0, Wikimedia Commons (https://oreil.ly/UJafx).

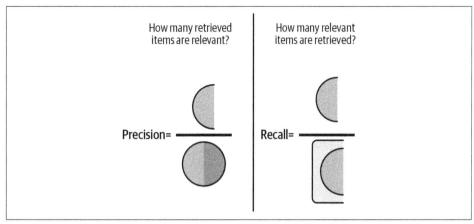

Figure 4-6. Illustration of precision versus recall.

With these terms, we can then construct various evaluations:

Confusion matrix
A summary of the TP/TN/FP/FN values in matrix form (as illustrated in Figure 4-7).

F1 score
Harmonic mean of *precision* and *recall.*

AUC (area under the ROC curve) and ROC (receiver operating characteristic)
The curve plots the true positive rate against the false positive rate at various thresholds.

		True status		
		No	Yes	Total
Predicted status	No	9432	138	9570
	Yes	235	195	430
	Total	9667	333	10000

Figure 4-7. Confusion matrix example.

Interview Tip: Domain-Specific Knowledge

Research the company where you are interviewing and imagine what is valued there on a business level. Doing so can help you engage better in interview questions about model evaluation metrics. For example, in a malware detection ML system, false positives are important to reduce because you don't want to create alert fatigue, which causes people to lose trust in the malware detection model itself.

Regression metrics

Regression metrics are used to measure the performance of regression models. Here are some terms and values to know:

- MAE: mean absolute error ($MAE \ (y, \hat{y}) \ = \ \frac{1}{n} \sum\limits_{i=1}^{n} \left| y_i - \hat{y}_i \right|$)
- MSE: mean squared error
- RMSE: root mean squared error
- R^2: R-squared

Clustering metrics

Clustering metrics are used to measure the performance of clustering models. Using clustering metrics may depend on whether you have ground truth labels or not. Here I assume you do not, but if you do, then classification metrics can also be used. Here is a list of terms to be aware of:

Silhouette coefficient
> Measures the cohesion of an item to other items in its cluster and separation with items in other clusters; ranges from -1 to 1

Calinski-Harabasz Index
> A score meant to determine the quality of clusters; when the score is higher, it means clusters are dense and well separated

Ranking metrics

Ranking metrics are used for recommender or ranking systems. Here are some terms to be aware of:

Mean reciprocal rank (MRR)
> Measures the accuracy of a ranking system by how high or low the first relevant document appears

Precision at K
> Calculates the proportion of recommended items at the top that are relevant

Normalized discounted cumulative gain (NDCG)
> Compares the importance/rank that the ML model predicted to the actual relevance

Now that you've decided on the metrics (and sometimes you'll want to use a few), you'll need to implement them with code. In common ML libraries in Python, there are already implementations of most of the metrics mentioned, so you don't have to implement them from scratch yourself. The following metrics implementations are good starting points:

- TensorFlow and Keras metrics (*https://oreil.ly/z6UD_*)
- Scikit-learn metrics (*https://oreil.ly/CyyXE*)
- MLlib metrics (*https://oreil.ly/-4ZdG*)

This list is not exhaustive, so take a look in the documentation of the library you are using. If the built-in implementations don't fit your specific needs for some reason, then you can write something custom. If this comes up in the interview, it's best to explain why. For example, if you wanted to mix and match a few different metrics from different libraries, you might have had to write some code to connect them all and aggregate them.

Trade-offs in Evaluation Metrics

For interviewers, it is important for you to demonstrate that you can think critically about ML evaluation metrics and various trade-offs. For example, using accuracy alone can hide a model's flaws with its predictions on a minority class (a category that has very few data points compared to the majority class) if the model is simply very good with prediction on the majority class. In that case, it would be good to supplement with more metrics, such as F1 score. However, at times you need to explicitly make a trade-off.

For example, in a medical model that predicts lung cancer from X-ray scan images, false negatives will have a very high impact. Hence, reducing false negatives is desirable. When false negatives are reduced, the recall metric is increased (see the previous section for a definition). But in some situations, on the way to reducing false negatives, the model may have accidentally learned to classify more patients as positive even if they do not have lung cancer. In other words, false positives have increased as an indirect result and decreased the model's precision.

Thus, it is important to decide on trade-offs between false positives and false negatives; in some cases, the juice could be worth the squeeze, and sometimes, it might not be. It will be helpful if you can discuss trade-offs like this when you answer interview questions.

 The interviewer can tell from your thoughtful answers that you can think critically about biases in the models and can select appropriate models and metrics, which makes you a more effective ML practitioner.

Additional Methods for Offline Evaluation

Using the model metrics I previously outlined, you can measure how effective the model has become at predicting previously unseen labels as compared to ground truth labels that were hidden from the model. Hopefully, you've experimented with a few tweaks to get here; even if your first model ended up being the best-performing one as measured by metrics, it's worth it to see what's not working. Your interviewer might ask about it, too!

Before the model is deployed, though, it's difficult to confirm that the model will indeed perform well live, in production. In this case, "live" means it's out in the world, similar to being "live on air." *Production* refers to software systems running with real inputs and outputs. There are many reasons why the model might perform poorly in production despite doing well on model metrics: data distribution in the real world is sometimes not captured by the training data, and there are edge cases and outliers, and so on.

These days, many employers look for experience with understanding how models might behave in production. This is different from a school or academic perspective because with real inputs, models behaving poorly will cause real losses to a business. For example, a poor fraud-detection model could cost a bank millions. A recommender system that keeps surfacing irrelevant or inappropriate content could cause customers to lose trust in a company. In some cases, the company could be sued. Your interviewers will be keen to see if this is something you are aware of and if you have given thought to how to prevent scenarios like these.

On the other hand, it's quite fulfilling to work in ML knowing that if the model is successful, it could be part of preventing losses of millions from fraud or could be working behind the scenes of your favorite music streaming app!

You can further evaluate the models before they go live in production and gauge if the models are indeed robust and can generalize to new data. Methods to do this include:

Perturbation tests[7]
> Introduce some noise or transform the test data. For example, for images, see if randomly adding some pixels will cause the model to be unable to predict the correct result.

Invariance tests
> Test if an ML model performs consistently in different conditions. For example, removing or changing certain inputs shouldn't lead to drastic changes in the output. If you remove one feature completely and the model makes different predictions, then you should consider investigating that feature. This is especially important if that feature is, or is related to, sensitive information, such as race or demographics.

Slice-based evaluation
> Test your model performance on various slices, or subgroups, of the test split. For example, your model might be performing well overall on metrics like accuracy and F1, but when you investigate, it is performing poorly on people over the age of 35 and people under the age of 15. This will be important to investigate and iterate on, especially if you've overlooked some groups while training.

For more on these evaluation techniques, please see *Designing Machine Learning Systems* (*https://oreil.ly/JVYBI*) by Chip Huyen (O'Reilly).

Model Versioning

The goal of model evaluation is to see whether a model is performing well enough, or if it's performing better than the baseline or another ML model. After each model training, you will have various model artifacts, such as the model definition, model parameters, data snapshot, and so on. When you want to pick out the model that has been performing well, it's more convenient if the output model artifacts can be easily retrieved. Having model versioning is more convenient than running the entire model training pipeline to regenerate the model artifacts, even if you know the specific hyperparameters that led to said model.

The tools used for experiment tracking (listed in "Experiment tracking" on page 140 earlier in this chapter) often support model versioning as well.

---

7 This terminology is used in Chip Huyen's book *Designing Machine Learning Systems* (O'Reilly), and I use the same terms for this section for convenience since there doesn't seem to be a unified terminology but more of a high-level grouping.

Sample Interview Questions on Model Evaluation

Now that we've gone through common techniques and considerations for model evaluation, let's look at some example interview questions.

Interview question 4-7: What is the ROC metric, and when is it useful?

Example answer

The ROC (receiver operating characteristic) curve can be used to evaluate a binary classification model. The curve plots the true positive rate against the false positive rate at various thresholds—the threshold being the probability between 0 and 1, above which the prediction is considered to be that class. For example, if the threshold is set to 0.6, then the probability predictions of the model that are above 0.6 probability of being class 1 will be labeled as class 1.

Using ROC can help us determine the trade-off in the true positive rate and the false positive rate at various thresholds, and we can then decide what is the optimal threshold to use.

Interview question 4-8: What is the difference between precision and recall; when would you use one over the other in a classification task?

Example answer

Precision measures the accuracy of the model at making correct predictions (quality), and *recall* measures the model's accuracy in terms of how many relevant items are predicted correctly (quantity). Mathematically, precision is TP / (TP + FP) while recall is TP / (TP + FN).

Precision can be more important than recall when it is more critical to reduce FPs and keep them low. One example is malware detection or email spam detection, where too many false positives can lead to user distrust. FPs in email spam detection can move legitimate business emails to the spam folder, causing delays and loss of business.

On the other hand, recall can be more important than precision in high-stakes predictions such as medical diagnostics. Increased recall means that there are fewer false negatives, even if that potentially causes some accidental FPs. In this situation, it's a higher priority to minimize the chances of missing true cases.

Interview question 4-9: What is the NDCG (normalized discounted cumulative gain), explained on a high level? What type of ML task is it used for?

Example answer

NDCG is used to measure the quality of ranking tasks, such as recommender systems, information retrieval, and search engines/applications. It compares the importance/rank that the ML model predicted to the actual relevance. If the model's predictions differ a lot from the actual (or ideal) relevance, such as showing products at the top of a shopping website that the customer isn't interested in, then the score will be lower. NDCG is calculated via the sum of the predicted relevance scores (DCG, or discounted cumulative gain) divided by the IDCG (ideal discounted cumulative gain). This is then normalized so that the result is between 0 and 1.

Summary

In this chapter, I walked through an overview of the ML modeling and training process and how each step relates to the ML interview. First, you defined the ML task and acquired suitable data. Next, you selected the model based on which algorithms were suitable for the task as a starting point. You also selected a baseline model, starting with something simple to compare any further ML models against, such as a heuristic-based method or an as-simple-as-possible model like logistic regression.

In all these steps, it's important to note in an interview how you *iterated* on the process to make the model better, which could even involve going back to a previous step, such as data acquisition. While answering interview questions about your experience with ML model training on your own projects, whether that's a school, personal, or work project, it's essential to talk about the trade-offs you faced and the reasons why you thought a certain technique would help.

Simply having a highly accurate model (as measured on the test set) isn't enough, as it matters a lot these days to employers that the ML candidate has exposure to how models might behave in production. If you are applying for an ML role that builds the production pipelines and infrastructure, then it's even more important. Finally, you reviewed how to evaluate the ML models and select the best one.

In the next chapter, I'll discuss the next major component of ML technical interviews: coding.

## CHAPTER 5

Technical Interview: Coding

In the previous chapters, I walked through the ML interview process and the ML algorithms and model training portions that are part of the technical interview. Technical interviews can ask for much more of candidates beyond ML algorithms, stats knowledge, and model training, though. This chapter will cover one of those pieces, which is the coding interview.

For jobs in machine learning, the kinds of coding that could be asked for will differ among companies and even among teams in the company. For example, when I was interviewing for data scientist and MLE roles, I got the following types of coding questions and tasks:

- Company 1: Python questions related to data manipulation in pandas
- Company 2: Python brainteaser questions ("LeetCode style") only
- Company 3: Data-related coding questions in SQL and Python Pandas
- Company 4: Take-home coding exercise with a real-life scenario to code

...and so on.

There is a large variance in what companies might ask in a coding round of interviews. From what I've seen personally and heard from colleagues working as software engineers and hiring managers of software engineers, the ML coding interviews are less standardized than the technical interviews for software engineering roles. On the bright side, interviewers for some ML roles don't always ask candidates the most difficult "LeetCode style" questions, aka "LeetCode hards,"[1] since the

---

1 A coding question labeled as hard (in terms of difficulty) on LeetCode, an online coding practice platform. Other difficulties at the time of writing were easy and medium.

candidate can be evaluated on their other skills, such as ML algorithm knowledge. This heavily depends on the role, though: for example, a candidate interviewing for an engineer title (such as MLE) at big tech gets the usual software engineering loop questions, which could include LeetCode hards. As usual, check with your recruiter.

As I mentioned in "The Three Pillars of Machine Learning Roles" on page 12, people working in ML are expected to clear both bars of programming and ML/stats. You aren't expected to be the most skilled coder who is even more experienced than the average candidate for software engineer roles, but you need to be good enough to easily work with a team.

You might encounter some teams where all you need is ML/stats knowledge, where you work with smaller scale data and never need to put things into production. Those companies may not test your coding skills during the interview process. But for this book, I tend to aim more toward ML roles where there is a blend of software engineering and ML since, without a way to distribute and serve the ML models, they don't become part of the products that we use so much in our day to day. ML itself doesn't make a Netflix recommender system, it's putting that model into production and being a part of the frontend experience that customers interact with that brings in the user delight and thus revenue from ML. (For more on interviews that test your knowledge of model deployment, see Chapter 6.)

In this chapter, I'll break down the common types of programming questions that show up in ML job interviews and walk through how to prepare:

- A learning roadmap if you don't know Python
- Python questions related to data
- Python brainteaser questions
- SQL questions related to data

Starting from Scratch: Learning Roadmap If You Don't Know Python

Feel free to skip this section if you already know Python! The reasons I focus on knowing Python are:

- Most, if not all, of the interviews for ML that I've been through assume you know Python to some extent. Most ML libraries you'll be using at work have an implementation in Python.
- For interviewing, even software engineers recommend using Python in language-agnostic interviews over other languages because of the speed (of coding) and abstractions. Instead of spending valuable interview time coding out from

scratch in C or C++, you could instead code just one or two lines in Python, which helps you focus on the important things in the interview.

- Often in an ML job, you'll be collaborating with other individuals and teams. Even if ML might be your main skill, the interviewers will be looking to see if you can write readable code that colleagues can read and use.

Given these reasons, here's a suggested roadmap to self-learn if you don't know any Python or if you're a little rusty.

Pick Up a Book or Course That's Easy to Understand

Find a book or course that focuses on practical code where you can immediately see the results.[2] Do the exercises in the book. Here are some resources I recommend:

- *Automate the Boring Stuff with Python* (*https://oreil.ly/DAwOt*) by Al Sweigart (No Starch Press): it's free online, and the exercises are related to day-to-day activities. It starts with the bare basics of Python, such as using it for math (2+2 is the first line of code in the book), so anyone can get started with it.
- For those who prefer video format, Al Sweigart has a playlist (*https://oreil.ly/JbMbT*) on YouTube that walks through his book in 15 video lessons.
- Learn Python, Data Viz, pandas and More, tutorials at Kaggle (*https://oreil.ly/lCzfX*).

Start with Easy Questions on LeetCode, HackerRank, or Your Platform of Choice

There are many similar online coding platforms, the most common (in North America) being LeetCode (*https://oreil.ly/-ghT4*) and HackerRank (*https://oreil.ly/QNx1z*). For simplicity, I will be using these two platforms the most as examples, but there might be other equivalents in your region or locale.

Two classic beginner questions are Fizz Buzz (*https://oreil.ly/b9O_W*) and Two Sum (*https://oreil.ly/0WEIZ*). Try them on your platform of choice; it's OK if you need to look at the answers during this early stage of learning. The goal is to understand the snippet of code—if you can understand this now, you can understand the harder ones later.[3]

---

2 I learned this through coding in the Ren'Py (*https://www.renpy.org*) game engine. Because it's based in Python and I could immediately see the results on the screen, I was able to viscerally understand what my code was doing. This was extremely helpful for a self-taught coder.

3 To take an analogy from learning musical instruments: if you can play it slowly, you can play it quickly.

Set a Measurable Target and Practice, Practice, Practice

Even trying to complete *one question a day* or one question every two days is helpful for a beginner. Keep a tracker in your journal or phone. Try for an hour, and if you get stuck, look at the answers and read them or find video explanations until you *understand*. You can redo the question after a few more days to see if the understanding stuck. Avoid using rote memorization since the interview likely won't have the exact same question, unless you're supremely lucky.

Try Out ML-Related Python Packages

After you become familiar with some of the basics in Python, start with these tutorials for using ML:

- CatBoost: "Tutorial" (*https://oreil.ly/LLHMA*)
- NumPy: "The Absolute Basics for Beginners" (*https://oreil.ly/t_q7L*)
- pandas: "10 Minutes to pandas" (*https://oreil.ly/BnmdV*)

The CatBoost tutorial (*https://oreil.ly/qTHUE*) can be a starting point for your first ML model! After this step, you can try using your own dataset or make modifications, try out other types of models, and build your own projects.

Now, I'll go through some tips for coding questions that may be asked during ML job interviews.

Coding Interview Success Tips

Before we head into the code portions of this chapter, here are some tips that you need to keep in mind. Your performance on the day of the interview is extremely important to optimize; no matter how well you've prepared, it doesn't matter if the results aren't apparent to the interviewer. I've seen many candidates neglect this, thereby letting their hard work go to waste. On the other hand, candidates that do well with these tips can make their performances disproportionately successful.

Think Out Loud

Even if you are the one coding, the interview is still a discussion between you and the interviewer. It's not always clear to the interviewer what your intent is for writing down a certain line of code. If you think out loud as you are typing, you can help the interviewer understand the direction you're taking, and even help yourself. An example of thinking out loud is: "I'm going to write some tests next, but I'm thinking about what to test..."

Even when you code an optimal solution, it usually isn't a great sign if the entire interview is spent mostly in silence. You don't have to (and shouldn't) fill up every moment with thoughts and conversation either, as long as you're providing enough information to your interviewer instead of just coding in silence.

Here are a couple of examples: I was interviewing a candidate who was very quiet during the entire interview. I asked some questions to prompt them to explain their code, but they might have been nervous and didn't provide any explanation. In the end, I couldn't provide help to guide them toward an optimal solution. In another interview, the candidate shared their thought process, so I was able to follow up with clarification questions before the candidate went down a rabbit hole. The candidate was able to get on the right track. Note that this doesn't mean you will be given a solution if you're thinking out loud, but rather, by increasing the conversation with the interviewer, the interviewer can provide you with better clarifications as you code.

Interviewer's Perspective

As an ML interviewer, I'm looking for candidates who could become my colleagues. If an interviewee can communicate clearly without getting others confused, then it's likely they can work with my team on our mutual projects and help them go more smoothly.

Control the Flow

As a candidate, you can actively shape the interview's conversational flow to help you concentrate while working out some code. If you do need a moment to focus, just let your interviewer know! I've used this line before when I was thinking of a solution: "I'll focus for two minutes or so while I try to come up with a solution, so I will be quiet for a little bit." This also works well for behavioral interview questions like "Tell me about a time you overcame a challenge on a team project." If you really don't have an answer off the top of your head, and your mind is blank, you can say something like, "I'm gathering my thoughts before responding," instead of making up something on the fly while you're nervous. The same applies during coding interviews; you can control the pace to help yourself perform your best, since the interviewer can't read your mind.

You should also keep track of time and not only rely on your interviewer to do so. As the interviewer, I've had to cut candidates short to move onto the next question when we've run out of time. As the candidate, you can clarify at the beginning of the interview how many questions you will be asked and roughly how much time you're expected to take for each one. Sometimes, the interviewer will offer this information to you directly, but not always. For example:

Candidate: "How many questions are there, and how long would you like me to take for each question?"

Interviewer: "The interview is an hour, and we have three questions for you to go through, so roughly 20 minutes each. But the first one is the easiest, and the last one is the most complex, so I'd say if you try for 10 to 15 minutes for the first question, that is pretty typical."

By asking one simple question, you get more information to help you pace yourself and control the flow of the interview! Now you won't get caught off guard if there are 10 minutes left and still a few more questions to go.

Interviewer's Perspective

I usually mention the number of interview questions close to the beginning of the interview. However, some of my fellow interviewers don't do this; to be fair, it's not a required step, and interviewers may not mention it for any number of reasons. For example, if the interview is starting late because there were some tech issues, then they may jump right in.

As the interviewer, I also try to work with the candidate to keep time. If time is running out, I will remind the candidate, but sometimes, if I see that they are really close to a solution, I might mention that we can take just a little more time on it. I won't purposely let the candidate unknowingly run out of time if I can help it. But interviewing others is also a skill; as the candidate, it's better if you also keep an eye on the flow to better suit your needs, not just let the interviewer dictate the entire pace.

Bonus tip: don't rush! Paraphrase the question to the interviewer to make sure you understand the question before you dive in.

Your Interviewer Can Help You Out

Similar to the "think out loud" tip is this advice: if you're stuck, let the interviewer know. They're usually not prevented from giving you tips. As a candidate, I've straight up asked for tips before! For example: "is there any specific direction you suggest that I take this question?" (I've cleared interviews where I've asked for simpler tips like this.) But I'm careful: each time I ask, I am aware that if I ask for too much help, it'll be bad for my interview evaluation compared to someone who asked fewer questions. Still, I'd rather get a small hint and be able to complete 30% more of the question than be stuck for a long time while the clock's ticking. Weigh your situation and your time. It's often better to ask your interviewer if you're on the right track than to go down a completely different rabbit hole.

"Most of the time, interviewers want candidates to pass the interview with flying colors! Thus, they ask questions to elicit the right responses so they have evidence the

---

candidate is ready for the role, as well as provide feedback and hints during technical interviews. Thus, the interviewer should be perceived as an ally, not a gatekeeper," says Eugene Yan, Senior Applied Scientist at Amazon.

Optimize Your Environment

This should go without saying, but if you're interviewing on a call, try to be in a quiet environment where there are no distracting background noises. If you have your video camera on, ensure the background isn't too distracting or use a virtual background. One interviewer told me that when they were interviewing someone, the candidate's partner wasn't fully dressed and was moving around in the bed behind the candidate. Not a great way to be remembered! Thanks to virtual backgrounds on Zoom, Microsoft Teams, and Google Meet, you can avoid this kind of situation.

In general, though, if I'm a candidate and I have no choice but to take an interview in a loud environment like a busy cafe, I mention that I may have to mute myself (on the call) because of background noise. In these situations, the interviewers have always been understanding. The main goal is for you to be able to speak clearly enough for them to hear; it can be awkward if you have to repeat yourself again and again.

If you are interviewing on site, make sure you take care of the basics: don't let yourself go hungry before interviews. If the company you're interviewing with is offering free lunch for you *after* the interview, but you don't have time to get snacks or breakfast on site, then try to make sure you eat something beforehand. In my case, I like to drink coffee every day, so I make sure I can grab it or buy it before the interview. Don't leave things up to chance; even if the company has a kitchenette and free snacks, it doesn't guarantee you can access them when you need them. I find it easier to just bring my own.

I also bring a water bottle to on-site interviews and try to sleep well the day before. Of course, that's not always possible, but try your best—you won't regret it.

Interviews Require Energy!

I mention all these tips because interviews require a lot of concentration and mental and physical energy. It's not just about your preparation on the technical topics; the entire interview, just like standardized exams, assesses your performance holistically. There are people who prepare a lot but perform poorly because of stress, nerves, or not enough sleep. There are people who prepare a bit less but perform better due to their good mental and physical state at the time of the interview. The one who performs better gets the job. It sounds unfair, but keep this in mind and do the best that you can.

Python Coding Interview: Data- and ML-Related Questions

Now, let's dive into the first type of programming/coding interview questions: data- and ML-related questions. These questions focus on using Python, such as using the NumPy and pandas libraries or ML libraries like XGBoost, to code up solutions to interview questions. The main difference between this type of question and the brain-teaser/LeetCode questions covered in the next subsection is that this type of question will relate more to what you'd be doing in your day-to-day role in an ML job.

Depending on the type of company you're interviewing for, these questions may be themed around the company's product. For example, a social media company could ask a series of questions on how you'd pull information about new user signups, how you'd extract the answers to how active the users have been, and how many users have churned (left) within the last week.

Sample Data- and ML-Related Interview and Questions

In this section, I'll walk you through an interview scenario and provide two sample data- and ML-related Python questions that might be asked in the interview. Note that the datasets given in these examples are intentionally small and simple for the purpose of understanding.

Scenario

On interview day, your interviewer sends you a link to a HackerRank (*https://oreil.ly/ NK22m*) interface. When you open it, you see an interface where you can write your code. You double-check with the interviewer that there are two questions in total during this one-hour interview and gauge that you should aim to spend 15 minutes on the first question and 30 minutes on the second one. The rest is buffer time and Q&A with the interviewer.

The interviewer copies and pastes the first question at the top of the page, which outlines the question in commented-out code. The coding interview interface may already have the question prepopulated, but in many data interviews I've been through at various types of companies, from big tech to startups, the question may not be on the sidebar but instead pasted into the coding area. As an interviewer, I'm speculating that this is more suitable for questions where you don't have to run the full script as well as for interviews that focus more on the back-and-forth discussion.

You double-check that you aren't expected to run the code fully, as the HackerRank environment doesn't happen to connect to an actual database. The interviewer confirms this.

Question 5-1 (a)

At *[the social media company that you're interviewing for]*, we are looking into user behavior. The data format we have is [sample data in *.json* format]. The data is provided in the following two *.json* objects (referred to as "tables" for convenience).

Table 1:

```
user_signups = {
  "user_signups": [
      { "user_id": 31876, "timestamp": "2023-05-14 09:18:15" },
      { "user_id": 59284, "timestamp": "2023-05-13 15:12:45" },
      { "user_id": 86729, "timestamp": "2023-06-18 09:03:30" },
  ]
}
```

Table 2:

```
user_logins = {
  "user_logins": [
      { "user_identifier": 31876, "login_time": "2023-05-15 10:28:15",
"logoff_time": "2023-07-15 13:47:30" },
      { "user_identifier": 31876, "login_time": "2023-06-17 15:12:45",
"logoff_time": "2023-07-17 18:31:20" },
      { "user_identifier": 31876, "login_time": "2023-06-20 09:03:30",
"logoff_time": "2023-07-20 12:17:10" },
      { "user_identifier": 59284, "login_time": "2023-05-16 14:49:10",
"logoff_time": "2023-07-16 18:02:45" },
      { "user_identifier": 59284, "login_time": "2023-05-18 09:33:25",
"logoff_time": "2023-07-18 12:48:15" },
      { "user_identifier": 59284, "login_time": "2023-06-19 14:06:40",
"logoff_time": "2023-07-19 16:34:50" },
      { "user_identifier": 59284, "login_time": "2023-06-21 08:20:05",
"logoff_time": "2023-07-21 11:36:25" },
      { "user_identifier": 59284, "login_time": "2023-07-23 15:28:50",
"logoff_time": "2023-07-23 18:44:40" },
      { "user_identifier": 86729, "login_time": "2023-06-18 10:48:30",
"logoff_time": "2023-07-18 10:58:20" },
      { "user_identifier": 86729, "login_time": "2023-06-19 13:31:05",
"logoff_time": "2023-07-19 15:50:40" },
      { "user_identifier": 86729, "login_time": "2023-06-21 10:10:25",
"logoff_time": "2023-06-21 12:21:15" }
  ]
}
```

Table 1 has the new user signup time:

- user_id
- timestamp

Table 2 has current accounts:

- user_identifier
- login_time
- logoff_time

Question: Given these two tables, which users' latest activity is beyond 60 days since signup?

Here are some things you should do as you begin to answer this first question:

- Confirm what each data type means if unclear: is user_id in Table 1 the same as user_identifier in Table 2? (For the example answer, we assume that it is.)
- Load up the *.json* format into your format of choice—for example, into a pandas DataFrame.
- Think out loud—explain your approach and thoughts as you code. Confirm the question if you're unsure; in this case, even if there are several columns, you don't need some of them in the end, or you could simplify the results.

The following code is an example answer for question 5-1 (a):

```python
# python

import json
import pandas as pd

user_signins_df = pd.DataFrame(user_signins["user_signins"]) ❶

user_logins_df = pd.DataFrame(user_logins["user_logins"])
latest_login_times = user_logins_df.groupby(
    'user_identifier')['login_time'].max() ❷

merged_df = user_signups_df.merge( ❸
    latest_login_times,
    left_on="user_id",
    right_on="user_identifier",
    how="inner"
    )


merged_df['timestamp'] = pd.to_datetime(merged_df['timestamp'])
```

```
merged_df['last_login_time'] = pd.to_datetime(merged_df['login_time'])

# merged_df
```

user_id	timestamp	login_time
31876	2023-05-14 09:18:15	2023-06-20 09:03:30
59284	2023-05-13 15:12:45	2023-07-23 15:28:50
86729	2023-06-18 09:03:30	2023-06-21 10:10:25

```
merged_df['time_between_signup_and_latest_login'] = \
merged_df['last_login_time'] - merged_df['timestamp'] ❹

# merged_df
```

user_id	timestamp	login_time	time_between_signup_and_latest_login
31876	2023-05-14 09:18:15	2023-06-20 09:03:30	36 days 23:45:15
59284	2023-05-13 15:12:45	2023-07-23 15:28:50	71 days 00:16:05
86729	2023-06-18 09:03:30	2023-06-21 10:10:25	3 days 01:06:55

```
filtered_users = merged_df[merged_df['time_between_signup_and_latest_login'] \
> pd.Timedelta(days=60)] ❺


filtered_user['user_id']
# Result: 59284
```

❶ Read in the .json objects as pandas DataFrames.

❷ For each user, get their latest login time, and store in a DataFrame named `latest_login_times`.

❸ Merge the two DataFrames. Now, for each user, it displays their signup time (timestamp) and latest login time (login_time). (Tip: if time allows in the interview, rename these columns to have clearer names.)

❹ Calculate the time between signup timestamp and the latest `login_time`, putting the results into a new column.

❺ Filter the users, keeping only the one(s) that have logged in over 60 days after signing up.

For the code samples in this book, sometimes the line breaks aren't as clean as what a code formatter would output, due to formatting for print books.

Question 5-1 (b)

Now, the interviewer pastes the second question into the HackerRank interface.

Suppose you have a new dataset, Table 3.

Table 3:

```
{
  "user_information": [
    {
      "user_id": "31876",
      "feature_id": "profile_completion",
      "feature_value": "55%"
    },
    {
      "user_id": "31876",
      "feature_id": "friend_connections",
      "feature_value": "127"
    },
    {
      "user_id": "31876",
      "feature_id": "posts",
      "feature_value": "42"
    },
    {
      "user_id": "31876",
      "feature_id": "saved_posts",
      "feature_value": "3"
    },
    {
      "user_id": "59284",
      "feature_id": "profile_completion",
      "feature_value": "92%"
    },
    {
      "user_id": "59284",
      "feature_id": "friend_connections",
      "feature_value": "95"
    },
    {
      "user_id": "59284",
      "feature_id": "posts",
      "feature_value": "63"
    },
    {
      "user_id": "59284",
      "feature_id": "saved_posts",
      "feature_value": "8"
    },
    {
      "user_id": "86729",
      "feature_id": "profile_completion",
```

```
      "feature_value": "75%"
    },
    {
      "user_id": "86729",
      "feature_id": "friend_connections",
      "feature_value": "58"
    },
    {
      "user_id": "86729",
      "feature_id": "posts",
      "feature_value": "31"
    },
    {
      "user_id": "86729",
      "feature_id": "saved_posts",
      "feature_value": "1"
    },
    {
      "user_id": "13985",
      "feature_id": "profile_completion",
      "feature_value": "45%"
    },
    {
      "user_id": "13985",
      "feature_id": "friend_connections",
      "feature_value": "43"
    },
    {
      "user_id": "13985",
      "feature_id": "posts",
      "feature_value": "19"
    },
    {
      "user_id": "13985",
      "feature_id": "saved_posts",
      "feature_value": "0"
    },
    {
      "user_id": "47021",
      "feature_id": "profile_completion",
      "feature_value": "65%"
    },
    {
      "user_id": "47021",
      "feature_id": "friend_connections",
      "feature_value": "73"
    },
    {
      "user_id": "47021",
      "feature_id": "posts",
      "feature_value": "37"
    },
```

```
    {
      "user_id": "47021",
      "feature_id": "saved_posts",
      "feature_value": "32"
    }
  ]
}
```

Question: Based on the tables in the previous question as well as this new table (Table 3), how would you approach building a predictive churn model with this toy data, assuming that the model can be run on much more data than this? Assume that the day the analysis is run is July 25, 2023. Create the churn indicators and feature table, and verbally describe how you would proceed with modeling.

Here are some tips for answering question 5-1 (b):

- You should analyze the data, even if it's a toy dataset, and walk through what you would do if it were larger.
- Define what it means that the user will stay or leave. Does the company have a definition of churned users? (For example, are they users who haven't logged on in 30 days?) Get clarity on anything that's unclear to you.
- Suggest some possible ways to find correlation—for example, if the user has a lower profile completion rate, are they more likely to churn? Also, outline and code out how you can test and confirm those assumptions in the dataset.
- For modeling, what are some low-effort baseline models you could try? Perhaps regression or a simple tree-based model?
- For a more complex model, what would you do?
- If you notice that your time is running out, tell the interviewer you'll give a quick high-level overview of how a complex model might work, and wrap it up.

For illustration, here's an example of what some rows of the table could look like after you load in the table form:

user_id	feature_id	feature_value
31876	profile_completion	55%
31876	friend_connections	127
31876	posts	42
31876	saved_posts	3
...		

The following code is the first part of an example answer for question 5-1 (b), which loads Table 3:

```python
# python

import pandas as pd

user_info_df = pd.DataFrame(user_info["user_information"])

user_info_df.head() # print top 5 rows
```

```
|user_id   |feature_id            |feature_value
|31876     |profile_completion    |55%
|31876     |friend_connections    |127
|31876     |posts                 |42
|31876     |saved_posts           |3
|59284     |profile_completion    |92%
```

The interviewer confirmed that if the user hasn't logged in for 30 days, then they can be considered as churned. Note that we assume the current date is July 25, 2023. You create a binary column that indicates churn. The following code is the second part of the answer for question 5-1 (b), creating a churn indicator:

```python
# python

import numpy as np

# add churn indicators

merged_df['churn_status'] = np.where(
    pd.to_datetime('2023-07-25') - merged_df['login_time'] >= pd.Timedelta(days=30),
    1,
    0
    )

# merged_df
```

```
|user_id |timestamp           |login_time          |time_between      |churn
                                                    _signup_and       _status
                                                    _latest_login
|31876   |2023-05-14 09:18:15 |2023-06-20 09:03:30 |36 days 23:45:15  |1
|59284   |2023-05-13 15:12:45 |2023-07-23 15:28:50 |71 days 00:16:05  |0
|86729   |2023-06-18 09:03:30 |2023-06-21 10:10:25 |3 days 01:06:55   |1
```

From here you can join it to the features table:

```python
# python

user_info_df["user_id"] = pd.to_numeric(user_info_df["user_id"])

features_df = user_info_df.merge(merged_df_2[["user_id", "churn_status"]],
                                  left_on="user_id", right_on="user_id")  ❶

# features_df
```

user_id	feature_id	feature_value	churn_status
31876	profile_completion	55%	1
31876	friend_connections	127	1
31876	posts	42	1
31876	saved_posts	3	1
59284	profile_completion	92%	0
59284	friend_connections	95	0
59284	posts	63	0
59284	saved_posts	8	0
86729	profile_completion	75%	1
86729	friend_connections	58	1
86729	posts	31	1
86729	saved_posts	1	1

❶ The DataFrame merged_df has your churn indicators, and now you join it to the table with features, features_df.

Next, you decide on a simple ML model, CatBoost, and proceed to convert this DataFrame to the required format (in this case, it's easier if the columns are the features).

An easy rules-based method could simply be that if a user doesn't log on for 20 days, they might already be likely to churn (not logged in for 30 days). It's kind of a simple "wait and see" rules-based approach, but it's an option. Another option is that they will likely churn if they have not logged in for 14 days and also have added no friends. Our guess is that if they have no friends at that point, then maybe they don't have an incentive to come back, so it's possible they'll churn.

 As mentioned in Chapter 4, this could be a place to discuss scaling the data so that the features with larger "numbers" don't throw off the scale of magnitude. Discuss cases if there are missing values (in this toy example, there aren't, but there likely are in the real world).

FAQs for Data- and ML-Focused Interviews

In the previous scenario, I walked through how a data- and ML-focused interview might go. I've been through many of these, sometimes as the interviewee and sometimes as the interviewer. Here are some additional observations and tips that I hope will help you.

FAQ: It seems like the interviews differ a lot. Should I try to practice on platforms such as HackerRank and CoderPad myself?
    A: The interview format might differ, but don't fret about it. Once you do a few, you'll get more used to the variety. For example, I've had interviews where I was expected to run the code correctly, and I've had others where best-effort pseudocode is fine. To use the Google interview example, coding in Google Docs,

of course you can't execute the code just like that. But if you aren't used to the syntax or make a lot of obvious mistakes, the interviewer can still tell, even if you don't need to run the code.

FAQ: *Thinking out loud seems distracting. What if I really can't do it?*
A: If you know thinking aloud will distract you, then you don't have to talk as frequently. However, I still recommend that when you're taking a natural pause, such as when you just finished defining a function, take that time in between to quickly summarize what you did and why. As an interviewer, even if I'm watching every single character the candidate is typing, I might have assumptions that are incorrect—I can't read minds! In summary, try to explain at least during a natural pause.

FAQ: *I don't have previous job experience working with data. How can I answer these questions well?*
A: I find that one big thing that people who work with data think about are the pros and cons of various algorithms. They also think about being more mindful of nuances in data. For example, going back to the interview scenario at the social media company, the interviewer might bring up that a tree-based model could work better on users with longer tenure, but it might not work so well for new users. It's good when interviewees are able to come up with a solution to the cons—for example, a solution could be to use this model only for users that have more than 30 days of activity.

As an example of nuances in data: if a table has a user ID as well as friend connections, but no information about how long the user has been using the social media platform, the numbers might not mean the same. Users who have used a platform longer might naturally have more friend connections. The significance of having 10 friends differs between a user who has been signed up for just a month and a user who has a tenure of one year, despite the same friend count.

The good news is that even without work experience in data, now that you know these main points, you can gain the same type of thinking via side projects. It sounds like a lot of requirements, but as a new grad, I was able to answer questions like this based on what I learned from school assignments in econometrics. As long as you've had some hands-on experience (which you should during your interview prep and in building your project portfolio), you can do it.

Resources for Data and ML Interview Questions

Here are some resources for further practicing data- and ML-related interview questions:

- NumPy exercises with solutions (*https://oreil.ly/ecEfI*) (10.6k stars on GitHub at the time of writing)

- pandas exercises (*https://oreil.ly/pzbxO*) (9.2k stars on GitHub at the time of writing)
- pandas practice with Google Colab (*https://oreil.ly/YqMzP*) (University of Berkeley)

 When googling interview questions about data and coding, I find that the search results favor the brainteaser-type questions if you search for "machine learning programming questions." The way I get around this is by specifying the Python library and then "exercises"—for example, "numpy programming exercises" or "pandas programming exercises."

Python Coding Interview: Brainteaser Questions

Now, on to the next type of programming question, which in this book I'll refer to as "brainteaser questions." They are also commonly known as "LeetCode questions" (people often abbreviate this as LC), coding challenges, and so on.

When searching for programming questions asked in ML-focused interviews, brainteaser-type questions pop up quite frequently in search engine results, though you know by now that it's not the only type of question that can be asked. The reasons these kinds of questions are important, though, are:

- They are more standardized.
- They are shared with the longer-established software developer/software engineer interview loop.
- For ML roles that heavily value software engineering skills, this type of question and interview loop overlap a lot with general software engineering interviews.
- Brainteaser questions are still used predominantly to assess a candidates' programming skills, even if in your real job the projects you work on will be more expansive than coding brainteasers.

 For those who are already familiar with this type of interview question, feel free to skip this section. It's aimed toward those who are new to the brainteaser/LeetCode question type and explains how to efficiently prepare for it—that is, work smart, not just hard. If you have heard of these patterns, then you know it's time to go practice and "grind LeetCode!"

Before I dive into providing advice and resources, here are some patterns to look out for as you tackle your preparation for brainteaser questions.

Patterns for Brainteaser Programming Questions

When you sign up for LeetCode or HackerRank, you'll be faced with hundreds of questions on the platforms. This can cause analysis paralysis: there are so many questions, what should I start with? This is often followed by overwhelm: there are hundreds of thousands of questions; can I really learn all of that?

Don't worry—you don't have to. Many of the questions quiz similar concepts or patterns. The more you start focusing on identifying the common patterns and understanding them from first principles, the more you can flexibly react to new questions, even if you haven't seen them before.

If there are one hundred questions, but they really test only 10 major patterns, it saves time to do two or three questions of each type initially (20 to 30 questions) instead of brute-forcing your interview preparation and doing all one hundred questions.

Feel free to skim this section; you don't have to fully understand everything in depth just yet. You can come back to review after you've started your interview preparation.

Here are some of the patterns to look out for:

- Array and string manipulation
- Sliding window
- Two pointers
- Fast and slow pointers
- Merge intervals
- Graph traversal, such as depth first search (DFS) and breadth-first search (BFS)

I'll cover the first three patterns in detail: array and string manipulation, sliding window, and two pointers. I've seen questions on those topics being asked the most across all data roles, while only job interviews that are more focused on software engineering might ask about additional concepts, such as graph traversal. I'll link to resources to help you prepare for those additional concepts later in this section.

Array and string manipulation

For many programming questions, you'll need to be able to manipulate an array, string, dictionary, or other data type. I'll break down this statement into two parts to explain some definitions. First, *arrays*, in this case, aren't literally limited to Python arrays (*https://oreil.ly/ncZpX*) or NumPy arrays; rather, this is a colloquial umbrella term. In the context of interviews, "arrays" could include Python lists and other iterable objects, which can be iterated over in a for loop. *Manipulation*, in this case, refers to tasks like updating, rearranging, and extracting the elements in the array to achieve the target outcome. This isn't a pattern in isolation; rather, you'll be using array and string manipulation skills in conjunction with other patterns like sliding window and two pointers.

Simple functions you should be able to use at ease for these questions are:

- len() (*https://oreil.ly/T0Etb*)
- sum() (*https://oreil.ly/BVbs0*)
- min() (*https://oreil.ly/NnOow*)
- max() (*https://oreil.ly/qwqK-*)
- enumerate() (*https://oreil.ly/7GTvF*)

Additionally, you might import modules such as collections (*https://oreil.ly/Dum4h*) or itertools (*https://oreil.ly/EEBfv*) or the built-in function sorted(), but these might be more trouble than they're worth if you aren't familiar with the syntax or if you can easily achieve the outcome with the simpler built-in functions (from Python documentation (*https://oreil.ly/I9XcU*)):

abs()	dir()	isinstance()	range()
aiter()	divmod()	issubclass()	repr()
all()	enumerate()	iter()	reversed()
any()	eval()	len()	round()
anext()	exec()	list()	set()
ascii()	filter()	locals()	setattr()
bin()	float()	map()	slice()
bool()	format()	max()	sorted()
breakpoint()	frozenset()	memoryview()	staticmethod()
bytearray()	getattr()	min()	str()
bytes()	globals()	next()	sum()
callable()	hasattr()	object()	super()
chr()	hash()	oct()	tuple()
classmethod()	help()	open()	type()
compile()	hex()	ord()	vars()
complex()	id()	pow()	zip()
delattr()	input()	print()	__import__()
dict()	int()	property()	

You should also familiarize yourself with common data types, which include the following (remember that this book focuses on Python):

Lists (https://oreil.ly/domv5)
You should be comfortable looping through and slicing and dicing these up with their indices. Grab elements A to B, grab the last three elements, and so on.

Strings (https://oreil.ly/u4moU)

You should be able to manipulate these like lists. Can you easily get the third letter? Grab the first one to three letters? The last letter? And so on.

Various numeric types (https://oreil.ly/JyA_n)

Does the interview question call for saving as int or float? Are there reasons for one or the other?

Dictionaries (https://oreil.ly/4CaPK)

These will help you to save something with a key-value pair and easily access it. They are also fast. For those who are used to other languages, this is similar to Java's HashMap.

Sets (https://oreil.ly/dAHtJ)

They're great if the interview question is focused on unique values.

Tuples (https://oreil.ly/u6kcb)

Great for when you want to return multiple results from your program in one go.

Generators (https://oreil.ly/UztZh)

Pretty useful in real life, these can really save on the memory required, reducing errors that might happen when running a test case that processes a large amount of data.

Arrays (https://oreil.ly/FkFsb)

I don't really use this Python "array" (not the same as a NumPy array) in interviews because using the previous data types has been enough for me. However, it might be useful to be aware of this implementation, which can be more efficient for large amounts of data and for numerical operations.

Note: my commentary on each of these datatypes isn't exhaustive but is what I've found useful during interviews.

 Depending on the role you're interviewing for, the difficulty of the questions may be much higher than the introductory summaries given in this book. It's recommended (even necessary) to practice a lot on online platforms like LeetCode if you're applying for an engineer role at big tech, which could include roles like MLE or ML software engineer. For folks starting out, do continue to build on the basics I introduce here.

Sliding window

Let's move on to the next pattern: *sliding window*. This pattern can be used for questions where you need to manipulate or aggregate a range of values (see Figure 5-1). Before I learned this pattern, I used to do these questions in a brute-force way: in each loop, I'd (for example) sum over the entire range. However, with this approach I soon ran into issues. It works on smaller data, but when the full range is large, my solution might time out and thus fail the test cases (on LeetCode). In interviews that provided test cases, this meant that I couldn't solve the question completely.

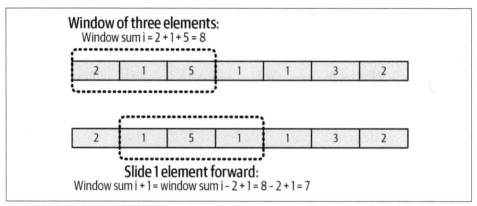

Figure 5-1. Illustration of sliding window.

The pattern helps you reuse the windows, or ranges, that are overlapping between each subsequent iteration in the loop. In the first iteration, you sum over everything in the required range in that first iteration. In the second iteration in the loop, instead of summing the second iteration's range from scratch, you can use the total from iteration 1, add the new number, and subtract the first number. This way, summing over a range becomes a simpler problem of working with only three numbers. When I applied this approach, I found that for many problems where I used to fail, test cases would now pass when running over a large range of numbers.

Now let's go through some sample questions, simplified for understanding. Note that many online platforms such as LeetCode will have some boilerplate code, such as pre-defined classes, for you to insert the code; for brevity I don't include the boiler-plate in the example questions and answers.

Question 5-2

Given the array of positive numbers [2, 1, 5, 1, 1, 3, 2] and the positive integer k = 3, find the maximum sum of any contiguous subarray of size k.

In this example, subarrays of size 3 are:

```
[2, 1, 5] → Sum: 8
[1, 5, 1] → Sum: 7
[5, 1, 1] → Sum: 7
[1, 1, 3] → Sum: 5
[1, 3, 2] → Sum: 6
```

The following code is an example answer for question 5-2:

```python
# python
def max_subarray_sum(arr: List[int], k: int):
    """
    :returns: int
    """
    results = []
    window_sum, window_start = 0, 0

    for window_end in range(len(arr)):
        window_sum += arr[end]                    ❶

        if window_end >= k-1:                      ❷
            results.append(window_sum)             ❸
            window_sum -= arr[window_start]        ❹
            window_start +=1

    return max(results)

test_arr = [2, 1, 5, 1, 1, 3, 2]
test_k=3
result = max_subarray_sum(test_arr, test_k)

# result: 8
```

❶ Add the new item after sliding the window (see Figure 5-1).

❷ For the first k elements, sum them all together in the first full `window_sum`. We use k-1 because the list/array is 0-indexed, meaning the positions start from 0, not 1.

❸ Once we start sliding the window, store the results in an array named `results`.

❹ Deduct the item no longer in the window after sliding (see Figure 5-1).

Depending on whether the input array is sorted or not, you may have different implementations. Always double-check your questions to see if they specify a sorted or unsorted input/output.

Two pointers

Two pointers is the next pattern I'll cover. Questions that follow this pattern can be solved by traversing through an array, list, string, and so on with two pointers (see Figure 5-2 in the example answer). Imagine a tortoise and a hare, each located at the opposite ends of a straight road, represented by the array. The tortoise and the hare each move toward each other in order to find the solution to the question, eventually meeting in the middle. There are other patterns as well; for example, one pointer could be fixed while the other moves.

To illustrate, let's look at an example of a two pointers interview question and some online resources for other relevant questions to practice with.

Question 5-3

From a *sorted* number array of unique numbers, locate a pair of numbers in the array that add up to a given target value. Return the indices (locations) of each number in the array. You may only use each number once—that is, you cannot add the same number with itself.

Here is the example input:

```
numbers = [2, 5, 7, 11, 16]
target = 16
```

The example target output is: [1, 3].

The numbers at indices 1 and 3, which are 5 and 11, add up to the target sum, 16.

Here's a simple explanation for understanding. First, I'll illustrate how the approach with two pointers works in Figure 5-2. In this example, the pointers start from the start and end of the array and move toward the middle so that the sum of the pointers' elements gets closer to the target sum.

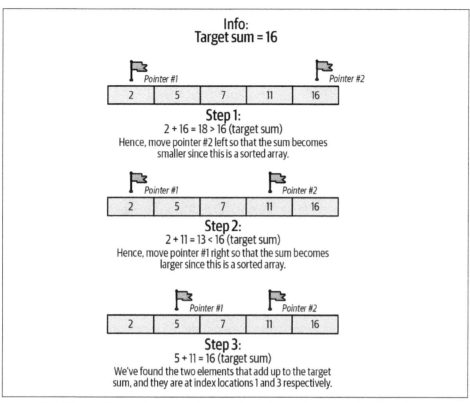

Figure 5-2. Illustration of the two pointer pattern for coding interview questions.

Here is the example code implementation:

```python
# python
import math

def get_pair_with_target_sum(numbers: List[int], target: int):
    """
    :returns: List[int]
    """
    start_ind, end_ind = 0, len(numbers) - 1    ❶

    test_num = math.inf

    while test_num != target_sum:    ❷

        start_num = numbers[start_ind]
        end_num = numbers[end_ind]
        test_num = start_num + end_num

        if test_num > target_sum:
            end_ind -= 1
```

```
      elif test_num < target_sum:
        start_ind += 1
      elif test_num == target_sum:
        return [start_ind, end_ind]

    if test_num == math.inf:
      return None

numbers = [2, 5, 7, 11, 16]
target = 16
result = get_pair_with_target_sum(numbers, target)

# result: [1,3]
```

❶ start_ind corresponds to pointer #1 (leftmost pointer) in Figure 5-2, while end_ind corresponds to pointer #2 (rightmost pointer).

❷ Keep iterating on the sum, moving the rightmost pointer left if the target sum is smaller and moving the leftmost pointer right if the target sum is larger, as illustrated in Figure 5-2.

If you are interviewing for roles for which the programming questions are harder, the interviewer might continue to ask if you can come up with how to optimize or speed up your initial solution. It's even better if you can come up with an optimized solution from the get-go! An example of further optimization is illustrated in the following code example.

The following code example is more streamlined, which simplifies the initial answer:

```python
# python
def get_pair_with_target_sum(numbers: List[int], target: int):
    """
    :returns: List[int]
    """
    pointer_1, pointer_2 = 0, len(numbers) - 1
    while(pointer_1 < pointer_2):
        current_sum = numbers[pointer_1] + numbers[pointer_2]
        if current_sum == target:
            return [pointer_1, pointer_2]
        if target > current_sum:
            pointer_1 += 1
        else:
            pointer_2 -= 1

numbers = [2, 5, 7, 11, 16]
target = 16
result = get_pair_with_target_sum(numbers, target)
```

```
# result: [1,3]
```

 Depending on the test cases, whether they are provided by the interviewer or are ones that you come up with, there might be assumptions about whether you sanitize the inputs or not. In question 5-3, I'll assume that the inputs passed in are positive integers, but sometimes there are trick questions, such as passing in negative numbers when your code assumes they are always positive inputs. Check with your interviewer and react accordingly.

Further Examples

Here are some online resources from LeetCode for relevant questions using this pattern:

- Two Sum (*https://oreil.ly/70iBt*)
- Move Zeroes (*https://oreil.ly/Bxzxr*)
- Is Subsequence (*https://oreil.ly/GcctB*)

Resources for Brainteaser Programming Questions

This section provides further resources for practicing for coding interviews.

Practice platforms for coding interviews

The following are common platforms for practicing LeetCode-style or brainteaser-style coding questions:

LeetCode (https://oreil.ly/1uqha)
   An online platform offering coding challenges and interview preparation resources for software engineers and developers

HackerRank (https://oreil.ly/ShS4w)
   An online platform offering online coding tests and technical interviews

Pramp (https://oreil.ly/sh_Bm)
   A free, online peer-to-peer platform for practicing technical interviews

Interviewing.io (https://oreil.ly/rguzR)
   Anonymous mock interviews with engineers from tech companies

Curated study resources for coding interviews

The following are popular and useful guides for this type of question; basically, they are the same resources you'd use for a regular software engineer interview loop:

- *Cracking the Coding Interview* (*https://oreil.ly/nf4lu*) by Gayle Laakmann McDowell: This book is considered one of the most popular introductions to big-tech-style coding interviews. It's focused on the software engineering interview loop, but if you are interviewing for ML roles with a lot of overlap with software engineering loops (such as some MLE roles, ML software engineer, etc.), then you will need to prepare for those interview loops as well.

- "How to Stand Out in a Python Coding Interview" (*https://oreil.ly/9pkXS*) by James Timmins.

Curated practice problems for coding interviews

For more patterns, you can check resources such as the LeetCode 75 Study Plan (*https://oreil.ly/YucsS*) for a full list of categories and read about them in resources such as the blog post "7 of the Most Important LeetCode Patterns for Coding Interviews" (*https://oreil.ly/_Yfud*) by Hunter Johnson.

Get Used to the Coding Environment

The company you're interviewing for may have different platforms that it uses to assess your coding: HackerRank, CoderPad, Codility, and so on. Most major platforms are pretty similar, so as a candidate, as long as you've had practice on one of them, you should be able to get used to the others without having actually used them.

Here's one scenario in which you'd benefit from practicing a little beforehand: Google requires that candidates code in Google Docs, so you can't run it; thus, take the time to ensure it's valid code. For candidates who might be used to autocomplete on online platforms and editors like Visual Studio Code (VS Code), this was a huge thing to get used to.

SQL Coding Interview: Data-Related Questions

People working in data will likely encounter SQL at some point in their careers. In every company I've worked with, I've had to use both Python and SQL. Therefore, many companies also test some data questions with SQL specifically, although you may be able to choose between Python and SQL for some questions.

Like the Python questions on data and ML, the SQL questions can be tied to the industry of the company or team you are interviewing for. For example, someone interviewing for a data scientist job on a large social media company's search team could get questions like the following:

- How many users made more than 10 searches over the past 14 days?

- What percentage of users got more than one search result type?

- You're asked to create an autocomplete feature for search. How would you do a simple version of this with SQL?

Here I've included a sample SQL interview question.

Question 5-4

For this question, you are given two tables.

Table 1 contains the product-level information as well as prices and quantities per product:

Product	Category	Price	Quantity
Product1	Category1	10.99	5
Product2	Category2	25.99	12
Product3	Category1	15.49	20
Product4	Category3	8.99	3
Product5	Category2	17.99	8

Table 2 contains the upcoming discounts:

Category	Discount
Category1	0.10
Category2	0.00
Category3	0.05
Category4	0.15
Category5	0.05

Write a query that gets, for each category, the total quantities and total discounted values (if all the items were sold while on sale), such as the following columns:

- category
- total_category_quantity
- total_discounted_values

The following code is an example answer for question 5-4:

```
-- SQL
SELECT
P.category AS category,
SUM(P.quantity) AS total_category_quantity,
SUM(P.quantity * P.price * (1-COALESCE(D.discount, 0)))
AS total_discounted_values
FROM TABLE_1 AS P
LEFT JOIN TABLE_2 AS D
ON A.CATEGORY = B.CATEGORY
GROUP BY P.CATEGORY
;
```

Resources for SQL Coding Interview Questions

The example given here is for you to get an idea of basic questions in SQL that test on joins. However, more advanced tables may include more tables, more complex tables, window functions (*https://oreil.ly/uyHg3*), subqueries, and so on. Use these resources to further your preparation:

- Learn SQL Basics (*https://oreil.ly/NEO3A*) (Coursera, UC Davis).
- SQL questions on LeetCode (*https://oreil.ly/Wkwrg*): as usual, you can (and should) start with the free questions first; there are a lot of them.
- "Advanced SQL Queries: Window Function Practice" (*https://oreil.ly/4EKy2*) (from O'Reilly; requires a sign-in).

Roadmaps for Preparing for Coding Interviews

Some of you may have experience with interviews and are already aware of the various types of questions that can be asked. When I was interviewing early on, I was caught off guard by so many different types of questions. For example, I focused on preparing for data- and ML-related Python questions but didn't realize there would be brainteaser questions that didn't use the common ML or stats Python libraries at all. From then on, I made sure to broaden the coverage of my interview preparation.

It was easier said than done, though. Whether you already know Python or SQL, the formats of these questions might still be confusing. The time limit is also a tough thing to perform well under without sufficient practice. Interviews are isolated events, and as I've mentioned, doing well in an interview is a separate skill. Someone who is very well prepared and experienced but is very nervous during the interview probably won't get selected. But a candidate who prepares smartly and performs well under pressure during the interview is more likely to get the job.

This book is about ML careers, so I won't comment much on whether interviews like this are the best system overall to gauge the performance of (especially experienced) folks in the industry who just haven't practiced LeetCode brainteasers in a while. But what I do know is that when I interview, I take the time to brush up on some of these questions and make a timeline for doing so. You may already know what to prepare based on what was covered in this chapter, but without putting your hands to the keyboard, you won't make that tangible progress toward getting a job offer.

Each time I job-seek, I make a list of what I should prepare and create a schedule for what and when to practice. Here, I've included example calendars that you can use either as a university student or as someone making a job transition, with some variations. I encourage you to fit the schedule to your own situation and get started. This chapter focuses on the programming interview preparation roadmap, but you can use the same format to prepare for all the interview types mentioned in this book (see Chapter 8 for a more general ML interview preparation roadmap).

Coding Interview Roadmap Example: Four Weeks, University Student

Overview: you're a student in the final year of your bachelor's or master's program. You have some familiarity with Python and don't know anything about SQL because you haven't taken courses that happened to use SQL. You learn from an informational interview with an alum working in the data field and from reading this book that you should know a little bit of SQL, in addition to practicing some Python brainteaser questions.

Optional, but encouraged: you also reach out to your program's academic adviser or the equivalent, asking them to put you in touch with alumni of the program who went into data science and/or machine learning. They give you the contacts of two alumni,[4] who you find on LinkedIn and reach out to. One of them doesn't respond, but you are able to have a call with the other one, who talks about how they prepared. You take down some notes and start making a plan.

The goal is to start applying for jobs and interviewing in four weeks (Table 5-1).

Table 5-1. Example roadmap for a university student with preparation time set aside between classes and assignments, totaling about two to three hours a day, for about 18 hours a week

Example roadmap						
Week 1: Planning						
Mon	Tue	Wed	Thur	Fri	Sat	Sun
Read ML interviews	Read ML interviews	Read ML interviews	[Busy with assignment due tomorrow][a]	[Busy with assignment due today]	Make interview prep schedule[b]	Make interview prep schedule
Week 2: Data and ML questions						
Mon	Tue	Wed	Thur	Fri	Sat	Sun
Refresh knowledge on NumPy and pandas	Practice problems on NumPy	Practice problems on NumPy	[Club activities]	Practice problems on pandas	Practice problems on pandas	[BBQ with friends]

---

4 I've had academic advisers who affected my career in incredible, life-changing, positive ways. You may be surprised at the amazing resources they can provide you with, if you just ask. On the other hand, I had a fear of academic advisers for two years after one said, "You will never recover from this," when I failed a few courses and I overheard a few of them complaining about students during their lunch break. No hard feelings but lesson learned—it takes effort to find the good ones, who are worth their weight in gold. I mention this to encourage you to talk to more of them, if available. The effort is worth it!

Example roadmap

Week 3: Brainteaser programming questions

Mon	Tue	Wed	Thur	Fri	Sat	Sun
3 questions on the sliding window pattern[c]	3 questions on the two pointers pattern	3 questions on [pattern]	[Busy with assignment due tomorrow]	[Busy with assignment due today]	Questions on array and string manipulation (overlaps with previous two categories)	Try 3 questions and time how long it takes

Week 4: Learn SQL from scratch

Mon	Tue	Wed	Thur	Fri	Sat	Sun
Watch SQL intro videos, skipping some of them	Watch SQL intro videos	Try 3 questions, looking at the solutions	Try 3 more questions, looking at the solutions	Try 2 new questions without looking at the solutions	[Relaxing]	[Relaxing]

Week 5: SQL practice questions + brainteasers, timed

Mon	Tue	Wed	Thur	Fri	Sat	Sun
Practice 5 NumPy/pandas questions without looking at the solutions	Practice 4 LeetCode questions in all main patterns without looking at the solutions	Look at the solutions for questions where you were previously stuck	Practice trying to do 3 LeetCode questions in 1 hour without looking at the solutions	Practice 3 SQL questions without looking at the solutions	Look at solutions to previous day's SQL questions to see if there are better ways to solve them	Catch up on incomplete tasks

[a] You'll see me put these assignments in this prep calendar, but that doesn't mean you're not doing assignments, preparing for exams, and socializing outside of this calendar. This schedule is for only two to three hours a day, and if you list school or personal stuff here, that means you can still afford to take away from interview-prep time for urgent matters, assignments, or social events.

[b] In this example, weeks 2–4 were filled out during this dedicated time during the planning week.

[c] You can pick 2 easy-difficulty questions to start with and 1 medium-difficulty question. You can spend 30 minutes to 1 hour on each question; if you're still stuck after an hour, then look at the solution.

The main reason that this roadmap can be relatively short is that I like to get out of the phase of only *consuming learning materials* as soon as possible. There are people who make less progress in twice the time because they don't start getting their hands on the keyboard and practicing questions. This is like trying to learn math through reading and not solving anything yourself.

I also make my roadmaps low pressure. If you can't do three questions, then do one. Just one for that day. You can even look at the solution on at least half of the preparation days. You can do this!

It *will* be painful the first few times you try practice problems and find that you are getting stuck. It *will* be tempting to go back to watching videos and reading books, hoping you'll find that essential, game-changing, instantly effective tip. *Don't get stuck in that trap.* The faster you start trying out practice problems and making mistakes, the faster you will learn. And, in my experience, the better you will retain the information.

In my own experience, after preparing in a fashion similar to this roadmap, I continued to iterate and improve after I started interviewing and failing some interviews. Maybe I needed to practice more medium-difficulty questions or get faster at identifying the coding pattern during the interview. But at least I got started, and failing interviews and getting better with each subsequent interview got me so much closer to my goal of landing an ML job than being stuck passively watching videos.

Coding Interview Roadmap Example: Six Months, Career Transition

All right. Say you're not a student, but you are working in a field outside of machine learning. In addition, you have a kid you are taking care of, a shared responsibility with your spouse.

Overview: you're interested in the ML/data field and have been reading a lot of online materials, and you stumbled upon this book. You want to start taking the leap but don't have much time and energy after work. You dedicate the time on weekends to family, but you're thinking of taking two to three hours each Saturday and one hour on Sunday to interview prep. You want to make the leap and be ready to interview in six months, a realistic and sustainable goal (Table 5-2).

Table 5-2. Roadmap for a full-time professional and parent with about four hours set aside weekly

	Week 1	Week 2	Week 3	Week 4
Month 1	Read ML interviews	Read ML interviews	Make study plan	Make study plan
Month 2	Learn about NumPy	Learn about pandas	Practice NumPy questions (look at solutions, then don't look)	Practice pandas questions (look at solutions, then don't look)
Month 3	Read about Python for LeetCode	Read about patterns, do 1 question per pattern	Do 2 questions for each pattern, easy difficulty	Do 2 questions for each pattern, medium difficulty
Month 4	Learn about SQL through videos	Learn about SQL through videos	Try 3 SQL questions with solutions	Try 5 SQL questions without solutions
Month 5	Do 3 questions a week	Do 3 questions a week	Do 3 questions a week	Do 3 questions a week
Month 6	Do 5 questions a week, timed	Do 5 questions a week, timed	Do 5 questions a week, timed	Do 5 questions a week, timed

Note that you will also need to schedule preparation time for the other sections in this book. So for example, if you are learning ML algorithms as well, that could also be a six-month roadmap. If you're working and only have two to three hours free on the weekend or one hour each weekday, then you can adjust and extend the time frame. It's all yours!

Coding Interview Roadmap: Create Your Own!

Now it's time to make your own roadmap. Feel free to include preparation for other types of interviews in your calendar as well. I wanted to emphasize preparation for programming interviews because it takes a lot of muscle memory to be able to quickly complete questions. See Chapter 8 for a blank template that you can use for coding preparation as well as for overall interview preparation.

Share your roadmaps with me in the comments section of the companion site (*https://susanshu.substack.com*)!

Summary

In this chapter, you read about the various types of coding interview questions: data- and ML-related, brainteasers, and SQL questions. You also learned about what interviewers are looking for in the coding interview and some tips on how to succeed: think out loud, clarify with your interviewer frequently, and communicate during the interview. Last, I provided some sample roadmaps for preparing for the coding interview and encouraged you to create one yourself based on your own target timeline.

## CHAPTER 6

Technical Interview: Model Deployment and End-to-End ML

In Chapters 3 and 4, you got an overview of important interview concepts related to ML algorithms, model training, and evaluation. For ML models to have an impact on users, whether they are your company's customers or internal users and fellow employees, the model needs to be *deployed*.

There are many levels of being deployed, but the most important thing is that the end goal for the model is achieved. If your model is being run manually and ad hoc every time the marketing team asks for new results, and that's working well, then that could be your level of deployment. Or, you could have a fully automated system where the model goes out to customers as part of an A/B test, without the person who trained the model needing to do anything beyond the model training. That could be the level of deployment in a situation where the end goal calls for it.

On that note, it's not required for ML professionals to know all the details of model deployment. If you're applying for one of the following jobs, however, it would be useful to brush up on the topics mentioned in this section. Roles that are likely to require deeper knowledge on model deployment include:

- Machine learning engineer that doesn't only do model training
- MLOps engineer
- Data scientist or MLE at a startup that doesn't have additional dedicated people working on ML deployment

Coincidentally, the more your job falls into this type of role, the higher the possibility that the interviews will also include the coding questions mentioned in Chapter 5 that overlap with software engineering interview loops.

On the other hand, you can likely skim through or skip this chapter if the company or team you're interested in has very defined roles, and the role you're applying for does not need to do hands-on deployment, or the jobs you're interested in are the following:

- Product data scientist
- Data scientist, applied scientist, MLE, and so on, that focuses on model development or other analytics

This chapter will walk through model deployment, model monitoring after deployment, and other end-to-end ML processes and tools. In addition, I will briefly summarize more advanced ML interview topics: systems design, technical deep dives on past projects, and product sense. This is so that you are aware of the topics and how to prepare for them if you do encounter them. The good news is that the more difficult variants are only expected at senior or staff+ levels, not at entry level.

Model Deployment

An analogy I've used for a model being deployed is that it's "live and on air." In ML roles, this is an important part of the machine learning lifecycle, as discussed in Chapter 1. Interviews for roles focused on ML deployment could touch on topics such as ML or software infrastructure (which facilitates the model serving), ML hypothesis testing, monitoring, model updates, and so on, once the model is deployed.

This is a type of ML experience that may be harder to gain through self-learning since when we build ML models as a side project, there may not be users to test them on in the first place. Thus, it's not often a priority in my experience when it comes to side projects.

Next, I'll outline some reasons why model deployment is important in industry and show you how to mentally connect from the model training and development work to the deployment work.

The Main Experience Gap for New Entrants into the ML Industry

The concepts of production and deployment were unfamiliar to me when I was starting out in the ML field. Hence, I include this section describing how I was first exposed to the concepts and how I bridged the gap from theoretical ML knowledge to standalone projects to full-fledged projects. I hope you find this story relatable and helpful.

During my master's program at the University of Toronto, I used Python on Jupyter Notebooks for some of my research projects. For these projects, I scraped and acquired data programmatically, wrote scripts to clean them, and analyzed the data. During this time, I used my laptop for computation: I installed Python packages directly on my laptop's local environment. During development, I was able to quickly make edits to my code since I was the only person working on it. I didn't back the code up apart from making copies locally on my laptop. After the ML model training and analysis were done, I created some visualizations and put them into a paper format with LaTeX, and that was the end of that project. I never ran any of those scripts again.

This is all suitable for a learning environment but very different from the working environment in industry. Many ML practitioners have shared their experiences shifting their mindsets, too: models now need to be *deployed*, able to be run, and easily modified by other colleagues, and the code needs to be backed up and rerun—often automatically!

Production is a spectrum, depending on the company where you're applying. For some teams, your main ML deliverable may be generating some plots after training the model once, and that could be similar to your experience in school or with a personal project. For other teams (and anecdotally, these jobs are more competitive), production could come with expectations for uptime and running for millions of users. In those cases, what works for a simple development environment likely will be different from production.

At my first job, the ML models I developed had to run for millions of users every day. Compared to my grad school projects that only had several thousand records, the computation that was required was very different, and I could no longer run it on my laptop. At that first job, I had to learn to remote session into our local cloud computation and work with code on a virtual machine. I also had to learn how to use version control so that the code could be backed up and easily shared with colleagues. I had to write tests so that new changes to the code could be automatically tested; this wasn't something I did in my school projects since I manually tested each change. Finally, my ML models at my first job had to be run with a scheduler so that it could generate predictions at least once a day—a far cry from my ML models at school that I ran only one time after the training process to generate the full results.

I share all of this to say, if you're able to gain some of this experience at school with collaborative projects that use version control (Git, GitHub, etc.), then you'll be able to speak more articulately about some of these skills. If you didn't have the opportunity to learn collaborative development, then it'll serve you well to skim some of this chapter regardless of the role you're applying for so that you can familiarize yourself with what you might need to learn on the job.

Nowadays, I recommend that candidates try deploying a simple web app with tools such as Streamlit (*https://streamlit.io*). In the past, I have deployed my side projects with Flask locally or on hosting sites like Heroku (*https://oreil.ly/D86D9*).

Should Data Scientists and MLEs Know This?

This type of question comes up a lot from job seekers, such as "Should A know Docker?" "Should B know Tableau?" For example:

- Should data scientists know Kubernetes?
- Should MLEs know the math behind ML algorithms?
- Should data scientists know Docker?

My answer: *you* have to make the decision for *your own situation* on whether you should learn technology X at this specific time in your ML career, and here's how.

Let's use Kubernetes as an example—you might be trying to figure out if you should know it. My opinion is that there's an order to things: first, know what's necessary for *the role you're applying for*. Use the methods outlined in Chapters 1 and 2 to see what part of the machine learning lifecycle you're interested in and then parse out via job postings whether the job you're applying for requires you to know Kubernetes. If the role doesn't require it, focus on preparing other core topics, such as model training and evaluation.

If the roles you're aiming for do require Kubernetes experience or other types of deployment knowledge, such as setting up Jenkins, GitHub actions, and general CI/CD, then definitely do some research and gain some hands-on experience with them in a toy project.

Going a step further, it's important to read through various trusted and relevant sources on the topic and gather a wide range of perspectives.

For example, Chip Huyen, author of *Designing Machine Learning Systems* (*https://oreil.ly/j9Obs*) (O'Reilly), wrote in a blog post, "Why Data Scientists Shouldn't Need to Know Kubernetes":

> Owning a data science project end-to-end allows faster execution and lower communication overhead. However, it'd only make sense if we have good tools to abstract away lower level infrastructure to help data scientists focus on actual data science instead of configuration files.[1]

---

[1] Chip Huyen, "Why Data Scientists Shouldn't Need to Know Kubernetes" (blog), September 13, 2021, *https://oreil.ly/6c35m*.

I also recommend Eugene Yan's blog post "Unpopular Opinion: Data Scientists Should be More End-to-End,"[2] in which he writes: "I'm trying to convince [readers] that end-to-end visibility, cohesion (i.e., reverse Conway's law), and ownership leads to better outcomes."[3] But he's not necessarily "pushing for data scientists/ML engineers to be full-stack and have in-depth knowledge of how to set up K8s, do PhD-level research, design front-end, etc.," he adds.

At this point, after looking at job postings and various trusted opinions, you might make a decision: "I don't need to learn Kubernetes *right now,* but it might be helpful *eventually.*"

Whether your conclusion is yes or no, I think the best kind of answer assumes that you can *reevaluate* the answer when circumstances change. As with all careers, whether you should know X, Y, or Z technology will be fluid! As your career grows, you might find yourself in one of the following situations:

- Moving into a startup and having to take on a broader range of responsibilities
- Wanting to get promoted, and it's required to have more experience in X
- Wanting to move laterally into another ML role that requires more experience in X

In those scenarios, you will eventually need to know X! But that doesn't mean you need to know it now. Since you might be short on time for interview prep, treat it as constrained optimization. You probably have a limited amount of energy, preparation time, and research time that you can spend finding an ideal job. You should prioritize the activities that give you the most optimized interview results. If that's learning Kubernetes, then focus on learning it. If that's model training, then focus on model training first and use the remaining time on other tasks.

End-to-End Machine Learning

End-to-end is a term used to refer to an entire workflow, the "ends" being the beginning and the end of the project or workflow. There's been discussion around whether ML practitioners should be more end-to-end, and you might be wondering whether you should be. To tie to the machine learning lifecycle, the answer is that you should know about multiple aspects of the lifecycle (refer back to Figure 1-5), not just one part of it.

---

2 Eugene Yan, "Unpopular Opinion: Data Scientists Should Be More End-to-End" (blog), August 2020, *https://oreil.ly/iUnlj.*

3 For more on Conway's law, see "Conway's Law," Wikipedia, updated October 2, 2023, *https://oreil.ly/wJIN7.*

A similar term in software engineering is *full-stack engineer* or *full-stack developer*, and sometimes full-stack data scientist, full-stack MLE, and the like also refer to those roles being responsible for more of the end-to-end ML process.

My answer is going to be similar to the "Should I know this?" question: look into your job role and see what's needed. Then determine what's a priority and what's most beneficial.

 As Eugene Yan writes in his blog post, "Unpopular Opinion: Data Scientists Should be More End-to-End," it's helpful to be *aware* of the end-to-end ML process, but you don't have to be an expert in every single thing.

Here's my own story of becoming more end-to-end over time, but not as an entry-level candidate. When I got my first DS/ML job, I didn't know much about model deployment at scale or tools like Docker or Kubernetes,[4] and I didn't know data engineering and SQL that well either. During that first job, I learned more about data engineering and SQL to an advanced level, and Docker to an intermediate level, but I still didn't know Kubernetes.

During my second job, which was at a startup, I was responsible for more of the machine learning lifecycle, so I needed to learn more about deploying models in a scaled-up manner. In that scenario, it made sense to catch up on those technologies and become even more end-to-end to better connect the ML workflow to the non-ML portion of our app stack. I've spoken on the benefit of being more end-to-end in my keynote at the O'Reilly AI Superstream: MLOps (*https://oreil.ly/pb83P*), which is that understanding the deployment process helps ML practitioners be more efficient at completing ML projects.

Overall, I think it's benefited my career to become more end-to-end. However, this has happened over the course of many years: I didn't know so much at the beginning of my ML career but instead picked up knowledge project by project, role by role. So don't worry too much about claims that you need to know X, Y, or Z: evaluate your situation by looking at the roles that you are most interested in and prioritize the top skills to succeed in those interviews. You can also quickly gain a high-level overview of other skills from books like this one before diving deeper. You can pick up new skills later on the job or through continued self-learning, as I did.

The following sections will cover cloud environments and local environments, model deployment technologies, cloud providers, and additional tooling. If you're already

---

4 For this example, you don't have to know how they work either. Later in this chapter, I'll give an overview of Docker and Kubernetes, so don't worry.

familiar with the concepts or feel that some sections aren't relevant for you right now, feel free to skip them. You can also come back to this chapter when the topics become more relevant.

Cloud Environments and Local Environments

In Chapter 4, I talked about model training and evaluation. What I didn't detail in that chapter is the development environment. Models are trained somewhere and evaluated somewhere. That environment could be a local machine (such as your MacBook Pro), a cloud virtual machine (VM), and so on.

Additionally, the environment where the models are trained usually differs from the production environment. For example, the model could be trained on a VM and bundled up as a pickle file, then copied over by a script to the production environment, which could be in a completely different Google Cloud Platform (GCP) namespace that the person training the model might not have personal access to.

Whether working on the cloud or locally, you have to be mindful of the handover between the model training and deployment. How are the model training artifacts being shipped over to production? What's the production process, and *where* is each step in the process happening? Is there even a production process? Knowing the basics of the types of locations that ML workflows are built on can help you with the tasks of streamlining, automating, or optimizing ML deployment. This isn't often asked about directly in interviews, but it's an important foundation for other model-deployment topics in your interviews.

Summary of local environments

When I first started out in data, it was already more common to train models on a remote or cloud environment or provision a cloud VM. However, there are some things that aren't running on beefy compute and can still commonly be done locally on your machine (depending where you work). These include:

- Connecting to a remote data store and running a Jupyter Notebook locally for ad hoc exploratory data analysis
- Doing a quick prototype of model training on a small sample of data but running the full training remotely
- Testing the ML service locally, if the company's tech stack is set up to run locally

Local machines are often a *development* environment only, unless you're a startup running a server off a single machine (very unlikely because of downtime or compute concerns). For this book, I won't discuss cases where a single local server is being run.

It is important to know how your *development* environment runs on a local machine, such as a laptop, so that you know how it can be replicated on your production environment, and vice versa. Setting up Docker (*https://oreil.ly/wsewB*) (to be covered later in this chapter) and dependency management like Pipenv (*https://oreil.ly/kIiKf*), Poetry (*https://oreil.ly/wPvpO*), and the like in Python are essential so that what runs on someone's laptop will run in production or even on another coworker's laptop!

Summary of cloud environments

While "cloud" has become the umbrella term for using remote servers managed by a third party, there are some nuances important to ML and different ways that cloud environments are deployed. Next, I'll walk through a few types of development environments.

Public cloud provider. *Public cloud* refers to cloud services from vendors such as GCP, Amazon Web Services (AWS), Microsoft Azure, and many more, which I'll cover more in "Overview of Cloud Providers" on page 203. What makes this service different from private cloud from the same vendor, however, is that hardware-wise, the same servers could run workloads from multiple companies—that is, they are *multitenant*. The upside of public cloud providers is their sheer convenience to set up, which makes public cloud a very popular choice for software companies.

Here are some additional considerations with using public cloud: because of the vast resources of large vendors, using public cloud can be generally secure, but for regulatory reasons, it might be the least ideal option. The process of migrating to the public cloud could cause downtime and disrupt day-to-day operations, which could be massively inconvenient. If you're preparing to work in a small to midsize company in ML, you're likely to use public or private cloud. If you're in a larger company in a highly regulated industry, you'll likely use on-premises or local cloud and/or work locally.

Public cloud became popular with the rise of platforms like AWS, prompting many companies to move workloads to cloud services from on-prem (on-premises) servers. However, many workflows or data stores still cannot be moved to the public cloud for regulatory reasons.

On-premises and private cloud. In some larger corporations, it's not uncommon to own servers and host on-premises platforms on them. When I worked at a large telecommunications company, it owned many servers itself. In fact, many of the servers that large public cloud providers use are leased from or owned by telecommunications companies. The company kept some servers for private use, and it had its own instances of GitLab (*https://oreil.ly/Osuho*) and other services. Many enterprise software solutions also offer self-hosted solutions that come with the benefits of having enterprise support. This is called *on-premises*.

The reasons for self-hosting many services include:

- The company owns the servers, and it's more secure than the same servers having exposure to the public cloud.

- It's easier in some cases for regulatory purposes, such as General Data Protection Regulation (GDPR), a European Union regulation on information privacy.

- Highly regulated industries like financial services and legal institutions have additional requirements for where the data is stored and if public cloud can be used to store personal identifiable information (PII).

Private cloud sits between public cloud and on-premises/local cloud. The vendor, such as AWS, that hosts the servers guarantees that the servers are dedicated to one enterprise customer only (single tenant),[5] as opposed to shared hardware that the public cloud uses. Companies might use a mix of all of these, including public cloud, depending on what is feasible and balancing trade-offs of costs, convenience, and regulations.

> If your role is not responsible for evaluating, setting up, or automating the deployment environments, the environments on which you are developing ML will not make a huge difference in your interview. When I worked on local cloud, it was slightly less convenient compared to private or public cloud (in my opinion) but overall required similar knowledge. If you've worked with one remote environment, you can work with another. However, if you're part of the MLOps platform team proper, you might be required to learn more about the underlying workings of the platforms you work with.

On the other hand, there's also been a phenomenon called *cloud repatriation*[6] where companies that have moved to public cloud services are now reevaluating and moving back to local cloud because of the various benefits of local cloud. In my observation, larger companies have more bandwidth to self-host local cloud instances because they have more staff and thus can afford to have dedicated staff to maintain those local servers and communicate with the vendor consultants on how to troubleshoot when things go wrong. When I was at a large company, one of its platform vendors was IBM; when there was an issue with our local instance of IBM's platform, one of the senior members on the data science team would call IBM and schedule a

---

5 "Selecting the Right Cloud for Workloads—Differences Between Public, Private, and Hybrid," Amazon Web Services, accessed October 24, 2023, *https://oreil.ly/KX5FE*.

6 Tytus Kurek, "What Is Cloud Repatriation?" *Ubuntu* (blog), March 17, 2023, *https://oreil.ly/2qcrO*.

meeting so that IBM could help troubleshoot. It was nice to have IBM support staff available around the clock, but as you can imagine, the costs for said support and consulting were high as well.

Smaller to midsize companies might find maintaining a local cloud cumbersome, costly, and too much of an overhead. Public or private cloud might remain the most common option for this type of company.

Overview of Model Deployment

After models are trained and ready, it's time to deploy them (to production)! At different types of companies, this process can be very different. There are various levels of production, as I mentioned earlier in this chapter, but the goal is for the model to be *useful*.

Here is a nonexhaustive list of examples of deployment, ranging from the least complex level to the most complex:[7]

- The ML model is stored somewhere and run ad hoc; results are saved locally.
- The ML model is stored and run ad hoc, but results are written to a central location.
- The ML model is stored somewhere and automatically run as a batch process, and results are written out.
- The ML model is wrapped in a simple web app such as Flask (*https://oreil.ly/QetyX*), and the app is spun up via a Docker container.
- The ML model is wrapped in a simple app and called via Google Cloud Functions (*https://oreil.ly/IEjDe*) or AWS Lambda (*https://oreil.ly/GRK30*).
- The ML model is served somewhere and orchestrated and managed by Kubernetes; almost everything is automated.

And so on.

Depending on the company you're interviewing with and its typical mode of deployment, there will be different expectations for you. If you're interviewing for a company with a mature tech or ML team, you'll likely be expected to know about the tools related to levels 5 and 6 in the preceding list. The company size is less the deciding factor than the maturity of the tech stack; when I was at a 200-person startup, our tech stack was working at level 6.

---

7 The order of least to most complex might depend on the exact tech stack and use case, but let's just use the order in this list for the sake of illustration.

This means that, in general, if you're in an ML role that is responsible for parts of the platform, deployment, and production lifecycle, you'll need to spend more time studying if you don't happen to have work experience in these technologies and tools. For ML teams with low maturity, such as those at levels 1–4, you might be juggling this role while also being the same person who trains the ML models.

As an ML team grows more mature, it'll become less useful for the same person to train the model and also build an automated platform. A person or team doing multiple things at once won't be able to focus on making the ML models the best they can be, especially as more and more models are needed as the company grows.

For example, an ecommerce company that started out making a simple forecasting model for inventory may want to develop models to recommend items in its newsletters. Then, the company may want to add a robust model for sales periods only. Or, perhaps fraudulent accounts were using the company's goods to obscure the flow of stolen money; someone at the company may issue a directive to create a fraud-detection model.

At the point where an ML team acquires more and more responsibilities, the team will become tired of duct tape (quick, ad hoc) fixes and want to start introducing some developer overhead, such as containerization and version control. Today, companies generally start with those right from the beginning, but only a few years ago, some teams with less mature software or ML teams might not have been using Docker, and you'd be surprised to learn that some companies and teams only started formalizing Git a few years ago (as of the time of writing in 2023). Nowadays, it's likely that knowledge about Docker and version control (such as Git) are more expected skills than before.

Introduction to Docker

Docker allows software applications and their dependencies to be wrapped up together and be *portable*—that is, with a Docker container, the same software should be able to run the same way on any compatible machine. On the other hand, running the same script on your colleague's system Python environment might work fine, but running the same script on your laptop might not work without the environment being *portable*. Thus, Docker also serves the purpose of making the environment independent of the infrastructure it's running on.

Containerization isn't new: in the past, VMs were pretty commonly used to address a similar problem—for example, someone working on a Linux machine wanting to test something on Windows could install a Windows VM, and vice versa. The downside is that the installations were entire operating systems, which is a lot of bloat just to test out something on another environment. With Docker containers, you don't need to install the entire OS (unless specifically desired). For example, you can have a

Docker image that specifies the Python environment;[8] the container uses the host's operating system but still provides the isolation from other parts of the host machine that VMs provide.

A *Docker image* is a read-only template with instructions for creating a *Docker container*.[9] So images are like a mold. The instructions that define this mold are in a *Dockerfile*. A Docker container is the runnable instance of an image, which you can create, start, stop, and so on. You can create multiple identical containers from one single image. For an example, see Figure 6-1.

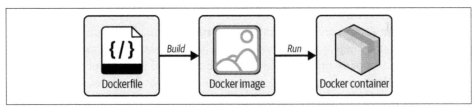

Figure 6-1. Dockerfile, Docker image, and Docker container.

How Much Docker Do You Need to Know?

As a person who primarily trains ML models but who has also set up end-to-end ML deployment infrastructure, I haven't been asked too much detail about the inner workings of Docker in interviews. I think the most important thing that I was often asked early in my career is whether I have practical, hands-on knowledge of *using* Docker. So even if you haven't used it previously, experimenting with it gives you a leg up on candidates who didn't have hands-on knowledge, ceteris paribus.

Orchestrating with Kubernetes

Modern web services are often expected by users to have high availability. Good practices like dockerization help package software in an easily portable manner, which help applications be released without downtime. However, that is only a piece of the puzzle; technologies like Kubernetes *orchestrate* containerized applications to run at the right place and the right times in an automated way. Of course, people (could it be you?) who are responsible for ML application orchestration will need to set up the automations and tweak the configurations and policies.[10]

---

8 "Containerize a Python Environment," Docker Docs, accessed October 24, 2023, *https://oreil.ly/fwWoP*.

9 "Docker Overview," Docker Docs, accessed October 24, 2023, *https://oreil.ly/JsMan*.

10 "Policies," Kubernetes Documentation, updated May 29, 2023, *https://oreil.ly/P37UZ*.

Note that the responsibilities of a job role that touches on orchestration could differ among companies. Some companies might have a DevOps engineer maintain the orchestration infrastructure. However, I've seen in many larger and more mature ML organizations that there are infrastructure engineers, MLOps engineers, and MLEs who might all be responsible for at least part of the uptime requirements for ML applications.

I've given an overview of Docker and Kubernetes in this book, but since I don't have sufficient space to cover as much as a DevOps/MLOps book could focus on, here are some additional resources from O'Reilly that I have found useful:

- *Kubernetes: Up and Running (https://oreil.ly/PgXCJ)* by Brendan Burns et al.
- *Kubernetes Best Practices (https://oreil.ly/K9HBS)* by Brendan Burns et al.

If all of this is completely new to you, don't worry. In my work experience, I've been able to learn most of the containerization and orchestration tools on the job. In fact, I'd say that hands-on learning on work projects within working hours has contributed to most of my knowledge in this space so far.

Additional Tooling to Know

Here I discuss a couple of other tools that are helpful to know about:

ML pipelines and platforms
Nowadays, there are many ML platforms that handle parts of the automation for ML workflows, and it's useful to be aware of them. If you happen to find out before the interview which platform(s) the company you're interviewing for uses, be sure to check out said platform's documentation page to find out common terminology and tools that the platform provides. These ML platforms can include Airflow, MLflow, Kubeflow, Mage, and the like.

CI/CD
In an organization where the software team is more automated and mature, you might need to know more about continuous integration, continuous delivery (CI/CD) tools and technologies. Having these tools set up allows for software to be automatically deployed when new commits are merged into the main branch (this is a simplified example for understanding). This reduces much of the manual work when updates need to be refreshed manually all the time. See Figure 6-2 for an example of automating updating the source code, creating the software

build,[11] testing, and deploying. Some tools for CI/CD, in combination with version control, could include Jenkins, GitHub actions, and GitLab CI/CD.

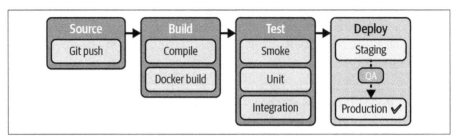

Figure 6-2. Sample flowchart of what is automated with CI/CD after a code change; source: "CI/CD Pipeline: A Gentle Introduction," Marko Anastasov, Semaphore (https://oreil.ly/SUkIQ).

On-Device Machine Learning

There are also specific fields in ML related to on-device deployment, or edge deployment. Techniques like quantization[12] make ML models smaller and efficient enough to run on mobile devices, IoT devices, and other types of edge devices. This requires a lot of additional considerations when it comes to deployment. This is a more advanced topic, so I encourage you to supplement your knowledge if you require it for interviews.

You can read more about on-device ML via the following resources:

- "On-Device Machine Learning" (*https://oreil.ly/n4riR*) by Google for Developers
- *AI and Machine Learning for On-Device Development* (*https://oreil.ly/HvZtW*) by Laurence Moroney (O'Reilly)
- "TensorFlow Lite: Solution for Running ML On-Device" (*https://oreil.ly/bk4dZ/*), a talk by Pete Warden and Nupur Garg (Google)

Interviews for Roles Focused on Model Training

Even if you are applying primarily for the roles that do ML model training, don't underestimate how some of this higher-level knowledge can help you in your interviews. Since there are many knowledgeable candidates in the ML training space, if you are tied on that front with another candidate, having more knowledge or experience with model deployment practices and collaborating cross-team could be a

---

11 Converting source code files into standalone software artifact(s), often called a *software build*, or simply a *build*.

12 "Quantization," Hugging Face, accessed October 24, 2023, *https://oreil.ly/L-RAZ*.

tiebreaker. However, you should prioritize the core ML training competencies in Chapters 3 and 4 if your role is less focused on ML operations.

As a personal anecdote, at some places where I've successfully gotten an offer, I've received feedback that the interviewers were impressed with how I connected the ML training to the deployment process. For example, during interviews I mentioned how I optimized ML inputs to ensure that the ML model could still run fast enough to satisfy the requirements in production. Candidates who are mindful of the end-to-end process can shorten the time it takes to go from ML model prototyping to being integrated into the company's product (such as a RecSys on a shopping site).

Therefore, in industry it's important for candidates to not treat the ML models as mere curiosity projects—using as much data at runtime as possible and requiring too long to iterate on or no way to debug. That works fine on a research or ad hoc basis where the entire model is run only at rarer intervals. But in production, where an outage or bug could cause the loss of revenue or user trust, it's important to prune some things and ensure the related scripts can be debugged.

Articulating my opinion and experiences on this matter helped set me apart from candidates who seemed to not take any responsibility for the usability of their ML models downstream.

Your Interview Varies Greatly with the Maturity of the Organization

For each role, the team's maturity and the organization's size will heavily influence what the day-to-day responsibilities of that job will look like (see Figure 1-3) and, in turn, how the interview questions are structured.

Consider the following: you applied for two MLE roles, one in a large organization and one in a midsize organization where a new ML team is being set up.

The large organization might have all of its CI/CD set up already, and all the automations, version control, containerization, and orchestration have long been completed, so the MLE hire will focus more on maintenance and optimization. Therefore, the interview questions might focus more on whether you know common bottlenecks and how to resolve them.

For the midsize organization where the ML team is just getting set up, the day-to-day role might be more about setting up the automated systems themselves, so you'd get more questions on how you work in an environment where you've set up something from scratch.

Model Monitoring

After the model is trained (via the process outlined in Chapter 4), you still have to deploy it to production. Before that, however, it is important to decide on and set up monitoring so that you can detect problems with the model in production as early as possible. For example, if the model is constantly rejecting loan applicants, you'll want someone on the ML team to be looking into why and potentially bringing it up with the business or product team. Other types of monitoring to set up could include an alert when the data pipeline is failing and so on.

In this section, I'll cover common setups for monitoring, such as dashboards and data quality checks. I'll also cover specific ML-related monitoring, such as accuracy-related metrics.

 Job candidates who don't have experience deploying ML models to production can mimic some of this experience by deploying some simple web apps, as mentioned earlier in this chapter.

Monitoring Setups

Here are a few common ways of monitoring ML models once they are live in production.

Dashboards

Dashboards are often the first step in monitoring. You might not have automated data quality checks yet, but many companies I've seen have at least some sort of dashboard to monitor ML predictions.

Here are some important considerations when you are creating dashboards for ML monitoring:

Keep the visualization as simple as possible.
    If it's too complicated, people will stop looking at it, which defeats the purpose of creating one.

Make the labels as clear as possible.
    Team members I've worked with and mentored in the past know that if the labels aren't there or aren't clear in any visualization, I will mention their importance in a code review. In particular, please don't forget the axis labels.

Show patterns well.

Sometimes the default scale can't show the differences or magnitude well enough; for example, sometimes the graph gets very cramped. You can use log transforms to make a graph more readable.

 Some of these points aren't determined during the interview but much earlier. For example, if you linked a GitHub portfolio on your resume, the interviewers might have looked at it. If the dashboards or graphs on the portfolio are horribly unclear and lack axis labels, then that already gives a negative impression before the interview even happens.

In terms of implementation, here are some common tools for visualization and monitoring:

- Custom dashboards: Seaborn (*https://oreil.ly/m-0-g*), Plotly (*https://plotly.com*), Matplotlib (*https://oreil.ly/s2smF*), and Bokeh (*http://bokeh.org*)
- End-to-end platforms: Amazon SageMaker dashboards (*https://oreil.ly/zuL3R*) and Google's Vertex AI monitoring (*https://oreil.ly/GEIlI*)
- Other business intelligence (BI) tools: Microsoft Power BI (*https://oreil.ly/dSwsq*), Tableau (*https://oreil.ly/xPRW6*), and Looker (*https://oreil.ly/Xokd6*)

Data quality checks

Since dashboards are something to check manually, you may want to add automated checks to save time and ensure accuracy. These checks could include checking for missing values in the incoming data or even checking for a distribution shift in the data.

Tools for data checks or data unit tests include:

- Great Expectations (*https://oreil.ly/OvPXL*) (see Figure 6-3)
- deequ (*https://oreil.ly/zIGqn*)
- dbt (*https://oreil.ly/WROHG*) (pipelines can include tests)

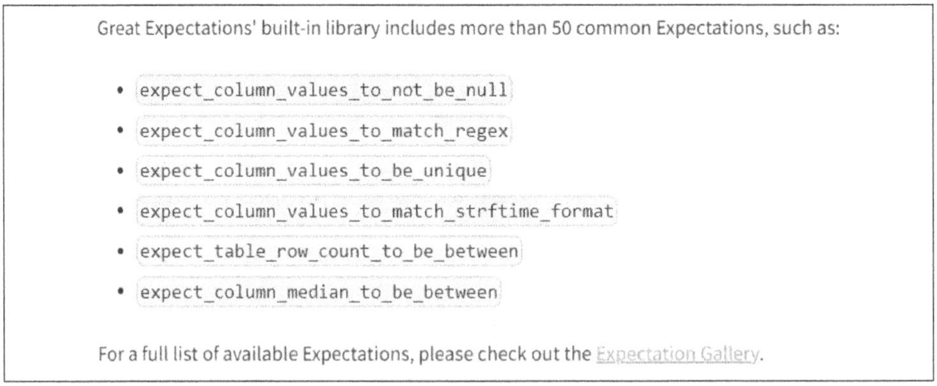

Great Expectations' built-in library includes more than 50 common Expectations, such as:

- `expect_column_values_to_not_be_null`
- `expect_column_values_to_match_regex`
- `expect_column_values_to_be_unique`
- `expect_column_values_to_match_strftime_format`
- `expect_table_row_count_to_be_between`
- `expect_column_median_to_be_between`

For a full list of available Expectations, please check out the Expectation Gallery.

Figure 6-3. Screenshot of Great Expectations' Expectations, which can test if data fulfills certain requirements.

Alerts

Now that you have automated the detection of data quality drops or shifts, you can set up alerts. An alert policy includes the logic for the alerts, such as: if the column starts having too many Null values, notify this Slack channel. Figure 6-4 shows an example of how a test would appear on Slack via Great Expectations (*https://oreil.ly/ UV9ey*).

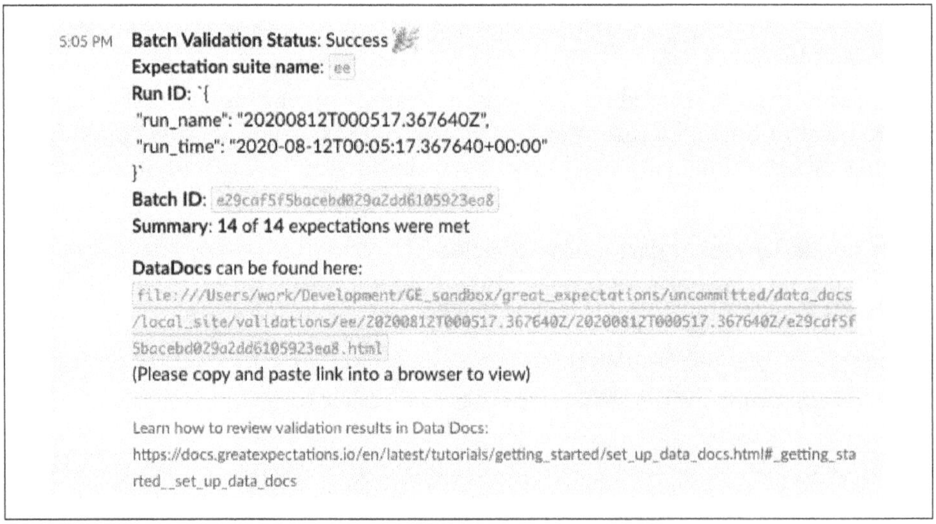

5:05 PM **Batch Validation Status: Success**
Expectation suite name: ee
Run ID: `{
  "run_name": "20200812T000517.367640Z",
  "run_time": "2020-08-12T00:05:17.367640+00:00"
}`
Batch ID: e29caf5f5bacebd029a2dd6105923ea8
Summary: 14 of 14 expectations were met

DataDocs can be found here:
file:///Users/work/Development/GE_sandbox/great_expectations/uncommitted/data_docs
/local_site/validations/ee/20200812T000517.367640Z/20200812T000517.367640Z/e29caf5f
5bacebd029a2dd6105923ea8.html
(Please copy and paste link into a browser to view)

Learn how to review validation results in Data Docs:
https://docs.greatexpectations.io/en/latest/tutorials/getting_started/set_up_data_docs.html#_getting_sta
rted__set_up_data_docs

Figure 6-4. Screenshot of Great Expectations' website: Slack notification example; source: Great Expectations documentation (https://oreil.ly/7Nozg).

ML-Related Monitoring Metrics

Previously, I discussed overall monitoring setups and data monitoring, and now I'll drill down on metrics that measure model performance itself, or the outputs and predictions of the models. This is often asked in interviews to determine how you would handle model performance changes. Here are some categories of metrics to use:

Accuracy-related metrics

You can monitor and track accuracy-related metrics, although this might require the entire feedback loop to be complete. For example, in a churn-prediction model, you might predict that one user will churn during this month's cycle. After a month, you then check if that prediction was indeed correct and do the same across all predictions in the month. If your model accuracy is lower than expected, then note that as something to investigate.

Prediction-related metrics

In cases where it's important for the model to react more quickly than you have the feedback loop for, you can monitor the prediction metrics as well. For example, if the model starts to predict an abnormally high volume of fraud alerts (you can determine the threshold beforehand), investigate if anything has changed. Since you have data quality checks set up from the previous step, that can be a good starting point. In other words, use the output of the models as an alarm and troubleshoot it via investigating the inputs or other factors, such as recent world events or sales.

Interview Tip: Don't Focus Only on Model Metrics

As mentioned at the beginning of this section, the ML model aims to improve something in the product itself, be it customer satisfaction, retention, or the like. Sometimes, the highest ML accuracy might achieve an incorrect result. For example, a RecSys might accurately predict clicks, but it turns out that the content being recommended is clickbait or illegal. User satisfaction and trust will end up going down if this behavior isn't quickly discovered and the model tweaked or replaced.

Overview of Cloud Providers

In this section, I'll give an overview of the big three cloud providers. In ML interviews, I don't think it makes a big difference which one you have experience with, as long as you have awareness of how they work. As an example, my first job used local cloud, but my second job, which primarily used GCP, was fine with that experience since it demonstrated that I could work with remote machines. My third job used a mix of AWS and GCP and didn't mind at all that I had only used GCP thus far, with small exposure to Azure.

Once you get used to the main components, each big three cloud provider's functionality generally has equivalents. I still often find myself googling something like "GCP [terminology] AWS equivalent," where [terminology] could be something like service accounts (*https://oreil.ly/cAi6q*) since they are called something else in AWS. I later found that they are simply called IAM roles (*https://oreil.ly/f5hTc*).

Of course, an employer might expect the candidate to come in without much time to onboard and get used to a new technology, simple as it is. In those situations, the candidate who has experience with the platform that the company uses could get priority. I consider those situations to be something out of the candidate's control and knowledge, and you shouldn't feel too bad if you suspect a case like this.

Cloud Services' Names May Change with Time

What's more important than the specific tool name is knowing what the tool does. I tried to include the most well-known cloud services at the time of writing, but new things are often being added, so I encourage you to take a look at each services' high-level homepage to see what's new. For example, Google Cloud Run only became available in 2019,[13] and Vertex AI was announced in 2021.[14] There are always more tools being built!

GCP

GCP (Google Cloud Platform) is Google's cloud offering. In my experience at multiple workplaces that use GCP, it's pretty easy to use (in my opinion). The main tools I've seen in a data science/ML workflow are (this is a nonexhaustive list):

Google Colab (https://oreil.ly/TH4I6)
> This is a popular solution for creating, hosting, and sharing Jupyter Notebooks. It can be used for R&D, exploratory data analysis, and model training.

Google Cloud Storage (GCS) (https://oreil.ly/36cYD) and buckets
> Used to store some inputs and outputs of model training.

Google Cloud databases (https://oreil.ly/XKsAe)
> Includes Cloud SQL, BigQuery, Bigtable, Firestore, and so on. These are analytical databases, sometimes used as a feature store for batch ML.

---

13 "Announcing Cloud Run, the Newest Member of Our Serverless Stack," *Google Cloud* (blog), April 9, 2019, *https://oreil.ly/f5hTc*.

14 Craig Wiley, "Google Cloud Unveils Vertex AI, One Platform, Every ML Tool You Need," Google Cloud (blog), May 18, 2021, *https://oreil.ly/hfL1h*.

Google Kubernetes Engine (GKE) (https://oreil.ly/C4WyB)
For larger-scale operations, this tool uses Kubernetes to orchestrate the ML deployments like autoscaling when more compute resources are needed.

Kubeflow on Google Cloud (https://oreil.ly/MU_jW)
You can run tools for model management on GCP, such as Kubeflow, MLflow, and so on.

Vertex AI (https://oreil.ly/YGf0I)
At the time of writing, this feature is undergoing some updates and changes, but its purpose is to be an end-to-end ML solution.

Of course, depending on the ML company you join, there can be a mix and match of tools since, at the end of the day, all these components are simply a means to an end. As I said before, you don't need to know all of them; I'm mentioning some of these tools to help you gain general name recognition and get a sense of what each tool does.

To get started with ML on Google's tech stack for free, you can use Google Colab's free tier, which is quite good, in my experience. Then, you can use GCP's free tier (*https://oreil.ly/PAhx9*), up to certain monthly quotas. Beyond that, there's also a free trial up to $300 in Cloud Billing credits (*https://oreil.ly/wnTr1*) (available at the time of writing).

Google provides a mix of free and paid ML courses; at the time of writing, here is their foundational courses page (*https://oreil.ly/KGEZn*) and their Machine Learning Engineer Learning Path (*https://oreil.ly/SVQZ2*). There's also the Google Cloud Skills Boost (*https://oreil.ly/mkFKt*): training services with video lectures and hands-on labs to GCP via Qwiklabs.

AWS

Amazon Web Services (AWS) is another very popular cloud platform, owned by Amazon. It has a host of ML-related features and services; here is a nonexhaustive list:

Amazon Simple Storage Service (S3) (https://oreil.ly/XaWmX)
Storage solution that can be used to store some inputs and outputs of model training.

Amazon Elastic Kubernetes Service (EKS) (https://oreil.ly/kwSLG)
Fully managed Kubernetes to orchestrate ML deployments like autoscaling when more compute resources are needed.

Amazon EC2 (https://oreil.ly/oNArn)
Compute layer on AWS used to provision VMs.

Amazon SageMaker (https://oreil.ly/i-BAn)
> Managed ML platform, model store, and feature store. It includes model version-ing (*https://oreil.ly/Ydcvj*), model monitoring dashboards (*https://oreil.ly/8YnQA*), and more.

To get started for free, use AWS free tier (*https://oreil.ly/Q8OOr*) (available at the time of writing). AWS has official free lessons to guide you through the platform.[15] The AWS Machine Learning Learning Plan (*https://oreil.ly/rinPk*) is also free (at the time of writing). I recommend getting a quick view via the official free courses first, since they are usually shorter, and focusing on what the providers themselves con-sider the most important parts to learn.

Microsoft Azure

Here is a nonexhaustive list of ML tools on Azure, Microsoft's cloud platform:

Azure Blob Storage (https://oreil.ly/b8jnH)
> Storage solution that can be used to store some inputs and outputs of model training

Azure Virtual Machines (https://oreil.ly/UrntN)
> The compute layer on Microsoft Azure

Azure Machine Learning (https://oreil.ly/ci02E)
> End-to-end platform for the ML lifecycle

To get started, you can use the free services (*https://oreil.ly/48cUE*) that are available on Azure. Azure has official free lessons on ML training on the Machine Learning for Data Scientists page (*https://oreil.ly/LVJ_s*).

Developer Best Practices for Interviews

During interviews, it's useful to see if candidates have experience working in a proper software environment. For entry-level candidates, I expect to be coaching and men-toring them on the tools they haven't used before. But I've seen a lot of people com-ing out of school who already have used tools like Git and have learned the process of getting code reviews in their school assignments or at their co-op intern placements, so to be realistic with you, the competition is pretty fierce out there. Even at the co-op/intern level, I've interviewed and mentored many candidates (for example, from the University of Waterloo, my alma mater) who have gained full-time-equivalent experience with the general developer tools described in this section.

---

15 For an overview of free and paid courses, see "Cloud Roles—Skill Builder," AWS Training and Certification, accessed October 24, 2023, *https://oreil.ly/f9jH-*.

This section is very useful for anyone working in ML, not just those focusing on model deployment.

Version Control

Any job candidate for an ML position should have some experience using version control. Most commonly, version control is done with Git (*https://git-scm.com*). Companies often use online platforms like GitHub (*https://github.com*) or GitLab (*https://oreil.ly/coJq7*) that support Git version control. The goal of version control is to be able to track changes to the code, roll back (reset) to a previous version of the code, and collaborate easily with other team members. When you're the only person working on the codebase (e.g., on your personal project), you might not see the point and instead use copy-paste to back up your code. However, when it comes to any larger codebase that two or more people work on, save yourself the headache and use version control.

In my personal view, spending a little time upfront setting up version control pays for itself exponentially; without version control, you could waste hundreds of hours trying to pass code between multiple people or panicking when the code breaks and you can't recover a past version that works. I'm shuddering thinking about it.

How Can I Self-Learn Version Control?

If you want to gain experience with version control outside of work, you can get started by putting some of your code on GitHub or GitLab. But don't stop with the initial code upload; try to learn to make changes with git-branch, git-commit, and so on. You can get started playing around with commands in the gittutorial.[16] In my experience learning Git, I learned the most from running the commands hands on. It's normal to be pretty confused about the commands initially; don't be afraid to test things out even if you're not sure (back up your code by a local copy-paste just in case, though). If you're afraid of messing up the code repository you're working on for school or work, you can create a test repository that you can freely mess up and test the commands however you want.

---

16 "gittutorial—A Tutorial Introduction to Git," Git, accessed October 24, 2023, *https://oreil.ly/C7KCS*.

Dependency Management

For ML roles that require the candidate to have strong software development skills, dependency management could be a topic of discussion during interviews. In development, it's a best practice to use some sort of tool for portability, but at a more granular, project level. This could be as simple as having set up Python dependency management, such as Poetry (*https://oreil.ly/nyt4A*) or Pipenv (*https://oreil.ly/Ev5kg*).

The list is nonexhaustive, but it shows that you can keep in mind code portability and working together as a team to ship software/ML solutions. Knowing dependency management best practices ties in with the section "Docker" earlier in this chapter, where it's useful to show that the candidate can integrate easily into a collaborative software development workflow with a team.

Code Review

When you make changes to production code at work, there's often a review process during which other team members can give you feedback. You'll need to demonstrate that the code works as intended and doesn't break anything; tests are a common way to do this.

Those who are new to the industry or fresh out of school are less likely to have gone through a code-review process. In the interview, this doesn't matter too much, but one thing behavioral interviews can test is whether a candidate can take feedback well. This is to prevent friction after the candidate joins the team and is part of code review; people who can take constructive feedback well and not make it personal will be easier to work with. It's out of scope for this book to talk more about ways to give and take feedback in code review, but I hope that you can see why some interview questions are designed to get an insight into how you might react in code reviews, a very common part of the ML/software workflow. To learn more, a useful starting point is the "Respectful Changes" page (*https://oreil.ly/w21h1*) from Chromium Docs and the "How to Write Code Review Comments" section (*https://oreil.ly/0xQBP*) of Google's Engineering Practices Documentation (*https://oreil.ly/bgso7*).

As a cautionary example, I've seen candidates respond noncollaboratively and with aggressive defensiveness when probed about a mistake or misunderstanding in an interview. Recently, I heard of a candidate who even emailed to further criticize the interviewers and insult the company when they couldn't answer the questions well. If a candidate reacts like that to a standardized, well-conducted, and professional one-hour interview, then how would they react to a code review? How would their coworkers who work day in and day out with that person feel if they can't even handle one hour of interaction? It's an easy way to not be hired, that's for sure.

Tests

In many coding teams, it's a best practice to write tests for code. In Python, you can use packages like pytest (*https://oreil.ly/pv2TP*) and unittest (PyUnit). It doesn't really matter which one you know; you can see a detailed comparison on the Pytest with Eric blog.[17]

In many coding interviews, a hidden requirement is that you include tests for your code. This could be the case even if it's not included in the description. For example, I've had live coding interviews on HackerRank or CoderPad that expected tests, but this wasn't mentioned, and I also had a take-home coding exercise that expected the candidate to proactively add tests.

 Just to be safe, mention some test cases during your coding interview. The interviewer will usually expect you to at least mention it; if it's out of scope to fully code out during the interview, they will let you know. If it's a take-home exercise, I highly recommend writing some tests for it.

On the interviewer side, I also expect interviewees either to ask if they should add tests or to proactively add them. Some interviewers who follow the same track as the software engineer interview track might even expect interviewees to use test-driven development (TDD),[18] although I've found that to be rarer. If the interviewers expect something specific such as TDD, then they will mention it in their interview brief.

Here are some resources for reading more about writing tests for ML workflows:

- "How to Unit Test Deep Learning: Tests in TensorFlow, Mocking and Test Coverage" (*https://oreil.ly/PBBge*) by Sergios Karagiannakos
- "Getting Started with Testing in Python" (*https://oreil.ly/tfkuh*) by Anthony Shaw

Additional Technical Interview Components

As you saw in Figure 1-1, there are additional interview types. Usually, they are more advanced components, assessing candidates on various combinations of ML, coding, training, and deployment (content that has been covered so far in Chapters 3, 4, and 5 and this chapter).

---

17 Eric Sales De Andrade, "Pytest vs Unittest (Honest Review of the Two Most Popular Python Testing Frameworks," Pytest with Eric (blog), updated October 24, 2023, *https://oreil.ly/rYCOR*.

18 "Test-Driven Development," Wikipedia, updated August 27, 2023, *https://oreil.ly/i5tPU*.

Additional types that you might commonly hear about are:

- Machine learning systems design interview
- Technical deep-dive interview
- Take-home exercises
- Product sense

I will briefly go through each of these interview types, so you are aware of how to prepare for them. I personally didn't need to prepare for these types of interviews when I was looking for my entry-level role, as ML theory and coding were sufficient. However, I have encountered more and more advanced interviews as I progressed to senior and staff+ roles. Each company may ask for only some of these or none at all, so what you encounter in your interviews will differ. For example, Meta asks MLE candidates systems design questions, not just candidates at the "senior" level.

Machine Learning Systems Design Interview

ML systems design interviews and questions ask you to design something in an often hypothetical scenario. This could include asking you to design a brand-new system from scratch or how you'd hypothetically design a known system. Examples include:

- "Imagine you are part of an ecommerce company's ML team. It is aiming to use ML to increase customer retention. Walk through your initial approaches and how you would accomplish this."
- "How would you introduce ML-powered restaurant recommendations on Google Maps?"
- "The online game our company is developing uses reinforcement learning to improve player experience. How would you design such a system?"

ML systems design questions are often open ended, with plenty of back-and-forth with the interviewer asking follow-up questions that they find interesting. ML systems design questions can be quite challenging for a couple of reasons:

They likely don't have a 100% correct answer.
> Since the questions are often about hypothetical scenarios, the questions themselves might also change on the fly. For example, I (as the candidate) might ask the interviewer, "How many daily users are we expecting for this ML system?" Given the same question, by design the interviewer might not have defined all the parameters of the scenario and makes up a plausible number on the spot. Lots of what you do during the ML systems design is merely estimation and back-of-the-envelope math, and there is often no correct tool to choose (e.g., for some scenarios, you could use either XGBoost or CatBoost).

ML systems design questions have high variance between each company, team, and interviewer.

Much of your performance depends not only on your initial design but also on how you can respond to open-ended questions that could go in any direction. The interviewer could be curious about how you'd deal with the speed of the ML inference, and you could spend another five minutes on that topic. Or, by chance, they might ask instead about how you'd ensure that data quality is high before training the models. Treat it like improv and be able to adjust to how the conversation is flowing between you and your interviewer.

Do yourself a favor and check the job posting to see what aspects you should focus on. Even in a scenario where the systems design questions ask you to design an end-to-end ML project, you can spend more time focusing on the core competencies of the position during the job interview. If you're interviewing for a data scientist position that trains and evaluates ML models, then elaborate more on that and less on the deployment. Don't ignore other aspects of the ML system if it's an end-to-end system question, though. If you're interviewing for an MLE position that focuses on deployment, spend a little more time on that instead of getting stuck in a rabbit hole about data engineering. If in doubt, ask your interviewer if you're focusing on the right thing and if they'd like to dive deeper on any topic.

> Depending on the interviewer, they may have different ideas of what kind of answer they want. Some interviewers want you to start with talking about the data and the specific features available, if they are continuous or categorical, etc. Some other interviewers might not focus as much on those details. As an interviewee, it's important to check in with the interviewer about the level of detail they're looking for.
>
> —Serena McDonnell, Lead Data Scientist, ex-Shopify

I won't provide further examples here, since they would build on and combine the information from the ML algorithm, ML evaluation, ML deployment, and coding interviews that we've already discussed in this book. For entry-level roles, if there are systems design questions, they will focus on skills that have been covered in the previous chapters. The most advanced systems design questions are mostly reserved for more senior and staff+ roles.

For greater depth on this subject, I recommend the following resources:

- "ML Systems Design Interview Guide" (*https://oreil.ly/QuMZw*) by Patrick Halina
- *Machine Learning System Design Interview* by Ali Aminian and Alex Xu (ByteByteGo)
- Search YouTube videos on example system design interviews for ML; this is a good example: "Harmful Content Removal: Machine Learning (System Design)

Staff Level Mentorship" (*https://oreil.ly/RsjeE*) by Interviewing.io. (This question is aimed at the L7 staff position.)

ML System Design Interview at Meta

At Meta, example questions include "design a personalized news ranking system," "design a product recommendation system," and so on. As you can see from the following breakdown, Meta is looking for an accumulation of the skills discussed in this book, not just a narrow subsection of them.

The signals the interviewer is looking for from candidates include:

Problem navigation
    Seeing if the candidate can organize the entire problem. Meta's interview prep guide highlights that candidates should connect the problem to the business context. (Refer to Chapter 4 and the section "Product Sense" on page 214.)

Training data
    How would you collect training data and evaluate the risks? (Refer to Chapter 4.)

Feature engineering
    How would you come up with relevant features for the ML task? (Refer to Chapter 4.)

Modeling
    How do you justify choosing a specific model? Explain the training process, and explain the risks and how you'd mitigate them. (Refer to Chapters 3 and 4.)

Evaluation and deployment
    How do you evaluate and deploy the model? How do you justify which metrics to monitor? (Refer to Chapters 4 and 6.)

You can read Meta's official resource in its software engineer ML full loop interview prep guide (*https://oreil.ly/MbOLH*), which can be found on its careers site (*https://oreil.ly/TkJnp*).

In Meta's interview prep guide, you'll see repeated mentions of expecting candidates to come up with potential risks and mitigations for the ML designs they propose. This is a useful pattern of thinking for all ML interviews and a sign of a more effective and thoughtful ML practitioner. A useful and important way to improve your discussion of possible risks is to read about AI biases because they are a big part of risks. Research from Timnit Gebru and Joy Buolamwini are good resources; for example, they investigate ML algorithms' accuracy disparities (*https://oreil.ly/db8Iq*) on gender and race (via skin type).[19] Meta's own blog on progress and learnings in AI fairness and transparency also mentions various risks and mitigations.[20] Meta's efforts include creating more datasets to "help researchers evaluate their computer vision and audio models for accuracy across a diverse set of ages, genders, skin tones, and ambient lighting conditions."

Technical Deep-Dive Interview

Technical deep-dive questions allow you to walk through something *you've designed and built* from scratch in the past, discussing the trade-offs and challenges you encountered along the way and how you addressed them. I have frequently seen this type of question grouped under behavioral questions that are related to past projects; for example, Shopify places a large emphasis on technical deep dives in its technical interview loop (*https://oreil.ly/c_F8P*).[21]

 There are many companies that do this type of interview, and I've heard it called many names: case study interviews (different from the consulting type of case studies), reverse systems design, retrospective systems design, and whatnot. I'm borrowing Shopify's term, *technical deep dive*, to refer to this kind of interview and interview questions in this book.

Depending on the interview phase and the interviewer, answering this type of question can require more technical explanation and a deeper dive than the usual behavioral interview, and it has the depth and volleying that systems design has. However, it *differs* from the regular systems design questions with plenty of preparation material online since those questions focus on hypothetical situations instead of something you actually built in a former job or project. Anecdotally, the more senior I get, the more questions I have gotten that are of the technical deep-dive variant.

---

19 Joy Buolamwini and Timnit Gebru, "Gender Shades: Intersectional Accuracy Disparities in Commercial Gender Classification," *Proceedings of the First Conference on Fairness, Accountability and Transparency* 81 (2018), 77–91, *https://oreil.ly/spsb7*.

20 "Meta's Progress and Learnings in AI Fairness and Transparency," *Meta* (blog), January 11, 2023, *https://oreil.ly/AOwku*.

21 Ashley Sawatsky, "Shopify's Technical Interview Process: What to Expect and How to Prepare," *Shopify Engineering* (blog), July 7, 2022, *https://oreil.ly/QaUfA*.

> ## Tips from an Interviewer's Perspective
>
> Here are important things to keep in mind while answering technical deep-dive questions:
>
> *Justify and understand trade-offs in the system.*
> Why did you choose BERT-cased over BERT-uncased? Why did you choose a basic Q-learning algorithm over a deep Q-network (DQN), or the other way around? Bring up analyses or benchmarks you ran during the time and be prepared to use them to justify your past choices.
>
> *Deeply understand the main components you were responsible for.*
> If you were responsible for training the model, be prepared to answer questions on the inner workings or even the mathematical foundations of those algorithms. For example, I've been asked how matrix factorization works, stemming from my project that used matrix factorization in the context of collaborative filtering. If you were responsible for the deployment infrastructure, such as in an MLE role, be prepared to answer more details on the Ops side.

Take-Home Exercise Tips

Sometimes, companies will provide an exercise or assessment for the candidate to do at home. These might be graded automatically, and a candidate would be passed or failed. There are also open-ended take-home exercises where the goal isn't to pass or fail the candidate by the exercise alone but to combine it with an interview discussion where the candidate walks the interviewers through their solutions.

The tips for ML algorithms and coding from previous chapters all apply:

- Make sure you can not only explain the algorithms but also the trade-offs as well as why and how you decided on your approach.

- Explain your thought process clearly to interviewers with docstrings in the code as well as verbally during the interviews.

- Write tests!

Product Sense

In data science and ML interviews, especially in big tech, a hidden requirement is that candidates possess some "product sense." This is an umbrella term some companies use to describe whether a job candidate has practical knowledge on how ML benefits the company's products.

This can be shown when speaking about ML products and when you research the company's products. It's important to understand common product objectives for ML, such as:

- Increase user convenience
- Decrease user churn
- Improve onboarding experience

This is becoming more well-known nowadays; if you look up "data science product sense" on a search engine, some guides will show up. However, many candidates don't think about preparing for this unless it's explicitly mentioned by the recruiter or during the hiring process. As an ML candidate, you can integrate product sense into your behavioral interviews, systems design interviews, technical deep dives, and so on. The way you would prepare is to borrow from product manager interviews.

 From an interviewer's perspective, I think of it this way. Does the candidate care only about model accuracy metrics, or do they also care about monthly average users of the product? Do they connect the ML they're building to the product?

Don't underestimate this—when I was starting out in the ML field, much more experienced people and successful peers recommended that I learn more about and understand the business side. This is one way that mentorship benefited my career: there is a lot of information that's not shared in question-bank-type interview guides. In turn, I have included as much of that latent information as possible in this book.

Here are some resources to get started:

- "The Ultimate Guide to Cracking Product Case Interviews for Data Scientists" (Part 1) (*https://oreil.ly/E83EC*) by Emma Ding
- Exponent videos on product sense, such as this "Meta/Facebook Product Manager Mock Interview" (*https://oreil.ly/pLj8E*)
- *Cracking the PM Interview* (*https://oreil.ly/ESol4*) by Gayle Laakmann McDowell and Jackie Bavaro (CareerCup)

Sample Interview Questions on MLOps

Here are some interview questions I've used to interview MLOps engineers and MLEs who work on infrastructure. These interview questions include sample answers to help provide inspiration for your own potential responses. I want to point out that these questions mostly hinge on asking about your experience; most likely, the MLOps engineer and MLE will share the core coding interview loop (Chapter 5) with other roles, and then the resume walk-through and technical deep-dive questions will include questions such as the ones I've given here. As I mentioned in Chapter 5, those roles that are more focused on operations might also have more specialized coding questions that are similar to questions asked of DevOps engineers. At the risk of repeating myself too much, it is best that you double-check the job posting and with your recruiter and hiring manager, if possible, on the focus and expectations of the interview.

For this chapter, it's especially important to note that your answers will differ depending on your own experience; these answers are only high-level, relatively generic examples to show you what an answer might look like. *Do not* use them as a real answer in your interviews unless you've done the tasks/projects mentioned in the example answers.

Interview question 6-1: Can you walk through an example where you improved the scalability of ML infrastructure?

Example answer

Using scaling on Kubernetes helped; for example, horizontal scaling helped distribute the same workload across more instances. In cases when the heavy load came from request volume, I used load balancing (*https://oreil.ly/g3E7F*) with the Google Kubernetes Engine. In the past, I've used autoscaling features in cloud platforms, such as when I was working with GCP.

Interview question 6-2: How do you handle the monitoring and performance tracking of ML models in production?

Example answer

For machine learning, I've learned that what's different between monitoring an ML application in production as opposed to an application without ML is the data and model-related monitoring. This includes monitoring for data drift, model accuracy and drifts, and so on. For this, I use tools such as Great Expectations or Alibi Detect (*https://oreil.ly/Lk4CR*). In particular, at my previous company we used Great Expectations to check for sudden large amounts of missing values or distribution shifts.

In addition, using those monitoring tools, I can create alerts and have recurring anomaly-detection jobs on those platforms to report errors or drifts. On the service availability side (more general, less ML specific), tools such as Grafana, ELK Stack (*https://oreil.ly/SwUDT*) (Elasticsearch, Logstash, and Kibana, aka Elastic Stack), and Prometheus are commonly used.

Interview question 6-3: What kind of CI/CD pipeline for ML models have you built, and how?

Example answer

I started by automating the steps involved in the ML pipeline, such as tidying up the scripts for data preprocessing, model training, and evaluation. Then I integrated those steps into a CI/CD pipeline with Jenkins (*https://oreil.ly/dvtoY*), triggering a pipeline run when there are changes to the code on our GitHub repo. This pipeline includes spinning up the environment, code linting, and testing, followed by automatic model deployment to a staging environment for further testing. Upon successful validation, the model is copied over to the production environment. These steps automated the deployment process, saving on manual deployment time and also allowing for quality control.

Summary

In this chapter, I walked through the ML roles who might be interviewed on specialized knowledge of their operations and infrastructure experience. Next, I discussed some levels and examples of end-to-end machine learning, which differ depending on the size and maturity of the data team.

You also read about different types of cloud environments, trade-offs between private and public cloud, and common tools for ML model deployment and orchestration. I then discussed some model monitoring setups once the model has been deployed. I gave a brief overview of the popular cloud providers, noting that most cloud providers have a similar toolkit, and if you use vendors that are not mentioned in this book, you'll likely still find the equivalent services (just named something else).

I brought up some developer best practices that are foundational for operations and software-heavy roles. Many of these things are naturally learned with work experience, but for folks with school or bootcamp experience, you can still demonstrate these skills with group projects or open source contributions.

Finally, I covered additional types of interviews for ML roles, such as systems design, technical deep dive, and product sense. In the next chapter, we'll move onto behavioral interviews and how to succeed at them.

## CHAPTER 7

Behavioral Interviews

The goal of an interview is to gauge whether a candidate is suitable for a specific role, and that includes whether they can fit well with the team. No matter how amazing a candidate is at technical skills, they cannot deliver projects if they don't collaborate well with colleagues to deliver said projects. The interview identifies a good candidate by several measures, with their ML/coding ability being important but not the entire picture that the interviewers are looking for. This chapter focuses on the interview questions designed to assess your fit on a team.

To put it another way: there is a minimum requirement for technical skills, and candidates at least need to know enough to clear the technical interviews. The bar is set here so that the hiring company is confident that the candidate can do a reasonably good job from a technical perspective. There is still variance among candidates who clear this bar; for example, some candidates might be expected to take slightly longer to onboard, but if the employer is expecting them to stay for a year or longer, slight differences in their programming skills aren't expected to make a large difference in the long run.

What then, separates all of the candidates who performed well in the technical interviews? Interviewers depend on additional measures, such as how well the candidates can communicate, how well they can collaborate with colleagues, whether they respond well to feedback, whether they have a growth mindset, and so on. For instance, a candidate who has decent technical skills that clear the bar, coupled with strong communication skills, may perform better in the end than a candidate with very strong technical skills that clear the bar by a large margin, but who is insufferable to work with.

Behavioral interviews are often the most important component of overall interviews. In my experience, most deal-breakers come when the candidate's values and past behavior do not align with the company's or team's principles—there is usually a higher bar for this relative to just technical or soft skills.

—Eugene Yan, Senior Applied Scientist at Amazon

Generally, as long as you are self-aware and use common sense in your modes of communication, your interview evaluation won't be affected. My point is: an easy way for a candidate to fail interviews is to show that they're difficult to work with. The hiring team knows that people who are arrogant, not self-aware, and so on are likely to be a net negative to the team and, therefore, not a good hire.

Behavioral Interview Questions and Responses

To measure all those factors that are not measured by the technical portions of the interviews, interviewers use *behavioral questions*. Behavioral questions can be asked in dedicated behavioral interview sessions, although they can also be asked during technical interviews interspersed with the technical questions. The terms "behavioral question" and "behavioral interview" may vary from region to region or from industry to industry. Generally, this type of interview will be about what is commonly referred to as *soft skills*.

 It's important to understand that possessing these soft skills directly affects your ability to contribute technically to an ML project, unless you run something like a one-person startup.

Here are some examples of what behavioral interviews and questions measure:

- Communication skills
- Collaboration and teamwork
- Leadership skills
- Conflict-resolution skills
- How the candidate responds to feedback
- How the candidate deals with uncertainty and learning new technologies/tools
- Whether the candidate is aware of how their technical work contributes to the business/products the hiring team is building—sometimes referred to as *product sense*

The questions might follow formats like these:

- "Tell me about a time when you…" For example, "Tell me about a time you navigated conflict within an ML project you were working on."
- "Describe a time you dealt with a tight deadline and how you responded to it."
- "What's an example of a successful presentation you had to give about an ML project, and what was your preparation process?"

The goal is to measure how you would act as a colleague based on your responses describing how you reacted to a similar situation in the past. Note that behavioral questions are often about your real past experiences; do not confuse them with hypothetical situations, such as, "If you had a conflict on your team in some fictional situation, what would you do?"

Hence, it is important to treat preparation for the behavioral interview as a crucial part of your ML interview preparation. You should start by taking an inventory of your past projects, past work experiences, and other relevant experiences.

Exercise

Note down some past experiences at work, volunteering, or school that you are proud of. These will serve as a foundation when you prepare for behavioral questions. You'll refine the topics on this list as we proceed through this chapter.

Use the STAR Method to Answer Behavioral Questions

In ML interviews, and in tech interviews in general, a well-known technique for structuring answers is the STAR method.[1] Having a structure ensures that you give the interviewer enough context, including a description of the situation you experienced in the past and the impacts of your actions. The STAR method is detailed in Table 7-1.

Table 7-1. The STAR method

Situation	Provide context about the situation where your example took place.
Task	Explain what task you were responsible for during your example.
Action	Explain the steps and actions you took to succeed in the situation in your example.
Result	Explain the result and outcomes that your actions led to.

---

[1] You can read more about the STAR Method in "Using the STAR Method for Your Next Behavioral Interview," MIT Career Advising and Professional Development, accessed October 24, 2023, *https://oreil.ly/wiO9h*.

Here's an example question and answer, with the answer following the STAR method:

Question

"Tell me about a time you ran into tough blockers [business speak for situations that cause progress to be blocked] on a project. How did you push past them?"

Answer

[*Situation*] I was working on project Y, which is to create a recommender system for our company's shopping website.

[*Task*] I was responsible for training the machine learning models to generate recommendations for users of the shopping site.

[*Action*] I collaborated with data engineering to gain access to the required data and started training a baseline model with XGBoost. In the process, I identified new data sources that would be beneficial to the models, and in the end, I iterated on two types of models: one that performed better on newer users and one for existing users.

[*Result*] The models were run online and compared against a control group in an online experiment. In the end, the ML-powered approach gained a 2x lift in engagement metrics over the baseline control group.

Here's what this answer did well:

- It avoided too much jargon.
- It mentioned the lift (improvement) of the ML models compared to the control group.

As an interviewer, I feel that more detail could have been given about the shopping site, but in a real situation, it's likely that the contextual information was covered in earlier questions where the interviewee already described their responsibilities in this project. In addition, as an interviewer, I will ask follow-up questions on points I want to learn more about, such as "What were the two types of models you trained?"

Enhance Your Answers with the Hero's Journey Method

Sometimes, using the STAR method isn't enough, especially when candidates follow the template robotically, making the answer to the interview question dry and unmemorable. I suggest using the hero's journey method to enhance answers constructed with the STAR method. The goal is to further describe the challenges you overcame and the immense efforts you made to succeed in the situation, thus making your answer more impactful.[2]

The hero's journey, or monomyth,[3] is a common story template that involves a hero who sets out on an adventure and undergoes various trials and tribulations. Finally, they emerge victorious and return home changed or transformed. Some examples in mainstream media include *The Lion King*, *The Hunger Games*, and *Star Wars*. When you think of those films, what part of the story do you remember the characters going through the most? It is usually the journey and the challenges they overcame rather than the initial scenes that set up the world and backstory or the final few scenes when the hero has returned and there are celebrations.

The structures of the films are also roughly set up this way: they might set the context with 15–20% of the scenes, spend 60–70% on the journey and challenges, and then take the final 10–15% for the uplifting and triumphant conclusion.

Of course, this structure varies from story to story. The main takeaway I want to highlight is that a good chunk of time is spent on the journey and challenges. That is why I suggest incorporating this structure on top of the STAR method. An exciting story with this format, as shown in Figure 7-1, will emphasize the description of the challenges encountered during the adventure, along with the original catalyst and the result.

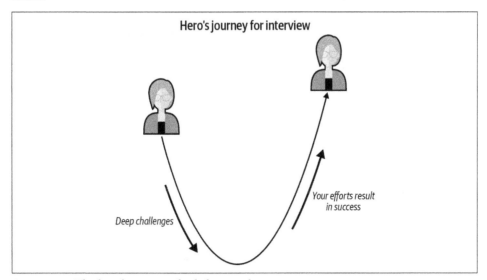

Figure 7-1. The hero's journey for behavioral interview questions.

---

2 I first saw a similar method mentioned in a video (*https://oreil.ly/K8GW9*) posted on "A Life Engineered" by Steve Huynh.

3 "Monomyth: The Hero's Journey," Berkeley ORIAS, accessed October 24, 2023, *https://oreil.ly/zjWAc*.

Now, I'll walk through an example of an answer to a behavioral question that isn't very memorable or impactful, despite following the STAR framework. Recall the example interview question in the previous section: "Tell me about a time you ran into tough blockers on a project. How did you push past them?"

I walked through an example answer using only the STAR method; here is an example of how to make this answer even better with the hero's journey:

[Situation]

I was working on project Y, which is to create a recommender system for our company's shopping website.

[Task]

I was responsible for training the machine learning models to generate recommendations for users of the shopping site.

[Action]

I collaborated with data engineering to gain access to the required data and started training a baseline model with XGBoost.

[Hero's journey, emphasis on challenge]

While training the XGBoost model, there was a catch: the model wasn't performing that well overall. I analyzed the results to find out further steps to investigate; the quality of the data sources was correct, so I ruled out a data quality issue. The dataset consisted of anonymized customer features, such as when they last accessed the shopping site and the values of their last purchases. However, the model wasn't able to capture further nuances of customer behavior because it wasn't in the data. I suggested that I'd need more telemetry data about customer behavior to my manager and the senior developer on the team, and they pointed out the clickstream dataset that I could use. After incorporating the new data, there was still some way to go. The new models were performing well on new customers but not as well on existing customers. Hence, I split out the data and used two models separately for each type of user depending on their account age, which was able to achieve the best overall performance.

[Result]

After I presented the detailed results of the model training to various senior members on the team as well as the product team, the models were approved to be run online. They were compared against a control group in an online experiment. In the end, the ML-powered approach gained a 2x lift in engagement metrics over the baseline control group.

Practice Out Loud—Theory Can Only Go So Far

I recommend practicing saying your answers to various behavioral questions out loud (you can find some examples in this chapter). When faced with real interviews, it's easy to freeze up and forget the STAR method or hero's journey. I recommend practicing with friends, and some peers have had good experience practicing on platforms like Pramp (*http://pramp.com*), which pairs you with a stranger for mock interviews (there are both free and paid options).

Best Practices and Feedback from an Interviewer's Perspective

Here are some of my comments as an interviewer on the example answer, which are also general best practices:

Describing the challenges you overcame helps build the interviewer's confidence in you as an interviewee.

As an interviewer, this answer, which adds the hero's journey method onto the STAR framework, describes much more about the challenges the interviewee faced when developing the ML models than the first example answer did. Why is this important to the interviewer? This type of answer can better exhibit that you are an employee who can dig yourself (and even your team) out of holes, and if you describe the depth of the hole (challenging situation) you've encountered in the past, the interviewer can be more confident that you can do the same if you join their company.

Challenges leave a stronger impression.

In addition, as an interviewer, when I hear and understand the extent of the difficulties the candidate encountered, I can better remember them. This also serves as an easy way to explain to coworkers why I'm vouching for this candidate, as opposed to candidates where everything seemed like smooth sailing for them. The interviewee who didn't describe their challenges in detail might have actually solved a more difficult problem than the interviewee who did, but (1) I wouldn't know, and thus (2), it leaves a smaller impression, and it's hard for me to describe it to my colleagues during a candidate-review survey.

Explain interactions and collaborations, giving credit when it's due.

This answer not only paints a better picture of the situation and challenges but also mentions the interviewee's teammates. Interviewers might get curious about whether the interviewee has skills involving cross-team communication, or at least communication with their manager or immediate peers. Because of the interview's time constraint, the interviewer might not have time to explicitly ask about the scope of the team. At worst, interviewers can become suspicious when the interviewee doesn't bring up any collaborators, due to patterns of interviewees claiming work that is not their own.

Explain the context and any specific terminology that the interviewer might not know.

A common mistake I've seen job candidates make is to jump right into the problem too quickly and not explain the context. When speaking to someone who works in the same company as you, expecting your coworker to have a certain level of familiarity makes sense, and you can often skip the explanation of what a word means. But as is often the case in interviews, you're likely speaking to someone at a different company. Instead of saying, "I was working on the ML model for MyShopping," say, "I was working on the ML model for MyShopping, which is the mobile app that customers can use to browse the store pages and make payments for their purchases." For interviewees who have not had work experience but are describing a school project, beware of using terms from your school without explaining them. For example, at the University of Toronto, computer science classes are labeled as CSC, such as CSC 110Y1, but at the University of Waterloo, they are labeled CS, such as CS 115. Explain any acronyms to your interviewer even if you think it should be easy to figure out what you are referring to.

Provide comparable technologies that are familiar to the interviewer to explain terminology.

Don't assume that everyone remembers the names of technologies and what they do. For example, when mentioning Trino, you can also mention that it used to be called Presto before it was rebranded. Or, if you are explaining how you used Airflow in a past project, you can mention that Airflow is a platform for creating and managing data workflows. In addition, you can mention that it has some similarity to MLflow or Dagster, and so on. Even better if you know that the company where you're interviewing uses a certain tool or technology and you use that technology to explain the way you used your tool, such as, "I was using Airflow, in a similar way to how you folks mentioned you use MLflow, which is…" In my experience, this connects very well with interviewers, and they know that I have been paying attention to our discussions and that I have researched their company beforehand or asked informative questions when on the call with their recruiter.

Adjust the level of detail depending on the audience.

It is important to be able to explain technical and nontechnical concepts with various levels of detail. In some interviews, namely the on-site final round, you might have an interview session or two with stakeholders like the product manager you'd be working with or the director of an organization that the ML team works closely with. I've encountered sessions like this, usually one hour each, in my experience interviewing for ML jobs. For interview sessions with product-oriented folks, I focus more on how my technical work ties into the product or how it affects the business rather than going down a rabbit hole of why I chose a certain ML evaluation metric. As an extension of this rule, when you are talking to interviewers who work directly in ML, still provide some context. For example, I don't have much experience with computer vision in my day job and will need to be reminded of certain acronyms in the computer vision space. It's possible that your interviewer needs a bit more explanation of reinforcement learning, if that's the domain you primarily have experience in, but the company or team you're interviewing for doesn't focus on it.

During behavioral interviews conducted by people who are ML experts, you should still provide context. One way to frame this is to remember they work for another company/team and that they might be an ML expert in another domain.

As illustrated in Figure 7-2, it doesn't just matter how much you know or how good your skills are; if your communication during the interview isn't getting through to the interviewer, then they won't know all your strengths and all the value that you can bring to their team. Spending time polishing up how you can use your communication as a conduit during the behavioral interview to help the interviewer understand you more has a very high ROI.

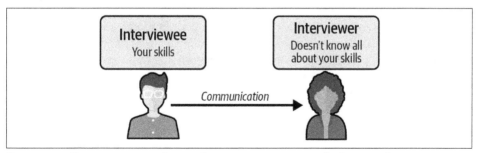

Figure 7-2. Communication during the interview is essential; if you can't communicate well, then no matter how brilliant your skills, that won't get across to the interviewer.

Common Behavioral Questions and Recommendations

Now that I've walked through how to structure your answers to behavioral interview questions, let's dive right into some common questions.

Questions About Communication Skills

1. Tell me about a time you had to help a teammate or colleague not on your immediate team understand a piece of code or design. How did you approach the situation?

Interviewer's perspective: one thing to think about is if the candidate tried to make their explanation from perspectives other than that of coworkers on their own team—for example, by providing more context.

2. Tell me about a time you had to present to nontechnical stakeholders. How did you prepare, and how did it go?

   Interviewer's perspective: asking a candidate how they prepared gives me, as an interviewer, better insight into what they value and whether they are observant about possible communication gaps. In addition, by asking how they prepared, it gives me insight into how they fill in perceived gaps in order to make the presentation a success.

3. Describe a time when you dealt with a frustrated teammate or manager. How did you handle the situation?

   Interviewer's perspective: it'd be nice for the candidate to bring up how they tried to resolve the conflict and how they approach situations where they'd need to meet in the middle. Their response to this question might also help me estimate how easy they are to work with in a tough or high-stress situation.

Questions About Collaboration and Teamwork

1. Tell me about a time you made a mistake and how you handled it.

   Interviewer's perspective: it's useful for me to learn how a candidate manages situations like making a mistake. Do they hide it at all costs? Do they make a situation worse by letting the consequences of the mistake build up? Or do they own up to the situation and come up with a solution? When you answer questions like this, try to communicate to the interviewer that you value collaboration and communication.

2. What was a time when you had a difficult conversation about a project? It could be with a teammate or person you are mentoring.

   Interviewer's perspective: of course, this question also touches on the communication aspect. From the teamwork aspect, I think it's useful to see if the person is the type to take ownership and responsibility as well as to find ways for the team to work better despite this difficult conversation and situation.

3. Tell me about a time you led a project.

   Interviewer's perspective: this is a free-form question, and answers can touch on some important aspects of a senior-level role. For junior folks, this is a good question to see how you treat your team members as a leader.

Questions on How You Respond to Feedback

1. Tell me about a time you received critical feedback.

2. What do you value the most about giving and receiving feedback? Give me an example for each.

3. If you were to change any decision you've made in the past, what would it be, and why?

Take Some Time to Think Through Your Answers

If you really are coming up blank for a question, it's OK to let the interviewer know that you need a few moments to think. My template for situations is this: "I'm taking a few moments to gather my thoughts for this question." I've never met any interviewer who had an issue with the candidate asking for a moment to prepare their answer. When I am interviewing others, I also respect the time, and I notice (anecdotally) that candidates who jump right into answering are more likely to have meandering answers. Taking a pause can help you perform much better, and it takes only a few seconds!

Questions on Dealing with Challenges and Learning New Skills

1. Tell me about a time where you dealt with high pressure, such as a tight deadline, and how you got through it.

2. Tell me about a time when you were unhappy with your job or project. What did you do to make the situation better? Is there anything you would have done differently, looking back?

3. In the past, have you needed to learn a new programming language (or other new skill) for a project? How did you ensure that it was effective? Walk through an example.

Interviewer's perspective: it's important to clarify the time frame and how what you learned contributed to the project. Bonus points for sharing the methods you use to get unstuck and recognizing when to ask for help. These are important skills for tech workers, not just in ML, as recognizing how to unblock yourself (including asking others after trying available solutions) can demonstrate a proactive approach to avoiding project delays.

This is not a clear-cut standard, but from my experience, it is not most important to be the "know-it-all" but rather to be someone who embraces a "beginner's mind" and learns quickly. This is essential to a long career in ML, and tech in general, since technologies change very quickly year over year.

Prepare a Few Scenarios and Reuse Them for Most Types of Behavioral Questions

There are many types of behavioral interviews, and it's impossible to memorize answers for all scenarios. I prepare a list of three to five past projects and reuse them for different situations. For example, I mentored and onboarded new team members onto a RecSys project in the past. I can use that example for leadership questions as well as communication-related questions. Then I prepare another scenario that I generally use to answer "how I dealt with a difficult situation" or "how do I deal with feedback" questions. Overall, I don't really use many scenarios, and I can quickly pivot a past scenario to fit the question that's asked. My advice is to treat interviews like improv and be able to adjust on the fly, instead of fully memorizing any answers. Memorizing can potentially sound unnatural.

Questions About the Company

1. How are you thinking about your career, and does the job posting fit your goals?

   Interviewer's perspective: the company wants to make sure your interests align. If the job doesn't interest you, it's more likely you'll leave sooner—that is, you're a flight risk.

2. Do you have some knowledge about the company, product, or team?

   Interviewer's perspective: spend 10 minutes reviewing the company website, a list of its products, and the job posting before the interviews, just to refresh your memory as part of interview prep.

Questions About Work Projects

1. Tell me about a time you built something from scratch.

2. Could you walk through the project you're most proud of?

   Note: these questions can be part of a technical interview, but they require a good behavioral interview structure to answer well.

3. Have you ever used data to improve a process or technology?

When You Don't Have a Past Scenario That Matches the Question, Substitute with Similar Experiences

If you really don't have an example that the question is asking about—for example, the question assumes you have mentored someone, but you have not formally done so—you should be truthful about what you think instead of making something up on the fly. What works for me is saying: "I don't really have an example of that scenario. However, I've helped onboard a teammate; could I talk about that experience?" Or: "Do you mean formally mentoring someone? I haven't been part of a formal program, but I have helped onboard and teach a new teammate about our codebase. Would that work?"

Free-Form Questions

1. What excites you at work?
2. What are some hobbies you have outside of work?

Behavioral Interview Best Practices

Now that you've seen some example questions, here's a summary of best practices for when you're answering behavioral interview questions:

I recommend reviewing the example questions and best practices when you are preparing your interview answers to help make sure you're covering your bases.

Make sure to pause occasionally during a longer answer or explanation.
Don't ramble on forever without giving your interviewer a moment to interject with questions. Now that more and more interviews are being conducted virtually, it is especially important to pause now and then so that your interviewer can respond. This helps create more natural conversation if you can't see the interviewers' body language.

Quickly summarize your interpretation of the question for the interviewer.
This can help check if you're understanding the question correctly and gives the interviewer a chance to correct any misunderstandings before you spend a lot of time answering the wrong thing. It takes a few seconds to summarize your understanding, but it can save minutes! In addition, I find that this creates a few moments for my brain to think, instead of trying to answer the question the

second after it's asked. Of course, if you notice that you are truly running low on time, you can skip this.

Clarify with your interviewer when in doubt.

As with the previous point, this is to make sure you're not going down a rabbit hole when you're unsure about something. I'd rather be safe than sorry and ask. Some folks avoid asking questions because they're worried it will make them seem unsure or unconfident, but I'd argue it's the opposite: by not confirming if you're still on the right track, it might give the impression that you are too high-strung to ask questions. A simple "Should I continue to talk about my approach to the model training, or did you want me to move on to the model evaluation?" should suffice.

Interviews are communication.

In interviews, the general rules of communication apply. Don't be rude (for no reason), don't put people down or ignore interviewers, and be professional. See one example of ignoring interviewers that should be avoided in Figure 7-3.

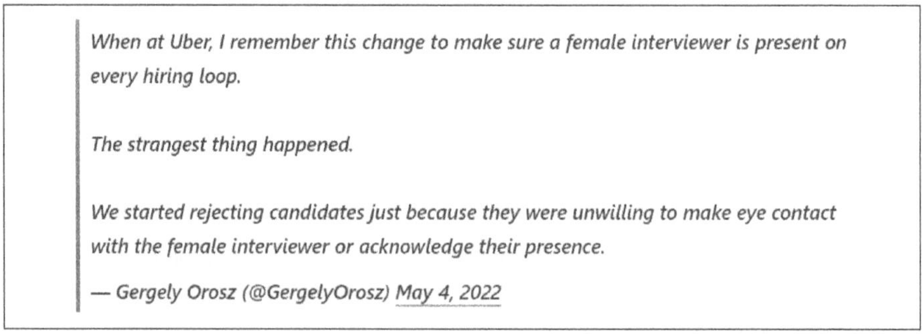

> When at Uber, I remember this change to make sure a female interviewer is present on every hiring loop.
>
> The strangest thing happened.
>
> We started rejecting candidates just because they were unwilling to make eye contact with the female interviewer or acknowledge their presence.
>
> — Gergely Orosz (@GergelyOrosz) May 4, 2022

Figure 7-3. Quote via Tweet from Gergely Orosz (full thread (https://oreil.ly/-pOmb)).

Find a way to use your past experience, no matter what it is.

You can find a way to connect your past experience with why you're here, at this ML job interview. Some people may think that mentioning their non-ML or non-tech skills is stretching the truth, but I feel that in many different fields, the transferable skills are very important.

How to Answer Behavioral Questions If You Don't Have Relevant Work Experience

If you're a student

Having a self-directed project, not just something where everything was handed to you, shows that you're, well, self-directed. This requires additional work, but you can make your own experience by defining your own project, such as a web app that serves ML predictions. You can break down the tasks required to build it and execute on them. These are often called *side projects* and don't require you to pay thousands of dollars or take another online course or bootcamp. You can use this experience to answer a good number of technical and behavioral questions.

If you worked in another field

You can certainly bring in transferable communication and leadership skills. If you've managed a kitchen, worked service jobs, or been a cashier, there are likely some memorable stories that serve as answers to behavioral questions like "tell me about a time you encountered a difficult situation at work." Don't ignore what you have.

Get creative—create your own experience

Once I had a mentoring call with a PhD candidate in English who had self-learned an impressive number of Python skills and was wondering how to showcase their skills formally. I recommended the same thing that I did myself: find a way to shoehorn data science or ML into a self-directed academic assignment. Being in the English program, they could easily find ways to apply NLP techniques within a formal school project. This amounted to hitting two birds with one stone: a great project to show-case on an ML resume that also counted for academic credit.

In my case, I used Python any chance I could for econometrics assignments during my master's degree studies, which was allowed (the options were to choose among Stata, R, or other tools). I had to go out of my way to do it since most of the instructional material was in Stata or R, and I googled how to translate instructions in those programs into Python. As you can see, this was great for answering not only technical questions but also behavioral questions on learning new skills and challenges I encountered.

Senior+ Behavioral Interview Tips

ML interviews for senior roles and higher levels, such as staff or principal, will also have behavioral interviews. I'll use "senior+" here to refer to those roles. The foundations of answering those questions generally follow all the principles in this chapter, but I'd like to point out certain differences.

Levels in Tech

Job titles and levels aren't standardized in the tech industry, as shown in Table 7-2. But as a rule of thumb, after the senior level come the staff and principal levels. At some companies, there might be only staff or only principal, or sometimes principal comes after staff, or it could even be flipped.

Table 7-2. Example of different titles in different tech companies as of 2019, from "The Career Path of Software Engineers and How to Navigate It" (https://oreil.ly/dOusN), a presentation by Nikolay Stoitsev, engineering manager at Uber

Uber	Google	Facebook
Software engineer	SWE 2	E3
Software engineer II	SWE 3	E4
Senior software engineer	Senior SWE	E5
Senior software engineer 2	Staff SWE	E6
Staff software engineer	Senior staff SWE	E7
Sr. staff software engineer	Principal engineer	E8
Principal engineer	Distinguished engineer	E9
	Google Fellow	

For each company, you can check *levels.fyi* as an unofficial source—emphasis on unofficial; it's still best to confirm with someone within the company, organization, or team.

Senior+ interviews will emphasize whether you can differentiate yourself from an entry-level hire, and you must demonstrate that in the interview. Examples of what a senior ML contributor will be responsible for include:

- Can you complete projects independently, and lead a team to do so?
- Are you able to find answers and unblock yourself in more difficult situations?
- Can you make your team more productive with developer leverage?[4]
- Are you able to mentor junior teammates?
- Do you understand the relationship between your organization and the product your company is building, and can you leverage that to succeed?
- Are you able to collaborate well with other teams and, in addition, build trust with stakeholders?

To succeed at interviews for senior+ roles, your answers to the interview questions will differ from those you prepared for an entry-level role. For example, at entry level, there might have been someone who assigned tasks to you, and it's OK if you didn't understand the entire rationale of why the API you were building helped the product. But at the senior level, your questions will be held to higher standards of

---

4 To learn more, see my blog post, "From Entry Level to Senior+ Developer—Multiply Impact with Developer Leverage," June 20, 2021, *https://oreil.ly/TOgB4*.

independence as well as idea creation (understanding the underlying reasons) and being able to be a multiplier for the team by helping everyone be more productive.

For staff and principal roles, you'll need to demonstrate all of the above, but at an even higher magnitude. Seniors might collaborate with their immediate team and a handful of adjacent teams, while staff+ jobs require building trust and relationships with the larger organization and other organizations. For example, staff+ roles may collaborate on a major product that the company produces with marketing, finance, product, and so on.

Specific Preparation Examples for Big Tech

If you are interviewing for some big tech companies, there are known ways to prepare. You'll need to put in additional effort to ensure your answers fit, but it will be effort well spent.

Knowing that each company has something it values makes it necessary to tailor your behavioral interview questions. For example, I went out of my way to make sure one of my commonly used behavioral interview questions for leadership could also cover the "Bias for Action" principle in the Amazon Leadership Principles.

The following are some examples.

Amazon

Amazon will tell every ML/DS interviewee to learn about its Amazon Leadership Principles (*https://oreil.ly/Zw9Nr*) and to demonstrate enough of those values in the interview.

At the time of writing, some of these principles are:

- Customer obsession
- Ownership
- Invent and simplify
- Learn and be curious
- Insist on highest standards
- Think big
- Bias for action
- Earn trust
- Have backbone; disagree and commit
- Deliver results

I recommend checking Amazon's official page (*https://oreil.ly/healj*) for the most up-to-date principles, as new ones (*https://oreil.ly/4kY5m*) are occasionally added.

Here are some example questions and related principles:

Insist on the highest standards
Tell me about the time when you raised the bar/standards of the team/project.

Learn and be curious
Tell me about a time when you made a better decision due to your curiosity.

Ownership
Tell me about a time you went above and beyond your normal responsibilities.

Note that these questions are similar to those asked elsewhere, but if you're interviewing at Amazon, map them to the closest Amazon Leadership Principle and make sure that you touch upon the principle in your answer.

> The unique part of my Amazon interview was how big of a portion the behavioral questions took. This made the behavioral interview stories preparation way more intense and valuable. The Leadership Principles are *very* important, even more so once you get into Amazon.
>
> —Ammar, Engineer at Amazon

Meta/Facebook

Meta has Six Core Values (*https://oreil.ly/rfkoO*). At the time of writing, they are:

- Move fast
- Focus on long-term impact
- Build awesome things
- Live in the future
- Be direct and respect your colleagues
- Meta, Metamates, me

To repeat the tips I previously mentioned, you'll have to weave these principles into your behavioral questions responses: you're not just listing them out.

Meta has five signals to assess during the behavioral interview. These are:

- Resolving conflict
- Growing continuously
- Embracing ambiguity

- Driving results
- Communicating effectively

These (five signals) focus areas were chosen as they are most important to thriving in Meta's work environment. So, when interviewing with Meta, place extra emphasis showing excellence in these areas.

—Igor, MLE at Meta

As usual, I recommend that you look at Meta's official page (*https://oreil.ly/vqORg*) to see the most up-to-date information on its core values and culture. A recruiter at Meta recommended looking at the resources on the Meta Career Profile (which you can create a profile for when invited to an interview). Publicly available resources recommended on the Meta Career Profile include:

- "Interviewing at Meta: The Keys to Success" (*https://oreil.ly/7Exl0*)
- "Software Engineer, Machine Learning Engineer: Full Loop Interview Prep Guide" (*https://oreil.ly/DIwaq*)
- "Five Ways to Grow Your Career at Meta" (*https://oreil.ly/kYbkY*)
- "Embracing Change to Evolve Her Engineering Journey" (*https://oreil.ly/80MTt*)
- "Opportunity and Trust: Growing an Engineering Career at Facebook" (*https://oreil.ly/XMPeH*)

Alphabet/Google

Google famously tries to gauge its interviewees' "Googleyness"[5] and has an "About" page post titled "Ten Things We Know to Be True" (*https://oreil.ly/1_aaE*) that lists several values important to Google.

Googleyness supposedly doesn't have one simple definition, but here is an example. Laszlo Block (former head of People Operations at Google and author of *Work Rules* (*https://oreil.ly/WEroL*)!) defined "Googleyness" as:

Attributes like enjoying fun (who doesn't), a certain dose of intellectual humility (it's hard to learn if you can't admit that you might be wrong), a strong measure of conscientiousness (we want owners, not employees), comfort with ambiguity (we don't know how our business will evolve, and navigating Google internally requires dealing with a lot of ambiguity), and evidence that you've taken some courageous or interesting paths in your life.

---

5 Mary Meisenzahl, "Google Made a Small but Important Change in 2017 to How It Thinks About 'Googleyness,' a Key Value It Looks for in New Hires," *Business Insider*, October 31, 2019, *https://oreil.ly/HKQ3X*.

Additional resources include an article from *Business Insider* that outlines 13 qualities that Google looks for in its employees (*https://oreil.ly/6HjNA*). In addition, traits like the ability to think logically, role-related knowledge and experience, and leadership will be important to weave into your behavioral interviews.[6].

> The reason they care about 'Googleyness' is because Google wants a lot of independence from their devs, even when they're more junior.
>
> —Engineer at Google (who reviewed this chapter)

Netflix

Netflix has its "culture deck" (*https://oreil.ly/UXQqD*). On the "Jobs and Culture" website are listed a few important values Netflix holds as a company. At the time of writing, they are:

- Valued behaviors (such as courage, communication, inclusion, etc.)
- Honest, productive feedback
- Dream team
- Freedom and responsibility
- Informed captains
- Disagree then commit
- Representation matters
- Artistic expression

For more elaboration on each of those points, I encourage you to look at Netflix's official web page (*https://oreil.ly/UXQqD*), which includes details on each of these values.

> The interview process (both technical and nontechnical) at Netflix is more team dependent, and the process is also more focused on the company values and cultural fit. This is why the culture deck at Netflix is so important. A great source to understand how Netflix operates is the book *No Rules Rules*.
>
> —Luis, ML Engineer at Netflix.

This is a nonexhaustive list of examples, but the hope is that you can see how to prepare for each different company. For each company, big or small, I recommend you do a quick search of its careers page to find out if there are values listed out like this; they could be in the rubric the interviewers are evaluating you on!

---

6 "How to Ace Your Google Behavioral Interview: A Guide," *Google Exponent* (blog), accessed October 24, 2023, *https://oreil.ly/kcsHf*

Spending the time to research this information is also an easy way to "guess" one of the guaranteed questions. For example, at Elastic (Elasticsearch), the values are called the Source Code (*https://oreil.ly/UkVY2*). In interviews, we ask if candidates are aware of it, and if so, which point in the Source Code is their favorite.

 A company that was acquired by another might use its new parent organization's rubrics. For example, when I was interviewing for Twitch (acquired by Amazon) a few years ago, Twitch recommended that I also look at the Amazon Leadership Principles, which was seconded by an Amazon employee I spoke to. Note that this might vary from team to team. Ask your recruiter when in doubt.

Summary

In this chapter, I discussed various ways to structure responses to behavioral interview questions, namely the STAR method and the hero's journey. Next, we looked at common categories of behavioral interview questions, with example questions for each. Then, we looked at various best practices for behavioral interview questions. Finally, we went over best practices for big tech, including specific examples from Amazon, Meta/Facebook, Alphabet/Google, and Netflix. I concluded with some tips on how you can tailor your behavioral interview answers to other companies.

## CHAPTER 8

Tying It All Together: Your Interview Roadmap

Now that you've gone through the entire ML interview process, it's time to create a plan. In Chapters 1 and 2, you learned about the many types of ML jobs and did a self-assessment of which one(s) might be more suitable for you. Based on that, you also learned about the skills you are expected to be stronger in. In the subsequent chapters, you learned about what types of questions are commonly asked in interviews. Are there any types that you need to prepare more for? The goal of this book is for you to start bridging the gap, not just read about bridging the gap.

To succeed in interviews and land the job, taking action will help you—not just thinking about taking action.

Interview Preparation Checklist

Follow this checklist to create a plan for your interview process. Refer back to relevant content or past exercises in this book to help you complete the checklist:

- Write down the parts of the ML lifecycle that you're interested in doing at work. See Figure 1-5 in Chapter 1 for a reminder of the ML lifecycle.

- Write down the skills that are required for that role and run the self-assessment of them in Chapter 2.

- Determine what types of interviews could be relevant for that role. Review the overview of the interview process in Chapter 1.

- Make sure your resume is tidied up, with bullet points relevant to the role you picked. Refer to Chapter 2 for more resume tips.

- Write down a time frame during which you're aiming to prepare for interviews and start applying. For example: I aim to prepare for interviews for three months and then start applying.

Now that you have these components in place, it's time to construct your roadmap.

Interview Roadmap Template

Table 8-1 includes a sample roadmap that you can reference while creating your own. Try writing down the overall plan but know that it's not set in stone. I recommend adjusting your plans on a weekly basis. Start by setting achievable goals within your target time frame. For example, if you want to read a nine-chapter ML book in a week, you'll need to aim for completing 1.3 chapters a day. Breaking down the tasks to the chapter or practice-question level can help you see at a glance what's feasible and what is not. At the end of the first week, if 1.3 chapters a day proved to be unreasonable, you can expand your timeline or spend more hours per day on preparation. If you were able to breeze through two chapters a day, you can adjust some of your projections on how much to read during the second week.

 In Chapter 5, you filled out a roadmap for programming preparation, which I felt was important to include separately because of the muscle memory and repetition that coding-interview preparations require. This chapter's roadmap focuses on the overall interview process, so it's a good time to add in any other ML-related study and preparation planning.

Table 8-1. Example roadmap; hours: between classes/assignments and evenings, two to three hours per day

Example roadmap						
Week 1: Planning						
Mon	Tue	Wed	Thur	Fri	Sat	Sun
Read ML interviews	Read ML interviews	Read ML interviews	[Busy with assignment due tomorrow][a]	[Busy with assignment due today]	Make interview prep schedule[b]	Make interview prep schedule
Week 2: Data and ML questions						
Mon	Tue	Wed	Thur	Fri	Sat	Sun
Refresh knowledge on NumPy and pandas	Practice problems on NumPy	Practice problems on NumPy	[Club activities]	Practice problems on pandas	Practice problems on pandas	[BBQ with friends]

Week 3: Brainteaser programming questions

Mon	Tue	Wed	Thur	Fri	Sat	Sun
3 questions on the sliding window pattern[c]	3 questions on the two pointers pattern	3 questions on [pattern]	[Busy with assignment due tomorrow]	[Busy with assignment due today]	Questions on array and string manipulation (overlaps with previous 2 categories)	Try 3 questions and time how long it takes

Week 4: Learn SQL from scratch

Mon	Tue	Wed	Thur	Fri	Sat	Sun
Watch SQL intro videos, skipping some of them	Watch SQL intro videos	Try 3 questions, looking at the solutions	Try 3 more questions, looking at the solutions	Try 2 new questions without looking at the solutions	[Relaxing]	[Relaxing]

Week 5: SQL practice questions + brainteasers, timed

Mon	Tue	Wed	Thur	Fri	Sat	Sun
Practice 5 NumPy/pandas questions without looking at the solutions	Practice 4 LeetCode questions in all main patterns without looking at the solutions	Look at the solutions for questions where you were previously stuck	Practice trying to do 3 LeetCode questions in 1 hour without looking at the solutions	Practice 3 SQL questions without looking at the solutions	Look at solutions to previous day's SQL questions to see if there are better ways to solve them	Catch up on incomplete tasks

[a] You'll see me put these assignments in this prep calendar, but that doesn't mean you're not doing assignments, preparing for exams, and socializing outside of this calendar. This schedule is for only two to three hours a day, and if you list school or personal stuff here, that means you can still afford to take away from interview-prep time for urgent matters, assignments, or social events.

[b] In this example, weeks 2–4 were filled out during this dedicated time during the planning week.

[c] You can pick two easy-difficulty questions to start with and one medium-difficulty question. You can spend 30 minutes to one hour on each question; if you're still stuck after an hour, then look at the solution.

Use the template in Table 8-2 to fill out your own roadmap. Take into consideration your other life commitments and energy. How many hours each day are you setting aside? (If you need more time than provided in the template, just add more rows and create your own version.)

Table 8-2. Interview preparation roadmap template—fill in your own!

Roadmap template						
Week 1						
Mon	Tue	Wed	Thur	Fri	Sat	Sun
Week 2						
Mon	Tue	Wed	Thur	Fri	Sat	Sun
Week 3						
Mon	Tue	Wed	Thur	Fri	Sat	Sun
Week 4						
Mon	Tue	Wed	Thur	Fri	Sat	Sun

Efficient Interview Preparation

In addition to writing about machine learning and tech careers, I've written about efficient time management and productivity since 2017. These are great skills to have in life, and they allow me to achieve more in less time. With the right time management skills, you can spend more time with loved ones, doing chores, playing video games, and enjoying life, all while hitting your career goals.

It's no different with interview preparation. Everyone wants to do more with the same amount of time or less. Competitors for the same ML job who are disciplined, efficient, and effective with their interview preparation will likely secure the positions over those who aren't.

Become a Better Learner

Here are the main tips I use to excel at learning, which I will discuss more in detail in the following sections. These tips are beneficial not only for preparing for interviews, but also for acclimating quickly to a new job and for getting fast promotions:

- Learn quickly by getting hands-on as soon as possible.
- Understand the system.
- It's not about a shorter time frame but progress per time spent.
- Recursively seek out knowledge gaps.

Get hands-on ASAP

Learning by osmosis doesn't work. Just watching endless YouTube videos or reading more Reddit posts and books won't work. I say this because I've done it before. It's fine to relax while doing surface-level browsing and reading, but if you want to move the needle, get hands-on as soon as possible in parallel to learning. Code a small neural network. Do a LeetCode question without looking at the solution. Figure out what you don't know and fill in that gap. Rinse and repeat.

When I was studying for the CFA Level 1 exam, I did mock exams before I finished reading all the materials. I'd get only 35% correct, but it helped me rapidly identify which materials I should read more and which I could skip altogether.

Understand the system

Standardized exams test how well you know the materials as well as how well you know the systems and structures of the exam itself. Even native English speakers fumble the IELTS (*https://www.ielts.org*) (International English Language Testing System) exam if they don't prepare at all because they're caught off guard by the question format. If you try to study for a university exam without looking at the course syllabus, you'll be at a severe disadvantage. In fact, you probably wouldn't prepare for an exam at school without checking the syllabus first. Job interviews are the same. Lots of candidates don't take detailed notes on what the recruiter says is going to be asked in the next rounds, and they don't follow up. I try to construct as detailed a picture as possible by asking clarification questions: "When you say coding interview, is that general Python, like LeetCode style, or focusing on data manipulation, such as with pandas?"

Progress per time spent equals efficiency

I've mentioned doing more with less. This doesn't mean I prepare for interviews in only a week while others take two weeks. Let me explain efficiency with a ratio: progress made toward goal / time spent.

If I'm spending five hours, that five hours better count. I don't enjoy doing something in ten hours that I could have done in five (though it happens). For people with a very limited amount of time to themselves each day, such as one hour, then it's even more important to increase the efficiency. Don't compare yourself to someone who has much more time available and can complete their preparations in a week.

Instead, with your one hour a day, focus on the right things, and you may be able to achieve your goal within a month's time instead of letting the time balloon to three months. Compare yourself to yourself and focus on your own time availability and your own goals. Don't waste time but do increase your efficiency when possible.

Iteratively fill in knowledge gaps

As you were reading this book, you might have come across terminologies you didn't fully understand. The same applies when you're researching for new job roles. Instead of ignoring these terms, note them down and learn the definitions. The next time you come across that term, you won't have the same question again!

Here's an example of iteratively filling in knowledge gaps when encountering a new term or technology, ChatGPT:

ChatGPT
GPT models: while reading up on these, came across the new term *transformers*

Transformers: reading up on this, came across the new terms *encoder/decoder* and *self-attention*

- Encoder/decoder: read up on this, seem to understand it for the most part
- Self-attention: read up on *attention*, seems to make sense

The goal is to dig as deep as you can until it ties back into the knowledge that you already have or until you acquire the knowledge. This is why foundational knowledge is important: you can use that building block to connect knowledge with new concepts for better understanding and knowledge retention.

Time Management and Accountability

Preparing for interviews is often an exercise in optimizing the results with constrained resources (time, energy, etc.). Good time management can help you maximize your outputs with the same amount of time spent. Accountability can help you do what you planned to do. Here are some tips on time management, which I will discuss in greater detail in the following sections:

- Block out time to focus.
- Use the Pomodoro Technique.
- Avoid burnout.
- Ask yourself: do you need an accountability buddy?

Focus time

I recommend blocking out time on your calendar specifically for interview preparation and protecting that time. Let's say you have Thursday evening after work blocked out to prepare—if some friends ask you to come out for a beer, you should probably say no, but you'll catch them next time. OK, unless it's a friend from out of town you see only once a year—then move Thursday to Friday; don't just forget about it!

I personally like blocks of one hour or more, ideally two to three hours since my brain takes 30 minutes to warm up. The essential thing is to block the times in advance as much as possible. If you try to block the time on the day of, it's much easier to let procrastination sweep you away.

Use the Pomodoro Technique

Here is how the Pomodoro Technique for time management works:

- Set a timer (the default is 25 minutes).
- Don't do *anything* apart from the task at hand during that time. Checking social media, reading unrelated emails, and the like are all not allowed. (Looking up terminology or websites directly related to the task is allowed.)
- After the timer is done, take a break (the default is five minutes).
- Repeat.

The reason I like setting a timer is because it increases the *efficiency* (progress per time spent). If I'm spending an hour on preparation, I might be able to complete two practice questions. If I'm fiddling on my phone or distracted, I might only complete one practice question in one hour! That's half the efficiency I could have had if I had just set a timer. Obviously, this can affect the amount of time required to prepare for interviews.

If you haven't tried using a focus timer (Pomodoro) yet, I highly recommend you give it a try to greatly increase your efficiency. If you're more of a go-with-the-flow person, and you've *tried out* timers and they don't work, then go with what you know works for you.

Do you need an accountability buddy?

In many cases, it's worth sharing your progress with someone, even if they're not preparing for interviews with you. I found that when my peers were working hard on interviews when I was in school, it was easy to also work harder, even if we weren't interviewing for the same companies. If you're preparing on your own, it's possible that in isolation, it will be more difficult to keep up your motivation. In that case, here are three options:

- Keep track of as much as you can on the roadmap and be your own accountability buddy.
- Tell a friend or family member about your progress. They don't have to know too much detail unless you want them to.
- Join study groups online in your community (e.g., alumni group).
- If you have hired a career coach, they can help you with accountability.

I've personally had great results with being my own accountability buddy. Having a visualization of my roadmap and calendar and filling it up feels great. I also like playing video games, so maybe something about being able to see the progress is very satisfying to me. The downside is that since I'm the only one in the know about my progress, I can start to procrastinate and keep adjusting my timelines: one week becomes two, becomes three… because there's no one who knows.

In the case of telling someone about your progress, it's easier to find someone around you who you can update. Here's an example of something you can send to a friend: "I've been preparing for interviews. Mind if I send you a quick message about it every week? You don't have to respond in detail. I just want to have some accountability." My friends have always been OK with this. At the end of a week, I might message them: "I did pretty well this week. I finished the two chapters and 10 questions I planned to do. However, I'm three questions short of the goal, and I'll do that next week."

You can try out different methods to see what works for you. As in the case of working out at home or at a gym, this is something that differs for each person, and you'll have your own strategies for how to get your preparation workouts in.

Avoid Burnout: It Is Costly

The reason why the Pomodoro Technique has time built in for breaks is genius. It's not just time management—it's also energy/focus management. Do you ever have those moments where you're working on a math problem for hours and you're really stuck? But then you go take a washroom break or a walk, and when you come back, you magically realize how to do it? This happened to me a lot when I was practicing LeetCode questions and would get stuck. I'd take a walk to clear my mind and come back to tackle the problem after being refreshed. Better yet, just call it a day and go to sleep. When I was in grad school, I called this the "sleep technique."

Sustained practice, via breaks, is the best way to avoid burnout. In an extreme example, if you let yourself burn out, you could be losing weeks or months of motivation. I've been there before—a few times—and it's not great; it set back my goals for a while because I couldn't get energized or motivated since I worked myself to the point of burnout when I was younger. It took months to recover. Our bodies aren't machines, and our brain gets tired after long usage. Take care of yourself and avoid overworking yourself if you can. Much like myself, though, I suspect that many people might not learn their limits until they actually reach them, and that's fine too. As long as you keep it in mind!

Impostor Syndrome

You may have heard the adage "Job postings are wishlists, not requirements."[1] If you are a person who is generally hesitant about applying for jobs where you meet about 60% of the qualifications, I encourage you to try applying to some of them. You may get better results than you had been expecting! If you are hesitant about jobs where you meet most of the qualifications and instead apply only for jobs you're overqualified for, take a step back and consider if this could be related to *impostor syndrome*. Remember that in a company with enough resources (i.e., midsize and up), the more entry level the job is, the more the team will expect to spend time to onboard and mentor you.

I've also experienced severe impostor syndrome,[2] and felt like I was not actually qualified for jobs (even jobs I was currently doing). One thing I've learned is to *zoom out* and look at the big picture. Who am I comparing myself to that is making me feel inadequate? Am I actually comparing myself to a broader group of people than I should be—for example, people with many more years of experience? If I'm surrounded by peers who all seem smarter than I am, perhaps that's a good thing rather than a bad thing (a phenomenon I experienced studying at a highly competitive master's program).

I recommend reading Eugene Yan's blog post on the same topic for tips to identify and manage impostor syndrome.[3] It's not something that will just go away; maybe it won't ever fully disappear since as you move up in your career, there are always new things to learn (and to feel like an impostor about!).

In short:

- You might be comparing yourself to a broader group of people who are doing better for reasons such as more years of experience. Stop comparing yourself to others like that or frame it as a good thing.

---

1 Alison Green, "Are the Requirements in Job Postings More like Wish Lists or Strict Requirements?" *Ask a Manager* (blog), February 18, 2016, *https://oreil.ly/i5osl*.

2 See my blog post "My Imposter Syndrome Stories, and Lessons I Learned," April 18, 2021, *https://oreil.ly/Ifblb*.

3 Eugene Yan, "How to Live with Chronic Imposter Syndrome," Susan Shu Chang (blog), April 11, 2021, *https://oreil.ly/3xJVp*.

- Write down a list of your own accomplishments and reflect on them often. You can also update the list and track it in a journal or brag document.[4]

Summary

In this chapter, you saw a summary checklist and roadmap for your own interview preparations. You also read about learning efficiently, managing time better, and avoiding burnout. Finally, I described possible impostor syndrome in an ML career and how to identify and manage it.

---

4 Julia Evans, "Get Your Work Recognized: Write a Brag Document" (blog), accessed October 24, 2023, *https://oreil.ly/AMCS1*.

## CHAPTER 9

Post-Interview and Follow-up

Since you've read to this point in the book, I hope you can apply what you have learned to your job search! It can be a game of persistence: while interviewing for one of my past roles, I applied to around 70 openings, and I got 10 recruiter interviews and two final-round interviews, which led to an offer. The interviews spanned several months, during which I kept running into new scenarios and questions.

You might have the same questions along your interviewing journey. Let's say you've gotten some interviews, and you're eagerly awaiting their response. *What should you do at this stage?* Of course, the ideal outcome is that you can smoothly move to the next stage, but statistically speaking, there will be times where you hear the unfortunate news that the hiring team has moved on with other candidates. *What should you do in this situation?*

In this chapter, I will go through the final steps, from post-interview to offer stage, covering FAQs that I've gotten from job candidates. I will lay out some scenarios that I've personally dealt with and that many job candidates have dealt with, too, and I will share advice to arrive at the best outcome. I'll also go through some tips for your first 30/60/90 days at a new ML job, to set yourself and your ML career up for success!

Post-Interview Steps

After the interview, I'm often just ready to relax and forget about it. But here are some actions I try to do (most of the time) after each interview to optimize my job search. To be honest, sometimes I don't complete every step, but I know that if I do them most of the time, that increases the chances that I will improve at job interviews and land that job!

Take Notes of What You Remember from the Interview

I like to take notes of what I remember of the questions and roughly how I responded. This helps me see what types of questions are being asked and if there are common patterns. An additional step you can do with this information is double-check the questions by googling resources like Reddit or Glassdoor to see if they coincide with what other candidates have been asked, and sometimes other job seekers will share how they answered.

I find that some companies with a very set interview process commonly reuse questions. But for companies that have more conversational interviews or give a take-home exam, it'll be harder to tell. Either way, if you can see ways to improve your answers on interview questions after the interview, that will help you perform even better if you encounter the same question or a similar one next time. It's easy to neglect this step, but if the next interviewer asks a similar question and you answer it poorly (again), causing you to fail the interview, wouldn't you really regret that?

Make Sure You're Not Missing Important Information

Ask the recruiter or hiring team what the next steps are and what the time frame is for when you should expect to hear back. Sometimes, the answer is that they don't know how long it will take, but that is valid, too. Just make sure you ask, whether during the interview, as a follow-up email, or in a call to the recruiter or hiring team.

Should You Send a Thank-You Email to the Interviewer?

I've been asked this question a lot, and when I was starting my first job, I also asked a friend/mentor about whether I should do it. As an interviewer who has now conducted many ML interviews, I'd say it doesn't really make a big difference. Sure, a simple and casual note is nice to read, but I'd say that the interview results really hinge on if the interview itself went well; a good thank-you note won't change your performance.

As a candidate, I do *sometimes* send a brief thank-you email. Now that I have experienced the other side as an interviewer, I know that they don't really make the candidate stand out too much. I have yet to meet someone on the interviewing team who's found simple, polite thank-you notes to be annoying, but if I ever get a follow-up note that's rude, then I'd rather the candidate didn't send anything at all.

Thank-You Note Template

If you really want to send a thank-you note, I suggest the following:

- Keep it short and simple.
- You can reiterate your excitement about the role.

- Do not try to explain away some mistake you made in the interview or be defensive about something. The interviewer might already have forgotten about it, and this only does more harm than good.

One suggestion to job seekers from a hiring manager is to not go the opposite direction and seem too desperate, such as by sending a very lengthy thank-you email that is overly thankful. Examples include exaggerations such as "This is an opportunity of a lifetime" or "It would be the greatest privilege to work for you." In an ideal world, the interviewer would take the email at face value and not judge the "desperateness" aspect of it, but in reality, these things do play a role.

 In your region, there may be other social norms that affect how verbose people are in professional correspondence or how much gratitude you show. I have worked for Canada- and US-based companies so my communication norms are North America centric. Do adjust accordingly!

Here's my personal interview thank-you note template—you should substitute the words in the brackets [ ] with your own situation:

> Hi [Xue-La], it was great to meet you [and the team] today during the interview. Thanks for taking the time to [answer my questions at the end about the work culture]; it made me more excited about [company name] and what you're building in [recommender systems]!
>
> Best,
>
> Susan

What Not to Do After the Interview

From a CTO and hiring manager in the fintech ML field: "One time after an interview, we received a long diatribe from the interviewee calling us unprofessional and that it was a waste of time."

The interview process was a standard process that the company conducted, with hundreds of candidates having gone through it, and the interview had multiple interviewers in that call. This candidate also seemed quite upset in the email that they weren't able to answer the questions, as well as exhibiting other rude behaviors. This interviewee was immediately dropped from the interview process.

How Long Should You Wait After the Interview for a Response Before Following Up?

Ideally, you've already been told when to expect a response from the recruiter and/or interviewers. If you haven't heard back, and they haven't told you when to expect a response, I think it's good to follow up after one business week. Some companies really do take months to hire, especially if the company is very large and bureaucratic. So even if you email after a week, they may not be able to give you a proper response right away, but at least you'll have started the post-interview conversation. Some companies also take only a week or less—those are usually startups.

What to Do Between Interviews

If you have a few interviews lined up, you may have some time in between several of them, whether that's between multistage interviews or interviews with different companies or for different roles. Or this could be the time after you get some responses, but you haven't accepted an offer yet. This is a fluid length of time, so you don't need to focus on separating the difference between "post-interview" and "between interviews," as there is some overlap.

How to Respond to Rejections

When I'm a job candidate myself, I know that rejection is an inevitable part of the process—getting those "unfortunately, we have decided to move on with other candidates…" emails. When it's a job I've been really hyped about and I anticipated a positive response, I give myself some time to feel upset and (reasonably) vent to trusted individuals, such as my friends or family. Generally, there's no reversing the situation, apart from being polite and professional. It's possible for a candidate to be a second pick, and if the first pick rejects the offer, you could be contacted again. But that will likely not happen for candidates who send an angry follow-up email.

You don't *have to* respond to a rejection if you don't feel like it, but especially for teams I interacted with more during the interview process, I will send an email as a courtesy since I already got to know those people.

Template for Rejection Responses

I often *don't* send an email back after an automated rejection email. However, if the email is from a recruiter after I've spoken to them or after I've passed more interview rounds and actually interacted more with the team, I will email to respond to a rejection. If I do, here's my template:

Hello [recruiter or hiring manager],

Thank you for the update, and for the time. It was good to meet you and the team and learn more about [COMPANY NAME] during the process. [Optional additional sentence here.]

Best,

Susan

Note: I usually add more (the optional additional sentence) only if I made it to the later rounds where I got to meet the team and had good rapport with them. I might also say something like "Let's keep in touch!" if I feel that we had good rapport. But I think this really depends on your personality.

 As usual, replace the text in the brackets [ ] with your own situation and keep in mind if your region values other types of communication, as I'm writing from a North American perspective.

A fellow ML professional mentioned that this is also when they ask for feedback (if applicable), and sometimes they do get it from the hiring team. I myself rarely have asked or received feedback after asking, which may be due to avoiding legal issues,[1] especially when it's a big company with processes to follow.

 When responding to rejections, it's best to stay professional, polite, and positive.

Job Applications Are a Funnel

In my experience, I don't get interviews for all the jobs I apply for, so it doesn't hurt to apply to more jobs that fit my ML skills and profile. As to whether you tailor the applications or not, keep in mind your effectiveness per application that was mentioned in Chapter 2.

Even if you feel that you are a little bit unqualified, still apply! Often, a successful candidate may not even have all the experience on the list. For example, I've seen many ML job descriptions mention Kubernetes, but as you've read in previous chapters, not all ML roles require in-depth experience in Kubernetes. Of course, you do still

---

1 "The Real Reason Why Big Companies Don't Give Feedback to Unsuccessful Applicants," *Forbes*, February 8, 2018, *https://oreil.ly/0V09R*.

need to fit a good amount of the expected experience or successfully persuade the hiring team that you are able to learn and contribute in a reasonable period of time.

You might have read or heard about this statistic: men apply for a job when they meet only 60% of the qualifications, but women apply only if they meet 100% of them.[2] This might be one of the ways that confidence manifests in fewer job applications from qualified candidates. If this is relatable to you, definitely take a look at whether you're underselling yourself.

So if you've received that dreaded rejection email, keep building that application funnel. Keep applying, keep browsing, and keep updating your resume! Use each rejection to help you increase your chances next time; otherwise, you may be spending more time than you need to on the process.

Network to Increase Your Interview Funnel

Each time you reach out for a referral, it won't always result in an interview. And not every interview will result in an offer. I've shared more about this in Chapter 2 as well as in a blog post, "Why Networking is like Investing in an Index Fund" (*https:// oreil.ly/q3h8g*), detailing how I met two final-round interviewers at the director level merely by attending some meetups and conferences. Networking and referrals are great ways to increase your effectiveness per application.

If you have the spare time and energy to go to just one event a month (or even every two months), it can really add up. I set a low-pressure goal to meet one new person per event. This is a long-term strategy, but sometimes you can reach out to folks for a job you're applying for and get a response if you made a good impression. Refer to Chapter 2 for some examples.

Update and Customize Your Resume and Test Variations

Sometimes, your resume really will make a big difference in reducing initial rejections. I've given people resume feedback before, and they've reported that the callbacks have increased. I've personally used this strategy when applying for different types of ML roles. Improvements to my resume have increased the number of interviews I received for jobs that were heavier on ML model development, and they also helped me avoid interview invitations for jobs that didn't match my skills.

---

2 Tara Sophia Mohr, "Why Women Don't Apply for Jobs Unless They're 100% Qualified," *Harvard Business Review*, November 2, 2021, *https://oreil.ly/z4VGh*.

As mentioned in Chapter 2, tailor your resume to the specific ML role you want; for example, for MLE, check if you should emphasize your ML model development skills or your Kubernetes skills. If you have space on your resume, you can emphasize both.

Steps of the Offer Stage

Now that you've gone through a few interviews, hopefully, you've gotten an offer! Even if your first offer might not turn out to be your ideal, I think it's a massive milestone. The first one can be the hardest!

Let Other Interviews-in-Progress Know You've Gotten an Offer

Sometimes, the timelines of other interviews are more delayed, but if you let other companies know that you've received an offer, there are places that are willing to expedite your interview process. Of course, this isn't guaranteed, but there is no harm done in letting other places know you have an offer. The best case is they'll expedite your process, and the worst case is that there's no change. These companies also now know that another company wants you; that could increase your value as a candidate since you have current external validation.

I don't cover much on negotiation in this book, so here are some articles that many have found useful:

- "Salary Negotiation: Make More Money, Be More Valued" from Kalzumeus Software (*https://oreil.ly/kCEaF*)
- "Exactly What to Say When Recruiters Ask You to Name the First Number… and Other Negotiation Word-for-Words" (*https://oreil.ly/8Fbm3*) from *interviewing.io (https://oreil.ly/hufqy)*

What to Do If the Offer Response Timeline Is Very Short

I'm going to be very honest here: a new job is a big career and life move, and it isn't something to trivialize. I often need a week—or a weekend at the very least—of uninterrupted time to think about the offer. Sometimes, you don't have the luxury of time and need a job immediately, and that's OK, too. Here, I'll outline my thought process when it comes to responding to an offer, assuming you are not in an urgent financial situation, in need of a visa quickly, or in some other type of personal situation. In those cases, you will probably have your own considerations for accepting a job offer, and the considerations I give here might not apply to your situation!

I personally ask for as many days as possible to decide—ideally, at least over a weekend. Let's say that you got an offer on Tuesday and they want a response by Thursday, but that's not enough time for you to research all the details and compare the offer. Here are some examples of what you can say:

- "I need to discuss the offer over the weekend with my family. Can I get back to you next Tuesday?"
- If you are still interviewing with other companies: "I need some more time since I'm also at the final stage of another interview. I'm very glad for the offer, and I'm very excited about this opportunity, but it wouldn't be right if I didn't double-check with the other company about their final details, too. I think I can know their decision by next Monday. Can I keep you posted by next Wednesday?"
- If you are relocating: "I want to take a little more time to research the area and cost of living before I can make a decision on this offer. Could I get back to you next Tuesday?"

Depending on your situation, there are many real and important reasons for you to do your due diligence and take some time before you sign the dotted line on a contract that could drastically change your day to day.

Understand Your Offer

Before making any decisions, I highly recommend understanding your offer holistically. The following are some aspects that might not come to mind immediately but are very important parts of your job offer, beyond the obvious base salary.

Workplace culture

Workplace culture is described as "a collection of attitudes, beliefs, and behaviors that make up the regular atmosphere in a work environment" by Indeed.[3] Work takes up a lot of time in our lives: at eight hours a day (not including transportation, if applicable), five days a week, about 24% of our week is spent at work. If we assume eight hours of sleep a day, and there are 16 waking hours in a day, then we spend 36% of our waking hours at work. So if the workplace culture isn't a fit with you and your values, the result could be mental and physical health issues that take a lot of money and time to fix. Is the ROI worth it? Is it worth your life?

Sometimes, it's hard to figure out what the real workplace culture is during the interview phase, but keep it in mind. Healthy workplace cultures could include behaviors like being fair, collaborative, and transparent, but unhealthy workplace cultures could foster bullying, discrimination, or illegal conduct. In North America, there are

---

3 Indeed Editorial Team, "What Is Work Culture? Definition, Elements, and Examples," Indeed, updated August 21, 2023, *https://oreil.ly/Dij-Y*.

protected classes,[4] laws that aim to protect against discrimination for a list of classes, such as race, age, sexual orientation and gender identity, veteran status, religion, and so on.[5] As a personal example, I am a relative minority in North America, and there are people similar to me who I know who have encountered hostile workplaces, so it's personally important to find companies with a work culture that is against sexual and gender-based harassment.

Work-life balance

An important question to ask yourself when assessing the offer is: can you spend time with those who are important to you? There's a saying that "20 years from now, the only people who will remember you worked late are your kids." There are also cases where people lament missing their kids' important milestones (like their first steps or other culturally important milestones) because of inflexibility at work. If you don't have kids, then substitute other loved ones[6] like parents, a significant other, your pet… you get the idea. The same logic can be extended to hobbies, such as creating art, socializing, going to music festivals, and the like.

Avoiding burnout is also important. *Burnout* is defined as "a syndrome conceptualized as resulting from chronic workplace stress that has not been successfully managed" by the World Health Organization, with effects including "feelings of energy depletion or exhaustion."[7] In the long run, the cost of burnout is probably higher than the temporary benefit of overworking. People often regret ruining their health, be it mental or physical, for work.

On the other hand, I have known someone who poured themselves into work as an escape from other things. There are also people who strongly believe in the company's mission and own more equity in the company, so working harder will give them more mental and financial fulfillment. Depending on your situation, evaluate these points of your job offer accordingly.

Base pay

This is the most obvious part of the offer: the monetary amount that you can see in your bank account every time you get paid. Base pay is often treated as one of the

---

4 See U.S. Equal Employment Opportunity Commission, "Who Is Protected from Employment Discrimination?" at *https://oreil.ly/AKD4a* or check your local government sites for any equivalents in your region.

5 These lists might have been updated since the time of writing, so do your due diligence.

6 The article "The Tail End" by Tim Urban has given me a life-changing perspective, and I highly recommend it; see Tim Urban, "The Tail End," *Wait but Why* (blog), December 11, 2015, *https://oreil.ly/sxXWk*.

7 "Burn-out an 'Occupational Phenomenon': International Classification of Diseases," World Health Organization, May 28, 2019, *https://oreil.ly/S8Xf1*.

most important parts of an offer, and rightfully so—money pays the bills and bails you out of catastrophic life events; it's harder to do that with fewer liquid funds.

For example, if you have restricted stock units (RSUs) in a public company, there are blackout periods (*https://oreil.ly/IETGI*)[8] for selling the stock, so you can't liquidate in the case of an emergency. Of course, if you have more savings, then it's fine to have less liquid base pay coming in. (More examples of non-base-pay options are discussed next.)

 For some regions, you can check Glassdoor or *levels.fyi* for average compensation. Do keep in mind that there might not be enough data for your specific situation, so take the numbers with a heavy grain of salt. For example, since I am Canadian, those sites don't often have enough data for me, and I get most compensation info by word of mouth from my mentors and network. Yes, people will share exact dollar figures if they trust you. Yes, you have to spend time to build that trust (refer back to Chapter 2).

Bonuses, stocks, and other kinds of compensation

Some companies may give you other kinds of compensation beyond base pay. Compensation you may commonly see includes RSUs, stock options, year-end bonuses, profit sharing, commissions, and so on. Be sure to check the value of these. For example, options are not the same as RSUs. At a previous workplace, even though I had a lot of options, they happened to end up being worth $0.

Some things you'll want to understand in an offer include the vesting period for stocks or options, how to exercise options, and so on. I'm not a financial expert, so you can read more about this in "Everything You Need to Know About Stock Options and RSUs" (*https://oreil.ly/RHNSD*) from the *Harvard Business Review*. Check online guides and/or ask an expert in your region for specific rules, laws, and taxes relevant to your area and employment situation.

Benefits

Your benefits might not be included in the base salary, but they could have a lot of monetary value. For example, I didn't even realize my company had contributed more than $10,000 to a retirement fund via employer matching in a year. I was aware of the employer matching but didn't actually calculate the dollar value when considering the offer. In hindsight, I absolutely should have. In the US, good health benefits

---

8 Christina Majaski, "Blackout Period: Definition, Purpose, Examples," Investopedia, updated April 15, 2021, *https://oreil.ly/65360*.

could literally mean thousands of dollars of savings for you. Maternity and parental leave could represent great peace of mind for you and your family.

Depending on your life stage, the list of relevant benefits could change with time. A personal example is that I didn't care much about health and dental benefits when I was younger, but after I started needing regular maintenance on a specific dental procedure, paying 20% of the treatment became more costly than paying 0% of it (my previous two jobs, respectively). My advice is to not underestimate the benefits.

Tying it all together

Now that you've taken a holistic look at the offer, think about what accepting the offer would mean for your life and career. I recommend always double-checking with the recruiter or hiring manager if you want to clarify anything. They already extended you an offer, and at this stage, they would rather answer your questions and adjust the offer (if reasonable) than spend dozens of hours on the interview process for another candidate. So don't worry about taking some time to look over the contract, ask questions, and do your due diligence.

Please Read Your Contract Carefully

I'll share a personal example here. I accepted a job offer where the hiring recruiter verbally mentioned an additional compensation component (on top of base pay) in my offer. However, it wasn't actually in the signed contract, and I naively assumed it would sort itself out. Fast-forward a few months, I finally asked about the compensation, and it turns out it was a mistake that it had been left out of the contract. This could have been avoided if I had asked the simple question before signing the contract! Thankfully, in my case, my manager quickly rectified the issue, but I may not have been so lucky without written proof. In addition, it might not have worked out if the hiring manager had left the company or if I had been assigned to a new manager in the meantime.

First 30/60/90 Days of Your New ML Job

So, after a lot of hard work going through the interview process, you've gotten an offer, or even a few—congratulations! Now you've accepted your job offer of choice and are starting the job!

There are lots of things you can do beyond onboarding that can benefit you during the first few months of your ML job. My formal education didn't teach me these things, and sometimes even past job experience won't make you aware of these helpful tips. The following actions have helped me greatly in my past jobs, and I think they are important to keep in mind during the first few months of your new ML job:

- Gain domain knowledge.
- Gain code familiarity.
- Meet relevant people.
- Help improve the onboarding documentation.
- Keep track of your achievements.

Now I'll walk through the details of each of these actions.

Gain Domain Knowledge

If you're a data scientist in banking, you'll onboard and learn about the banking products you're working with and how they work. If you're an MLE in ecommerce and recommender systems, you'll need to make sure you understand what the customers value and what the business values. If you don't understand these points well, you might end up developing models or infrastructure that don't fit what the company is trying to optimize for, making your job performance seem poorer than it actually is.

On the other hand, understanding the goals well will help you build ML more efficiently. Who knows, this could make the difference in how long it takes for you to get a promotion (if you're aiming for that)!

Gain Code Knowledge

I think this is the action that is least overlooked, as in an ML role, it's pretty much a guarantee that you'll be onboarded to the code and data or receive some training. But for the sake of completeness, here's what I make sure to do:

- Be able to set up the development environment.
- Check the permissions that are required and request them (or ask a manager to request them).
- Skim through the main projects and code repositories.

If there are libraries you aren't familiar with, ask a coworker if they are being used. If they are, then you can ask your manager if there's part of the onboarding process that trains you on those. The reason why I mention checking first is because lots of companies and teams have some legacy code that might not need to be changed, and thus you don't have to worry too much about it. For example, at one of my workplaces, a few folders and jobs ran on Scala, and I checked with my manager if they were being used because I was curious. It turns out that those jobs were being phased out, so I didn't need to worry too much about them at the time; focusing on familiarizing myself with the Python and shell scripts was more important.

Meet Relevant People

Companies are made up of people, even in tech where we work with code and machines. On the technical side, reach out to your principal, staff-level colleagues and other peers who are responsible for similar technical aspects as you. This can help when you are stuck on something because you know whom to reach out to to get unstuck. For example, as a result of reaching out to people early on as a new hire, I became much more effective at my job. When I didn't know how to track down a data source, I had a Rolodex of people to message or a list of documents to read (that were written and sent to me by humans).

If you are working on a specific family of products, such as a recommender system on a social media feed, then know who is making decisions about the product. Reach out to the product manager or relevant person(s). Don't underestimate reaching out to nontechnical folks; sometimes you are stuck not because of a code or data issue or a bug but because of some product logic that you didn't know.

As a new hire, set up 30-minute coffee chats (virtual or in person) with people on your team and organization. This can help you get to know them and onboard faster as they can share important context with you.

Once you finish a coffee chat with someone, ask who they suggest you meet with next. You can then set up a coffee chat with that person!

Help Improve the Onboarding Documentation

During onboarding at all companies I've worked for, there were always documents to follow and sometimes meetings with a coworker or manager to walk through the code, data, and projects. On documentation webpages, there can sometimes be broken links or outdated descriptions that your onboarding buddy tells you about verbally. Make a change to those docs; it's a great way to start contributing, and if your documentation is stored in a code repository (e.g., Markdown files on GitHub that are rendered on an internal Wiki page), then it's an easy pull request (PR) you can make in your first week, or even on your first day.

Keep Track of Your Achievements

As you get settled in, keep your long-term growth in mind. This means noting down anything you've done in preparation for performance reviews and promotion processes. One great resource is Julia Evans' brag document (*https://oreil.ly/YMc9d*), which is a document where you keep track of what you've accomplished at work.

Update it regularly, and it will be a great resource for the future you as you keep making your way in the ML field!

Summary

In this chapter, I discussed some post-interview FAQs such as following up, responding to rejections, and so on. I also walked through the common considerations and components of a job offer, which I hope can provide perspective. Next, I provided some tips for when you start your first ML job to help you succeed during the first few months.

Congrats on making it this far! Now I hope you can put what you've learned into practice. If there's one thing I want for you to take away, it's for you to learn to adjust and find your own footing. It's like bouldering (I don't even really boulder): when you grasp another handhold, the way you keep balance and grip will be different from how someone else does because they have different leg strength and different grips (Figure 9-1). And this ML career is the boulder we're all on, tackling in our own way. Best of luck; I'm rooting for you!

Figure 9-1. Finding your own ML career path is a bit like bouldering; photo by yns plt (https://oreil.ly/YxBVG) on Unsplash (https://oreil.ly/Rvf7P).

Epilogue

ML interviews aren't easy, and apart from everything I've detailed in this book, they also require grit and perseverance. Such qualities will get you far in your ML career. I'd love to hear your success stories; be sure to take a look at the companion site (*https://oreil.ly/o8EwV*) for additional discussion and bonus material that didn't fit into this book!

Going forward, there will be lots to explore, and you'll be excited to find what you can enable with ML and data. Beyond that, you may look into growing further in your career and becoming a technical leader or manager. I'm continuing to write about my own growth journey from entering the field and how I grew from entry level to principal level on my Substack (*https://oreil.ly/NKQMn*) and LinkedIn (*https://oreil.ly/lBihq*), so those resources may help you on your journey as well.

Index

About the Author

Susan Shu Chang is a principal data scientist at Elastic (of Elasticsearch), with previous ML experience in fintech, telecommunications, and social platforms. Susan is an international speaker, with talks at six PyCons worldwide and keynotes at Data Day Texas, PyCon DE & PyData Berlin, and O'Reilly's AI Superstream. She writes about machine learning career growth in her newsletter, *susanshu.substack.com*. In her free time she leads a team of game developers under Quill Game Studios, with multiple games released on consoles and Steam.

Colophon

The animal on the cover of *Machine Learning Interviews* is the short-beaked common dolphin (*Delphinus delphis*). With an average population of six million, these dolphins are one of the most abundant cetaceans worldwide.

Short-beaked common dolphins are about 6 feet long and approximately 170 pounds. Males tend to be slightly larger than females. They have round foreheads (known as melons); a moderately long rostrum with 50 to 60 small, sharp, interlocking teeth; and a sleek body with a tall, triangular dorsal fin in the middle of their back. They have a dark gray cape along their back and white bellies. On their sides, they have a distinct hourglass pattern that is gray, yellow, or gold in the front and a darker gray in the back.

There are large social groups of short-beaked common dolphins across the globe, ranging in size from hundreds to thousands. They prefer to live in tropical to cool water and are typically found around underwater ridges, seamounts, and continental shelves where upwelling (deep, cold, nutrient-rich water that rises toward the surface) occurs, which results in abundant prey. Their typical diet consists of schooling fish and cephalopods.

While these dolphins are considered a species of least concern, they are threatened by commercial fishing gear and suffer high mortality rates due to drift gillnet fishing operations. Many of the animals on O'Reilly covers are endangered; all of them are important to the world.

The cover illustration is by Karen Montgomery, based on an antique line engraving from *British Quadrupeds*. The series design is by Edie Freedman, Ellie Volckhausen, and Karen Montgomery. The cover fonts are Gilroy Semibold and Guardian Sans. The text font is Adobe Minion Pro; the heading font is Adobe Myriad Condensed; and the code font is Dalton Maag's Ubuntu Mono.

Printed in the USA
CPSIA information can be obtained
at www.ICGtesting.com
JSHW061457091223
53550JS00008B/9

9 781098 146542